D1046838

No Child Left Alone

No Child Left Alone

Getting the Government Out of Parenting

Abby W. Schachter

Encounter Books
New York · London

© 2016 by Abby W. Schachter

All rights reserved. No part of this publication may be reproduced, stored in a retrieval system, or transmitted, in any form or by any means, electronic, mechanical, photocopying, recording, or otherwise, without the prior written permission of Encounter Books, 900 Broadway, Suite 601, New York, New York 10003.

First American edition published in 2016 by Encounter Books, an activity of Encounter for Culture and Education, Inc., a nonprofit, tax-exempt corporation.
Encounter Books website address: www.encounterbooks.com

"There Is a Tree That Stands," by Itsik Manger, translated by Leonard Wolf, from *The Penguin Book of Modern Yiddish Verse*, edited by Irving Howe, Ruth R. Wisse, and Khone Shmeruk, copyright © 1987 by Irving Howe, Ruth Wisse, and Khone Shmeruk. Used by permission of Viking Books, an imprint of Penguin Publishing Group, a division of Penguin Random House LLC.

Manufactured in the United States and printed on acid-free paper. The paper used in this publication meets the minimum requirements of ANSI/NISO Z39.48–1992 (R 1997) (*Permanence of Paper*).

FIRST AMERICAN EDITION

LIBRARY OF CONGRESS CATALOGING-IN-PUBLICATION DATA

Names: Schachter, Abby W., 1969– author.
Title: No child left alone : getting the government out of parenting / by Abby W. Schachter.
Description: New York : Encounter Books, [2016] | Includes bibliographical references and index. | Description based on print version record and CIP data provided by publisher; resource not viewed.
Identifiers: LCCN 2015044908 (print) | LCCN 2015041108 (ebook) | ISBN 9781594038624 (Ebook) | ISBN 9781594038617 (hardcover : alk. paper)
Subjects: LCSH: Child welfare—United States. | Children—Government policy—United States. | Family policy—United States. | Parenting—United States. | Parents—United States.
Classification: LCC HV741 (print) | LCC HV741 .S347 2016 (ebook) | DDC 362.7/25610973—dc23
LC record available at http://lccn.loc.gov/2015044908

PRODUCED BY WILSTED & TAYLOR PUBLISHING SERVICES

To my parents,

Ruth and Leonard Wisse,

and to my husband,

Ben Schachter

Contents

Foreword   ix
Lenore Skenazy

Introduction   1

1. **Arresting Captain Mommy**   27
   *Criminalizing parents for raising
   independent, self-assured children*

2. **Breast Is Best, *or Else***   61
   *Advocating for breastfeeding
   isn't enough—it has to be
   the law*

3. **Daycare Nannies**   91
   *Too few child-care centers that
   cost too much—the result of
   too many regulations*

4. **School Statists**   121
   Obsessed with health and fat shaming

5. The War on Fun   147
   Banning play, toys, and games

6. Obesity Police   181
   Kids taken into state custody
   because they're fat and other
   child-welfare woes

Conclusion   217

Acknowledgments   233

Notes   234

Selected Bibliography   263

Index   266

Foreword

CAPTAIN MOMMY \\'kap-tən 'mäm-ee\ *n. idiom*
Mother who encounters and resists the excessive intrusion
into family life, most often through the use of overly expansive
definitions of the state's role in protecting children. *Example:
Lenore Skenazy, founder of the Free-Range Kids movement, is the
first Captain Mommy.*

CAPTAIN DADDY \\'kap-tən 'däd-ee\ *n. idiom*
Male version of a Captain Mommy.

"I'D LIKE TO LET my kids walk to school, but ..."

But what?

You're the parent! They're your kids! You want to give them
the freedom you loved—to walk, explore, stay home, go out, or
even, once in a while, to get lost or goof up. To do things on
their own.

But ...

As Captain Mommy knows all too well, it's no longer
straightforward.

For the first five years after I founded the Free-Range Kids
movement, parents who wanted to let their kids walk to school
would end that sentence with, "but I don't want them to get
kidnapped." Fair enough ... even though the chances of that
happening are so outlandishly small, that if for some reason you
actually WANTED your child to be kidnapped by a stranger,

do you know how long you'd have to keep him outside, unsupervised, for that to be statistically likely to happen?

About 750,000 years. (And after the first 100,000, you really couldn't even call him a "kid" anymore.) But that's for another book.

Suffice it to say that a few years ago, the "I'd like my kids to
walk" sentence started ending differently: "... but I don't want
to get arrested."

Fear of predators had been supplanted by fear of the police.

The stories, after all, were in the news: "I let my nine-year-
old play in the park and was thrown in jail for negligence." "I let
my kids eleven, nine, and five play in the playground across the
street from me, and I was put on the state's child-abuse registry." "I let my two-year-old wait in the car while I ran in to get
her life jacket and was charged with child endangerment. And
yes, I get the irony."

Real stories.

The problem seemed to be twofold. First, the government is
made up of human beings. Humans who watch TV, read Facebook, hear about childhood crimes and tragedies, and end up
just as outraged as the rest of us. Problem Number Two is this:
They feel that they can prevent all these sad tales from ever
happening again if only they passed some more laws.

So they do. And now in 19 states, you can't let your kid wait
in the car while you go run a short errand. In British Columbia,
the Supreme Court ruled that it is illegal to let your child stay
home alone as a "latchkey kid" until age 10, because—the judge
mused—what if the house caught on fire? In Rhode Island,
four legislators proposed a law that would make it a crime to
let any child below 7th grade—age 12!—off the school bus in
the afternoon unless there was an adult waiting to walk the kid
home.

That law was, mercifully, shelved, thanks to reality seeping in: Do we really think an 11-year-old can't walk a block home by herself? Do we really want parents quitting their jobs to stand out at the school bus stop every afternoon at three? While we're at it, do we really have to think in terms of the least likely, most horrific possibility—a carjacking! a house fire! a kidnapping!—every time we make any decision regarding what parents and kids should legally be allowed to do? If so, wouldn't that mean criminalizing any parent who drives her kid to the mall? After all, car rides can be deadly, too. Where does the obsession with safety stop?

That's the overarching question our good Captain addresses here, and the one we all have to consider unless we want to pursue absolute safety, which requires constant surveillance, un-fettered intervention, and a farewell to freedom for parents and for kids.

Which doesn't sound so great when you put it that way.

So start the charge, Captain. It's time for a revolution.

—LENORE SKENAZY,
founder of the book, blog, and
movement Free-Range Kids

No Child Left Alone

Introduction

Of all tyrannies, a tyranny sincerely exercised for the good of its victims may be the most oppressive. It may be better to live under robber barons than under omnipotent moral busybodies. The robber baron's cruelty may sometimes sleep, his cupidity may at some point be satiated; but those who torment us for our own good will torment us without end, for they do so with the approval of their own conscience.

—C. S. LEWIS[1]

DO YOU WANT TO SEE government operating as if it can and should raise your kids for you? Try enrolling your child in state-licensed daycare. When our eldest daughter was 18 months old and started at the local preschool, the intrusion into our family's decisions started almost immediately with strict rules about which foods I could send from home and how I should prepare and portion fruits and vegetables. My husband and I would joke by singing "Peel Me a Grape"!

I used to inquire about the reasons behind each of these policies. The answer was always the same, whether it was an issue of safety or hygiene, cleanliness or health: The state says so.

As the years passed, the rules piled up. No plastic bags. We had to provide multiple sippy cups because once a cup is proffered it cannot be used again. Requirements for daily sunscreen slathering, and a state mandate that all uneaten food be thrown out lest anything become "hazardous" over the course of the

1

day—these are just a few of Pennsylvania's daycare decrees. We got used to all that. It was annoying but tolerable, until I had my fourth kid.

When my son's caregiver inquired what she should know about him, I asked for exactly one thing: Please swaddle him for every nap. Swaddling means snugly or tightly wrapping baby in a blanket. It keeps them feeling safe and secure, and it is the only baby advice we followed. Harvey Karp, author of *Happiest Baby on the Block*, is a genius! It had worked for our three daughters, so we were sticking to it with our baby boy. No can do, the daycare lady said apologetically. The state doesn't allow us to swaddle.

I was shocked. In the three years since my third child began daycare, Pennsylvania, along with several other states, had changed the regulations to include a ban on swaddling. The reason is safety, because there have been cases of babies suffocating when covered by thick, loose blankets, and the overarching threat of SIDS. This is less common now that we're all taught to sleep babies on their backs, but it is still a danger, though there are no reported cases of babies suffocating due to loose blankets at daycare, certainly not in Pennsylvania (I checked). But I wasn't thinking about any of that when I learned about the new rules. As a mother, I want to do what works, and what worked for my other three kids—whether sleeping at daycare or at home—was wrapping them tightly in a blanket, like a burrito. Around the same time, Dr. Karp took up the cause as well, telling the *Washington Post* that banning swaddling in daycare was misguided. "We know it increases sleep and reduces crying," Karp said. "Those are extremely important goals."[2] Amen, brother.

I demanded to know what I could do and was told that a doctor's waiver would allow the daycare workers to wrap my son. I tried one pediatrician at my kids' practice, and she refused because the American Academy of Pediatrics doesn't recom-

mend swaddling after two months. I eventually found a pediatrician who signed the waiver and became my instant hero.
With the waiver, my boy was wrapped for naps. I was happier,
my son slept more, and the daycare workers had an easier time
caring for my baby.

After four kids you'd think I would be used to this sort of
bureaucratic intrusion into my personal decision-making. And
up to a point I was. But more and more government-mandated
parenting started getting under my skin.

I was fed up. And when push came to shove, I fought for
my rights. But how many other parents would do the same?

Lots, it turns out. Mine was only the most personal instance
what turns out to be a much more widespread phenomenon of
the authorities getting between parents and their kids. I had
joined the ranks of the Captain Mommy Squad, protectors of
parental rights, defenders of personal family authority.

I'm a journalist, along with being a parent, so, as part of my
job blogging and writing, I started paying attention to similar
stories. What I found was that I didn't know the half of it. Too
many parents have had run-ins with government nannies just
for exercising their own judgment. These parents are facing far
more dramatic situations than my own. Indeed, they make up
a whole subpopulation of persecuted moms and dads who are
willing to stand up for their right to raise their own kids. These
are the Captain Mommies and Daddies.

There have been banner headlines about a rash of "criminal"
moms and dads. Danielle and Alexander Meitiv got in trouble
with police and child protective services for allowing their two
kids to walk home alone. Nicole Gainey, a 34-year-old mother
of two, was arrested on a charge of felony child neglect for allowing her seven-year-old son, Dominic, to walk alone to the
playground less than a half-mile from her home in Port Lu-
cie, Florida. South Carolina single-mom Debra Harrell was

arrested for letting her nine-year-old daughter, Regina, play unattended in a nearby park while she worked. And a mom from Scottsdale, Arizona, was arrested and her kids taken into state custody after leaving two of them alone in a car while she interviewed for a job. Nothing happened to any of these children, and yet the state decided to punish the parents.

There are kids who have been threatened with suspension for contravening the school zero-tolerance policy for bringing parent-packed herbal drinks to school because the beverage may contain trace amounts of alcohol. And since I make my kids' lunch every day I was especially upset to read about a four-year-old in North Carolina who had her home-packed lunch confiscated. It seems her turkey and cheese sandwich, banana, potato chips, and apple juice didn't meet the standards set by the U.S. Department of Agriculture, as understood by the school's government-empowered food inspector. "What got me so mad is, number one, don't tell my kid I'm not packing her lunch box properly," mom Heather Parker railed to the newspapers.[3]

Parents have begun to feel disrespected by their kids' schools. In Cumberland County, Tennessee, Jim Howe was arrested at his kids' school when he complained about the policy banning *walking* into the building to pick up his children, instead of driving up. One principal threatened a visit from child protective services if a mom continued to allow her daughter to ride the city bus to school. Other parents have gotten intrusive letters telling them their kids are getting fat.

One dad was given a citation from police for disorderly conduct because he argued with officers who reprimanded him for taking his kids to frolic on the banks of a local frozen river.

ALARMED BY THIS EVIDENCE of a growing society-wide campaign to preempt individual parenting choices and criminalize choices that do not conform to state standards, I started following up with phone calls. I spoke to a mom in Atlanta who described how at her kids' private school, the board had just been forced to accept a new rule that all parent volunteers henceforth be "mandated reporters." Parents were now supposed to be on the lookout for any "inappropriate" behavior among staff and students and report it to the authorities. The mom and I both wondered why any parent would want to become an unpaid agent of child protective services? Shouldn't mandated reporters be trained and if so, why would parents do that simply to chaperone a trip to the zoo? Why should they be forced to? Then the hysteria over mandated reporters hit even closer to home when Pennsylvania passed new rules requiring more people to serve as mandated reporters in response to the Jerry Sandusky child-abuse scandal, and my college-professor husband was himself forced to become one, an unpaid—but legally liable—agent of the government (with no special training for what he should be looking for, mind you).

I spoke to a mom who was insulted and yelled at by a New York City police officer after her daughter and a friend's son *almost* stepped into an intersection when the light was red. Now, if the kids had been blocks ahead of their mothers, and, God forbid, they'd gotten hurt, I would have expected the verbal lashing they received. But the children didn't even get a full step off the curb before an idling driver blasted his horn and the moms themselves lunged for their kids, yelling at them to step back and wait for the light to turn. The kids were so scared by the ruckus they were clutching at their moms even as the officer made a beeline for the parents and began berating them. The officer accused them of neglecting their kids and threatened them as if a terrible accident had taken place. But, again, *nothing* had actually happened.

I wrote a column for the Pittsburgh *Tribune Review* about a monkey-shaped teething toy that was recalled by the Consumer Product Safety Commission because a few babies had gagged on the tail. But here again no one was injured. Come over to my house any night of the week, and you can see my baby gag on teething toys, spoons, and his fingers. Will the CPSC be issuing a recall for those as well?

In each of these cases, the state is intervening in choices and decisions that used to be up to parents. Whether to allow children to go unchaperoned to the local pizza shop or what drinks or food to send to school were choices that used to be left to mom and dad. Not anymore. Now the state's safety, hygiene, and health standards dictate, and their judgment might or might not coincide with yours. Indeed, when it comes to childhood, there is hardly any area of life that is left entirely up to individual parents.

But wait, as the TV infomercial says, there's more! As *No Child Left Alone* will chronicle, the nanny state is

- taking kids from their parents (and in some cases parents have been charged) for the crime of the children being obese;
- criminalizing parents for allowing their kids some unsupervised time outside;
- pressuring all women to breastfeed and mandating that every employer encourage breastfeeding at work;
- putting every public-school kid on a diet;
- collecting health data on students, and, in certain states, harassing parents about their children's weight;
- banning running at playgrounds;
- banning certain games and some types of play at public school;
- driving up the cost of daycare with burdensome regulations and certification rules, which puts safe, clean daycare out of the reach of low- and middle-income families.

One assumption driving this government intervention is that the only way to serve the so-called best interests of the child is to rely on state control. As the author of *Paranoid Parenting*, University of Kent sociology professor emeritus Frank Furedi, puts it, "[United Kingdom government] initiatives are underpinned by the assumption that parents cannot be trusted and must be subject to constant surveillance."[4] But this is not the way the United States Supreme Court has defined the rights of parents.

In *Meyer v. Nebraska* (1923), the court held that parents have a right to raise their children free from interference and that the right to raise a child as a parent sees fit is a liberty granted by the Fourteenth Amendment. This right is not unlimited, however. A parent has the right to "bring up children . . . according to the dictates of his own conscience," the Court said, but it is within the power of the state to obligate a parent to educate his or her child.

It is not as if there's been no tension between parents' rights and government dictates since that court decision nearly a century ago. But this is the first time government has ever taken such an interventionist, prescriptive approach to imposing its own standards for childrearing.

Politicians at all levels of government talk about what they will do to "protect," to "shelter," to "improve the lives of," and "support" "our" children. But does this really improve kids' lives, or does it just assert control? It is also true that regulation raises costs. For every legislative act of "child protection" there is a financial cost to parents and taxpayers. My problem is that a reasonable balance between the interests of necessary regulation and government oversight on the one hand and the rights of families and the effect on the marketplace on the other doesn't seem to be part of the state's calculations when it comes to children. It is also difficult to justify government's one-size-fits-all solutions when most problems affect only a tiny fraction of the population. This is public policy that serves only the interests of those who are exceptions to the rule.

These realizations changed the way I thought about raising my kids. Before, I was Mama. Now I am Captain Mommy, on guard against overprotective, overbearing, nannying authorities trying to take my choices away. And I've discovered that many other parents feel the same. Moreover, parents aren't the only ones who have noticed this problem.

Dana Mack's sociological study *The Assault on Parenthood*[5] seems to have been the first popular book to assert that a combination of psychologists, public servants, and public-school educators have been working against and getting between parents and their kids. "The African proverb 'It takes a whole village to raise a child,'" Mack complains, "seems to serve as a rallying call for the establishment of a communal authority to set new standards and methods of child-rearing." Government has only gotten more involved in the business of parenting since Mack's book was first published in 1997.

From the academy, too, comes a condemnation of dictating behavior to parents. In their book *Practical Wisdom: The Right Way to Do the Right Thing*, evolutionary psychologist Barry Schwartz and political scientist Kenneth Sharpe write, "Anybody who has raised a child ... knows the limits of rules and principles." They explain:

> We can't live without them, but not a day goes by when we don't have to bend one, or make an exception, or balance them when they conflict. We're always solving the ethical puzzles or quandaries that are embedded in our practices because most of our choices involve interpreting rules, or balancing clashing principles or aims, or choosing between better and worse.[6]

As the authors show, the problems arise when these rules are written and administered by government, which does not allow for individual discretion in balancing competing principles or applying the consequences and punishments associated with breaking the rules.

And from the legal realm there's Harvey Silverglate's *Three Felonies a Day*, in which the lawyer and civil-liberties crusader argues that the rules have become so complex and cumbersome that just about everyone breaks the law every day. "Wrongful prosecution of innocent conduct that is twisted into a felony charge has wrecked many an innocent life and career. Whole families have been devastated," Silverglate says.[7]

Philip K. Howard, corporate lawyer, Common Good[8] crusader, and author of such titles as *The Rule of Nobody* and *Death of Common Sense*, couldn't agree more. "Instead of defining the edges of wrongful conduct, protecting a broad zone of individual empowerment, modern law sees its role as telling people what to do and how to do it."[9]

Silverglate does have an optimistic view of the possibilities for reform, however, because the problem is so common, as we'll see throughout this book. "Vague laws threaten Americans from all walks of life and all points on the political spectrum," Silverglate contends. "Yet that depressing fact is actually encouraging, because it suggests the possibility of a broad coalition in support of much needed legal reforms, beginning with the basic principle that, absent a clearly stated prohibition, people must not be punished for conduct that is not intuitively criminal, evil, or antisocial."[10] To this argument I would add that parents must be allowed to raise their children by their lights, especially when there is no public impact on their private childrearing choices.

• • •

THE MORE I LEARNED, the more outraged and curious I became. I am convinced that parents who feel the same way have
to hear about each other. In every chapter, you'll learn all the
ways government is interfering in the private lives of families,
and you'll meet the many other Captain Mommies and Captain Daddies who have been shocked by the invasion of the
nanny state and who are fighting hard to get the government
out of parenting. The reason they are so passionate is that we've
all been mugged by the reality of the nanny state stepping between us and our kids.

My friend Lenore Skenazy, the godmother of all Captain
Mommies, is highlighted in Chapter 1, "Arresting Captain
Mommy." She was attacked as the worst mother in America for
allowing her nine-year-old son to ride the New York City subway by himself. And from that one act of unwitting defiance,
she became the mommy of a movement. In her book, *Free-
Range Kids: How to Raise Safe, Self-Reliant Children (Without
Going Nuts with Worry)*, Skenazy argues that children have to
be left to do things on their own, and she focuses much of her
work these days blogging, writing, and speaking on changing
parents' behavior. But she also recognizes that overbearing government and health and safety regulatory roadblocks do more
harm than good.

One of Skenazy's crusades is the defense of parents who
are criminalized for leaving kids unattended in cars for reasonably short periods of time. She calls this type of worry—when
the authorities react as if the worst-case scenario has actually
occurred—"worst-first" thinking. For parents, the result is often
trouble with the police, thousands of dollars in legal fees, and
perhaps even jail. Just like Nicole Gainey.

What has changed about our notions of safety on the one
hand and of allowing parents authority over their own children
on the other? Why is the state choosing to criminalize behav-

ior that was so recently commonplace, and when no harm has come to the child? Do we really demand that law enforcement prevent any bad thing from happening to anyone ever? Or that police punish those who make bad decisions that *could have* led to bad outcomes?

After a New Jersey mom was arrested for leaving her toddler in the car unattended for no more than 10 minutes,[11] attorney Scott Greenfield explained the extent of the problem at his criminal defense blog called *Simple Justice*, and he explained why this is an issue for the justice system.

> This isn't to argue that parents should not do what they can to avoid risks to their children's welfare.... Not leaving a kid in the car alone just isn't that hard to do, and for the most part, parents aren't inclined to do it.... This isn't a matter of parenting "best practices," but whether the failure to adhere to a bubble-wrapped vision of child-rearing forms the basis for criminal prosecution, for inclusion on the child-abuse registry, for loss of civil rights, perhaps career, home and even the right to remain parent to a child.[12]

For the "crime" of doing things that most of our parents did without incident at one time or another, and in cases when nothing happened to the child, more and more of today's moms and dads are prosecuted every year.

This type of overreaction by authorities to potential dangers that haven't produced harm is one of several themes running through *No Child Left Alone*.

There is a difference, after all, between parental anxiety about risks and dangers to our children and government safety policies. The latter, at least, are meant to be based on larger-scale, more objective calculations of risks versus costs.

The motivating force behind government intervention is

an ambiguous and unworkable definition of what it means to keep children safe, healthy, and protected. Current definitions of hygiene and safety assume that private decisions, preferences, and behavior can and should be government mandated, all in the name of the public "good." In extreme cases, parents have been criminalized and penalized for perfectly lawful, common-sense behavior.

In the 2014 best-seller *All Joy and No Fun: The Paradox of Modern Parenthood*, Jennifer Senior chronicled the insecurity, anxiety, and stress among some of today's parents beleaguered by chronic overscheduling, obsessing about the future, having too many expectations. But she failed to diagnose one major influence working against them: the anxieties of the nanny state. Parents have been harassed, threatened, and arrested for attempting to give their kids some level of freedom and independence.

The good news is that when some parents find themselves on the receiving end of a nanny-state lashing, they start fighting to change the status quo. After being threatened with arrest for allowing her kid to walk to soccer practice alone, a Mississippi mom I interviewed explained how she'd since become an advocate for safer streets and more sidewalks.

GOVERNMENTAL OVERREACTIONS to potential dangers and unreasonable standards for children's health and safety will be discussed at length in Chapter 2, "Breast Is Best, *or Else*"; Chapter 3, "Daycare Nannies"; and Chapter 4, "School Statists."

Government has become so convinced it knows the best way to feed a baby that employers are now mandated to encourage breastfeeding among their employees; government welfare benefits are enhanced and extended to low-income women who exclusively breastfeed; and formula is under lock and key at some public hospitals. Meanwhile, family traditions aren't good enough in a world that requires an authoritative standard.

In some cases, people find themselves suddenly at odds with the nanny state. In response to a New York City breastfeeding mandate, a Chicago-area mother named Faten Abdallah said, "I would hate the government or hospital to mandate what I think is a freedom of choice." Another Captain Mommy is born.

The health and safety stakes have become discouragingly high. Continuous monitoring is a hallmark of state-approved care for young children outside the home. High-level certification for daycare workers is becoming the norm. The result is that many parents who want to find a licensed daycare can't afford the tuition.

Philip K. Howard has spent years decrying the rise of regulation and all the associated costs that come with those rules. His books chronicle the negative impact of all this bureaucracy and state micro-management: We have a system where even those in leadership positions do not have individual discretion to make decisions.

Daycare workers have little flexibility to set standards that work for the children in their care or their parents. Our tolerance for risk is so low that public policy is driven by exactly the wrong incentives. And the nanny-state way of mitigating risk at daycare means increasing the rules to eliminate any potential hazard and then falsely "guaranteeing" that the daycare can be made into a perfect utopia of safety and hygiene.

Often state rules have been adopted through federally funded groups meant to provide guidance and advice. But when local regulators need to write rules for local conditions, they often turn to what seems like an easy fix; they adopt wholesale guidelines with the federal government's seal of approval. These then become the law of the land.

This disconnect between the rule-writers and the regulated has produced more and more precise, limiting, and proscriptive daycare rules, including banning plastic bags, mandating teeth brushing, and regulating how far apart coat hooks should be spaced. What, however, do any of these standards have to do with providing a safe, warm place for children while their parents work? Do these rules actually improve the quality of care?

Daycare workers are left with a series of checklists. Their primary task becomes to comply with state standards, rather than to care for small children. Not only does this hurt parental discretion and authority (Why can't I ask my daycare to swaddle my baby? Why can't I go down the street to find another daycare that will swaddle my boy?), it also has a negative consequence for those who are being regulated. "Rules are aides, allies, guides and checks," argue Schwartz and Sharpe. "But too much reliance on rules can squeeze out the judgment that is necessary to do our work well."[13]

Public school is another active battleground in the war between overbearing authorities and independent-minded parents. In 1996, a school allowed child protective services personnel to interview a boy without his parents' presence or knowledge (this is still legal). The parents sued and lost. Judge Melinda Harmon summarized why with this chilling statement: "Parents give up their rights when they drop the children off at public school." In the intervening years, there has been a growing awareness that perhaps this isn't what parents want or expect for their kids.

This power struggle was the subject of a 2012 movie starring Maggie Gyllenhaal and Viola Davis called *Won't Back Down*. The movie's synopsis reads, "Two determined mothers, one a teacher, look to transform their children's failing inner city school. Facing a powerful and entrenched bureaucracy, they risk everything to make a difference in the education and future of their children."

The movie represents a shift in the perception of good guys and bad guys when it comes to school. Whereas decades of films portrayed teachers and administrators as the heroes of these movies, now movies like *Won't Back Down* portray parents as the good guys fighting obstructive authority.

The film depicted a fight over curriculum and quality education, but meanwhile government do-gooders are forcing parents and schools to conform to rules and regulations that reach far beyond what happens in the classroom. Chapter 4 will relate recent fights over food and health standards at public schools.

New lunch menus have put every public-school kid on a restricted-calorie diet, while two dozen states collect students' height and weight statistics in order to track potential health problems. In the most aggressive cases, states have required schools to send letters home to parents warning that children may be at risk of or already suffering from obesity. When, however, did it become the state's responsibility to monitor students' body mass indexes? And what are the broader implications of these policies? Do they even work? And should public schools really be diverting their time and energy from education to these concerns?

Parents have been especially upset to discover that schools are now required by law to collect weight and height information on their children. In some states the policy is to inform parents about potential problems, which has made for some angry Captain Mommies and Captain Daddies.

THE GOVERNMENT has access to students through public schools and argues that, for the good of all children, it must impose its standards. Obesity is the current obsession. The combination of access and the current orthodoxy of government as the sole authority for combatting obesity led to a rejiggering of what government deems a "balanced diet" (now a plate instead of a pyramid).

This "plate" reflects nutritional preferences that are highly debatable. Take fat, for example. Government guidelines proscribe fat across the board, while some nutritionists counter that fat is especially important for children. As for dairy, the federal food plate includes a portion that critics insist is a U.S. Department of Agriculture gift to dairy producers more than it is truly necessary for overall health. Notwithstanding these disagreements, federal dietary guidelines aren't in themselves a bad idea. The trouble comes when advice morphs into law.

The USDA didn't just revamp the National School Lunch Program; it came up with a variety of new rules and mandates about how the foods should be prepared (no frying in oil, for example) and how much of each food children should be allowed (severe portion control). It has put schools in the position of having to shoulder a heavier and heavier burden of the costs—both financial and bureaucratic—for managing and enforcing their rules. The folks who have to implement the new rules were especially upset about the cost of enforcement. Just as additional safety and health prescriptions make daycare more expensive, these types of regulations result in increased costs for schools.

At the same time, because this is a federal government program it has to be implemented without exception across all schools and populations, even though the problems the new menus are meant to combat may not be prevalent at every school. The nanny state doesn't do nuance, you see. Not only is menu flexibility out of the question, but schools are discouraging parents from providing kids homemade lunches as well. The cost and complexity of compliance, meanwhile, means that taking the healthy step of cooking the food to order at school is just about impossible.

This isn't the first time Washington has committed itself to the problem of children's health. John F. Kennedy made it a priority even before he took office, penning a passionate affirmation of the need for physical health among the young and defending the necessity of government intervention. The difference between Kennedy in 1960 and the current crop of government do-gooders is that the solutions Kennedy supported were much simpler than those of today. He also, far more than is currently the case, placed the burden for success on individuals and families working *together* with government.

"A single look at the packed parking lot of the average high school will tell us what has happened to the traditional hike to school that helped to build young bodies," Kennedy wrote.[14] The solution he proposed required government help.

> The physical fitness of our youth should be made a direct responsibility of the Department of Health, Education and Welfare. This department should conduct— through its Office of Education and the National Institutes of Health—research into the development of a physical fitness program for the nation's public schools. The results of this research shall be made freely available to all who are interested. In addition, the Department of Health, Education and Welfare should use all its existing facilities to attack the lack of youth fitness as a major health problem.[15]

Kennedy may have argued that government has an important role in teaching American children how to live a healthy life, but he was equally persuasive about the role of adults and parents.

> No matter how vigorous the leadership of government, we can fully restore the physical soundness of our nation only if every American is willing to assume

responsibility for his own fitness and the fitness of his children. . . . All of us must consider our own responsibilities for the physical vigor of our children and of the young men and women of our community. We do not want our children to become a generation of spectators. Rather, we want each of them to be a participant in the vigorous life.[16]

The vigorous life of children and all the roadblocks that the nanny state erects to prevent it is the focus of Chapter 5, "The War on Fun." As a recent article by Hanna Rosin in *The Atlantic* argued, there is harm done to kids by overprotective parents *and* government management of playgrounds, games, and independent play. Her central thesis was that parents who bubble-wrap their kids hurt them by never letting them learn self-sufficiency, which requires skills like how to manage risk and deal with failure. As correct as she may be, however, it is nearly impossible for parents to fight the urge to be overprotective when the law says they should be doing just that. And what else are parents to understand from playground signs banning running and sledding?

In his book *No Fear: Growing Up in a Risk-Averse Society*, Tim Gill, who writes about these problems in Great Britain, has noticed that America's litigation culture is making matters even worse here.

In America, the compensation culture is a reality, and a major cause of risk aversion. Fear of liability is grounded not just in misperception or misinformation, but in fundamental differences in the way the legal system handles litigation. . . . US liability cases are conducted in front of juries, and may involve class action and punitive damages, all of which raise the stakes for defendants.[17]

Gill is absolutely correct. There is a practical reason why municipal playgrounds have, in many places, made the jungle-gyms lower to the ground and replaced concrete with rubber matting. Using taxpayer funds to remove hazards from the local park is much cheaper than settling lawsuits.

Fear of litigation isn't the only trend working against kids and parents. Frank Furedi and Gill both argue that freedom is being sacrificed on the altar of safety and health. Furedi chronicles the changes over the last decade.

> Society as a whole does not take children's freedom seriously ... [b]ecause Western societies actually regard parents who allow their children to pursue an independent outdoor life as irresponsible. In 2001, when I published my book ... I was genuinely surprised to discover that virtually all experiences associated with childhood came with a health warning.... But since the turn of the century, the regime of child protection has become steadily more pervasive and intrusive. The relentless erosion of children's freedom has been paralleled by the constant tendency to politicise parenting.[18]

Gill says that state intervention to protect children from risk is actually limiting the experiences of all children. I got a terrific education on these issues when I spoke to Mike Lanza, a Captain Daddy in California who has been building a community devoted to the proposition that children need to be outside, enjoying free play as much as possible. His book *Playborhood* argues for parent-made outdoor shareable play spaces for local kids. Lanza has had his own run-ins with local authorities who question his parenting choices. But he remains steadfast in his commitment to the quality of life necessary for his kids to thrive.

It feels like there is a government agency uniquely focused

on preventing parents from encouraging kids to have fun: the Consumer Product Safety Commission. Of course, the CPSC is supposed to help consumers uncover hidden dangers in consumer products. But like many regulators, the definitions have gotten much broader and the mandate much more expansive. Indeed, the CPSC isn't even satisfied with recalling and banning toys and games anymore. Now the agency has decided that protecting children requires suing private business owners who don't do what they want, even if their products aren't for children! CPSC has also gotten into the business of hectoring parents about how precisely they ought to use some products, as if we who have children couldn't get along without the anxiety-inducing warnings and advisories of Uncle Sam.

The list of CPSC "hasty responses" is long and varied—pajamas, baby baths, desk toys—and the list of consequences—killing business, worrying parents, wasting taxpayer money—is also impressive.

GETTING TO KNOW this community of subversive parents who don't like the government telling them how to raise their kids, and who are fighting for their rights, has raised important questions for me: How did we get here? How did this kind of overbearing authority become part of our fabric? I read a piece that offered a possible explanation. In his 2006 *Los Angeles Times* op-ed, Daniel Gilbert, a professor of psychology at Harvard University and the author of *Stumbling on Happiness*, describes how societal changes often happen slowly enough that most parents just aren't paying attention.

> The human brain is exquisitely sensitive to changes in light, sound, temperature, pressure, size, weight and just about everything else. But if the rate of change is slow enough, the change will go undetected. If the low

hum of a refrigerator were to increase in pitch over the course of several weeks, the appliance could be singing soprano by the end of the month and no one would be the wiser. . . . Culturally, we haven't noticed that laws, rules, bureaucracy was moving against parents' authority because it was happening in small ways over a long period of time. But when it happens in Technicolor (i.e., banning sledding or arresting parents) then the outcry is immediate from some quarters because it is blatantly contra the cultural norm that no one noticed had changed.[19]

I find Gilbert's explanation persuasive. I don't think the effort to dictate and organize parents' lives is coordinated or centrally controlled. This is a systemic change that has been going on for decades across the country, incrementally, and for a variety of intended purposes. The nanny state has blossomed because of real changes to our social culture. But though there may have been real problems, what seems clear by now is that government solutions just aren't effective. Moreover, these remedies may do more harm than good.

I went looking to see how bad the problem is for parents. It can be pretty bad. In the worst case scenarios, parents can lose custody of their children. Chapter 6, "Obesity Police," explores what happens when the government takes kids away from their parents—because the kids are considered obese.

In the name of combating obesity, doctors and legal experts assert that the state can do a better job than mom or dad. There are multiple problems with this proposed solution, however. First, should the category of neglect be expanded to include allowing your child to overeat? Second, should this be an appropriate area of concern for child welfare services? As happens so often with regulations, definitions are expanded to the point that they now include whole categories of behavior that never used to be considered legitimate targets of action. This is certainly what has happened with obesity. Perhaps we should include the other conditions for which parents can be accused of neglect: self-harm, anorexia, depression, drug abuse, drinking excessively, bullying.

There is a fundamental flaw in the fact that child-welfare bureaucrats see families as separate individuals in conflict rather than as a homogeneous unit deserving of help as a whole. So often, in cases of obese kids, the parents are also obese. Why don't these parents deserve the same care and protection? Instead, the child-welfare system can seem almost predatory.

Expanding the mandate of child-welfare services has been a near constant trend since the inception of the first child-welfare program. Indeed, it is a common problem in the welfare state. As David Boaz, executive director of the libertarian CATO Institute, explains, "Bureaucracies are notoriously unwilling to become victims of their own success. So, true to form, the public health authorities broadened their mandate and kept on going. They launched informational and regulatory crusades against such health problems as smoking, venereal disease, AIDS, and obesity. Pick up any newspaper and you're apt to find a story about these 'public health crises.' Those are all health problems, to be sure, but are they really *public* health problems?"[20]

When it comes to obesity, the problem is astonishingly complex, and there is no proven remedy. I will review the history of child welfare with an eye toward understanding the pediatric obesity problem.

Boaz doesn't even agree that obesity is a matter for public policy consideration. "Let's start using honest language," he advises. A "legitimate public health issue," Boaz explains, involves "consumption of a collective good (air or water) and/or the communication of disease to parties who had not consented to put themselves at risk. . . . [O]besity [is a] health problem . . . [a] *widespread* health problem . . . [but] not [a] public health problem."[21]

WHILE WRITING this book, I've been asked too many times to count whether my attitude about overbearing government includes favoring parental choice as it relates to vaccines. The answer is no.

My view on vaccines mirrors my attitude about government intervention in general. I believe strongly in reasonable, effective, limited government involvement in the lives of private citizens, and only for public problems and crises that are in fact amenable to government-implemented solutions.

I'm a mom of four children, all of whom were vaccinated. I want everyone else to vaccinate their kids as well. And when the government mandates vaccines, everyone's kids are protected. What is called "herd immunity" only works against contagious diseases like measles and whooping cough when more than 92 percent of the population is vaccinated. Parents who refuse to vaccinate choose to endanger others' kids as well as newborns and those who are immunocompromised, and I want the government to penalize them. And yet, as Jimmy Kimmel noted in March 2015, the culture in some places, like Los Angeles, where he lives, has become inverted. Kimmel quipped, "Parents here are more afraid of gluten than they are of smallpox, and as a result, we've got measles, measles are back."[22]

Kimmel was reacting to a health crisis triggered in December 2014 at Disneyland in Anaheim, California, when more than 100 people who were exposed to measles subsequently got sick. "The rate of growth [in measles cases] gives us a good idea about the percentage of people in the population who are immune," explained Maimuna Majumder, a research fellow at Boston Children's Hospital. A preliminary analysis "indicates that substandard vaccination compliance is likely to blame for the 2015 measles outbreak," Majumder and her coauthors concluded in their research letter for *JAMA Pediatrics*.[23]

Measles, mumps, whooping cough, and other preventable illnesses have returned to the United States because of concentrations of parents opting not to immunize their kids and a compliant government allowing them to get away with it. It took the crisis in 2015 to get politicians and the public at large to focus pressure on what had by then proven to be too-lenient rules for opting out of the medically recommended vaccination schedule. States like California are finally rewriting legislation to reduce the number of acceptable personal exemptions in the hopes of stemming the tide.

What I find hard to understand is why in such a clear case of necessary government intervention, so many states and localities choose to be hands-off and allow parents not to vaccinate their children. Even President Obama opted for a more laid-back approach in the response to the measles outbreak, with White House Spokesman Josh Earnest telling reporters, "People should evaluate this for themselves with a bias toward good science and toward the advice of our public health professionals." This is exactly the wrong place for government to be lenient, and it is especially maddening given the opposite situation in just about every other area of childrearing.

Now contrast the laissez-faire attitude toward vaccines with the harsh regulations that govern cases of pediatric obesity. The people who are hurt by obesity are the ones who are obese. The people who are hurt from low vaccination rates also include everyone in the population who is at risk of getting sick.

President Kennedy got this distinction exactly right.

We do not live in a regimented society where men are forced to live their lives in the interest of the state. We are, all of us, as free to direct the activities of our bodies as we are to pursue the objects of our thought. But if we are to retain this freedom, for ourselves and for generations to come, then we must also be willing to work for the physical toughness on which the courage and intelligence and skill of man so largely depend.[24]

How are parents to reconcile their own parenting values with those of an overbearing government? Many are fighting to remain independent, responsible parents, refusing to accept the yoke of an oppressive nanny state. We are living in a moment of great anxiety, but too often, in response, the state decides that personal decisions are better made by government fiat. I aim to celebrate the many Captain Mommies and Daddies out there who are working to reject government-issued parenting standards and are taking authority and responsibility for raising their own children. It will take a broad revolution to change the way we treat parents. *No Child Left Alone* will show that the change has already begun.

There Is a Tree That Stands
(Oyfn Veg Shteyt a Boym)
ITSIK MANGER

There is a tree that stands
And bows beside the road.
All its birds have fled away,
Leaving not a bird.

The tree, abandoned to the storm,
Stands there all alone:
Three birds east, and three birds
    west—
The others south have flown.

To my mother then, I say,
"If you won't meddle, please,
I'll turn myself into a bird
Right before your eyes.

All winter, I'll sit on the tree
And sing him lullabies,
I'll rock him and console him
With lovely melodies."

Tearfully, my mother says,
"Don't take any chances.
God forbid, up in the tree
You'll freeze among the branches."

"Mother, what a shame to spoil
Your eyes with tears," I said,
Then, on the instant, I transformed
Myself into a bird.

My mother cried, "Oh, Itsik, love . . .
In the name of God,
Take a little scarf with you
To keep from catching cold.

And dear, put your galoshes on,
The winter's cold and aching.
Be sure to wear your fleece-lined cap;
Woe's me, my heart is breaking.

And, pretty fool, be sure to take
Your woolen underwear
And put it on, unless you mean
To lie a corpse somewhere."

I try to fly, but I can't move . . .
Too many, many things
My mother's piled on her weak bird
And loaded down my wings.

I look into my mother's eyes
And, sadly, there I see
The love that won't let me become
The bird I want to be.

CHAPTER 1

Arresting Captain Mommy

Criminalizing parents for raising independent, self-assured children

THOUGH IT WAS WRITTEN in the 1930s, this poem by Yiddish poet Itsik Manger perfectly presents the helicopter parent of the late 20th and early 21st centuries. Manger's description of a stereotypical overprotective Jewish mother easily fits the mold of a generation's worth of American parents who "protect" their kids so well the children have been prevented from enduring any minimal risks or responsibility that would also surely broaden their lives.

As I complete this manuscript, Manger's poem provokes a very different image and in some ways a more discouraging one. Individuals can change their individual parenting styles or techniques. But when a larger entity intrudes, change can become more difficult to effectuate. In the 2015 version of the poem, the parent replaces the son and the mother becomes the nanny state, issuing rules, conditions, and definitions for the proper care of children that supersede parental authority and squash children's independence and self-reliance. And while there has been some backlash from moms and dads against helicopter parenting—the no failure, no risk, no independence variety—along with many parents who never would or could ascribe to that philosophy in the first place, the police, child protective service workers, school administrators, and others in authority assert the state's right to punish parents for breaking its norms and laws.

The irony is that whether you are a helicopter parent, like the mother in this poem, or if you ignore, reject, or want to break out of this mold, too often some representative of our intrusive, overprotective government comes along to impose a whole separate legal standard of safety and care. As we'll see in this chapter, the results are punishment for parents and a variety of negative consequences for children.

THE GODMOTHER OF ALL CAPTAIN MOMMIES

Lenore Skenazy decided to let her nine-year-old son Izzy ride the New York City subway alone. She wanted to allow her son a small taste of freedom and independence, while managing her own worry that something terrible might happen to him. A simple act of parental discretion turned into a movement, and Skenazy was reborn as the godmother of all Captain Mommies. What Skenazy uncovered goes beyond the single phenomenon—now all too common—of parents harassed by authorities for deciding to let kids be out in the world alone. Her decision regarding her son exposes the real conflict that exists between families and the nanny state and the harm that it causes the kids, their parents, and society at large.

The number of stories detailing mothers, fathers and guardians who have been harassed, threatened, humiliated, and arrested for allowing their kids to be alone and do for themselves is nearly endless. The adults affected by the overreach of police, judges, medical, educational, and social-service personnel come from the lower, middle, and upper classes. They are married and single. They are men and women. In other words, this is happening everywhere and to everyone.

The consequences for an adult range from the inconvenience of having to explain to a child why police were threatening and scary, to spending thousands on bail and lawyers' fees, to being removed from your home and family. The psychological impact on adults is important, but the emotional and psychological impact on kids created a problem for society when those same children mature into adulthood.

The adults and the kids lose trust in the people who are charged with keeping us safe and healthy, and the kids are kept from developing necessary life skills like self-reliance, creativity, intuition, and grit. The overreaction of the nanny state to young people who are allowed to operate independently feeds the already overly developed anxiety of too many parents regarding their kids' freedom. Moreover, look at any bookstore's shelf of current titles on education, child development, sociology, and public policy, and you'll see one analysis after another of why deficiencies of these characteristics in our children is hurtful to us all.

Consider the best-seller *How Children Succeed: Grit, Curiosity, and the Hidden Power of Character*, in which author Paul Tough shows that character matters more than intelligence when it comes to kids' academic and life success. He focuses on what the research shows regarding teaching children self-reliance and self-control and what some schools are doing to try to incorporate those ideas into their curricula. But what about what happens beyond these few schools (Tough profiles two), when everyone else—the vast majority of schools, not to mention police departments and legislators—are actually working against parents who might want to promote these characteristics in their kids?

Tough is a fan of psychologist Angela Duckworth, who argues that grit is what educators should be teaching.

So far, the best idea I've heard about building grit in kids is something called growth mindset. This is an idea developed at Stanford University by Carol Dweck, and it is the belief that the ability to learn is not fixed. That it can change with your effort. Dr. Dweck has shown that when kids read and learn about the brain and how it changes and grows in response to challenge, they're much more likely to persevere when they fail because they don't believe that failure is a permanent condition.[1]

Parents who offer their kids some freedoms may not be doing so due to any understanding of such direct developmental effects. Certainly Skenazy wasn't trying to teach her boy anything like Dr. Dweck's lessons on perseverance and its importance to future success. Skenazy was giving her son the opportunity that she'd had when she was a kid, namely the chance to rely on oneself for limited periods of time and learn about how the world works. Yet in 2007 Skenazy caused an uproar when she wrote a newspaper column about allowing Izzy to ride the subway by himself. After her initial decision to let Izzy off his previously tight parental leash, she endured numerous phone conversations with the police to defend her choice. And as she explained it to me, she now believes that society is "criminalizing things that used to be perfectly OK, such as punishing parents for trying to raise independent children, [something that] used to be a value and now is worth a hefty fine or a stint in lock-up."

After Izzy got home without incident the first time, Skenazy allowed him to ride alone again, this time on the Long Island Rail Road (LIRR). The security officers on his train weren't happy. As she described it, the conductor wouldn't listen to her son and radioed ahead to the next station, where the conductor held up the train until the cops came—the very stop where Izzy was getting off and his friend's family was waiting on the platform to pick him up. The officer wouldn't allow Izzy or the family to leave until he'd spoken to Skenazy.

Fluke, you say? No, because a couple of months later, when Izzy again rode the LIRR, Skenazy got another call requiring her to vouch for her son again. This time, the officer complained bitterly about the dangers of children riding alone, even though, as Skenazy pointed out, the LIRR rules state that any child over eight is allowed to ride the train unsupervised. "That doesn't matter ma'am, what if someone tried to take him," moaned the officer. To which Skenazy replied, "This is 5pm on a Thursday and I think that if anything bad was happening to [my son] the police would try to help him." The officer only replied argumentatively, "What if two people were trying to abduct him?"

Such experiences reveal that the current default standard is that nothing is safe enough, says Skenazy, and police "are often in agreement that anything could happen." Skenazy started a blog called *Free-Range Kids*, wrote a book, and became an advocate for changing the parental culture around allowing kids some freedom. She did a TV show and has appeared as a guest on dozens of interview programs and talk shows. At first she was talking mostly about changing the parenting culture. But now she spends a lot of time talking about reforming the law. What changed is that her experience with the police has been repeated over and over and over again by parents across the country and with far worse results.

Too often, authorities such as the local police or security officers impose rules of safety divorced from any real danger, by following what they perceive to be rules written so broadly as to be applicable to entirely innocent situations. In many cases, the police seem more worried about "what could happen" than even the most helicoptering parent, often overreacting in situations where nothing—*nothing*—has happened.

Such conflicts have visited injustice on some parents and

have turned others into parental-rights vigilantes—a.k.a. Captain Mommies.

In July 2014, Debra Harrell of North Augusta, South Carolina, was booked for "unlawful conduct" toward a child for allowing her nine-year-old daughter to play at the playground near her home and her mother's job. The cause of the complaint was another mother at the playground, who upon hearing from the girl that she'd been dropped off while her mother worked, decided it was best to call police to protect the girl. Did she need protection? According to other parents, indeed, she did. Lesa Lamback, who enjoys the park with her family, told a reporter that "you cannot just leave your child alone at a public place, especially. This day and time, you never know who's around. Good, bad, it's just not safe."[2]

Skenazy has actually done the research, however. Given today's crime statistics on abduction, as she explained to the *New Yorker*, it would take some effort to get your kid snatched away. "If you actually wanted your child to be kidnapped, how long would you have to keep him outside for him to be abducted by a stranger?" she asked Lizzie Widdicombe, her interviewer. "Seven hundred and fifty thousand years," Skenazy said.[3]

The day of the alleged infraction regarding Harrell's daughter, the playground was full of people; it was fine weather; and the girl could have walked the short distance home, where she had a key. Or she could have gone (and did go) to her mother's job at McDonald's to check in and have lunch. No matter. According to a lot of people, that isn't good enough—children have to be watched every second, because you can't know what might happen. What did happen as a result of alerting the police was bad enough, however. The girl was put into state custody because of her mother's arrest. The mother was fired from her job for being in trouble with the law. (Her job was subsequently reinstated because of all the publicity.) Then the mother had to fight the charges, and a fund to help her was established. A lot of time and effort was taken up by the local criminal-justice and social-services authorities in order to find a solution to a nonproblem. Nothing had happened to the girl, which is a recurring theme in these cases.

PUNISHMENT WITHOUT A CRIME

Distance often doesn't matter, as was evident with the arrest of 33-year-old Nicole Gainey. She was charged with child neglect in July 2014 after letting her seven-year-old son walk 800 meters from home to the local park. "I'm totally dumbfounded by this whole situation," Gainey told a local TV station.[4] "I honestly didn't think I was doing anything wrong. I was letting him go play." Gainey added that she planned to fight the felony charge. And fight she should, given that, at the time he was approached by police, Gainey's son had a cell phone to call his mother, and he was playing with other kids whom he knew and who knew him.

Even when a parent is right on top of her kids, the law sees something out of the ordinary. A 2011 news item out of Houston, Texas, reported that one Tammy Cooper "was arrested and charged with child endangerment and child abandonment after her neighbor told police Cooper's children, ages 6 and 9, had been abandoned."[5] In reality, the children were playing on the front lawn.

"After police arrived, Cooper told authorities that she had been sitting outside in a lawn chair watching her children the entire time." No matter. She was handcuffed in front of her kids, even as the children pleaded with the police officer not to take their mom away. Cooper's husband was away serving in the military at the time. Cooper was charged with "abandoning a child" even though she was with her children the whole time.

Cooper was reborn a Captain Mommy as she sued the LaPorte police department. According to her complaint, she "spent 18 hours in custody" and spent "over $7,000 in court and legal fees" before the unsubstantiated felony charges against her were dismissed. "The incident also led to an investigation by Child Protective Services, requiring Cooper to take her children to the CPS office in Houston," where her children "were separated from her and interrogated by child abuse investigators. CPS found no cause for concern regarding the well-being of Cooper's children and dropped the investigation."[6] As of December 2014, Cooper was still waiting for her case to go to trial so she could get her day in court. "I was hoping for some good news for Christmas but no!" she wrote on her Facebook page. "So I continue to be strong and pray for trial!! It must be nice to be all powerful and above the law to continue to keep this case from going to trial."

A mom in Connecticut was charged with "risk of injury to a minor" and "failure to appear" after, according to Manchester's police blotter, "she allowed her seven-year and 11-year old children to walk down to Spruce Street to buy pizza unsupervised."

From the Johnson City, Tennessee, police blotter of June 7, 2012: "April L Lawson … 27 … was arrested by officers of the Johnson City Police Department and charged with child neglect. The arrest stems from a 911 call in reference to a missing child. During the investigation, officers discovered that Lawson had allowed her two children, ages 8 and 5, to walk to the playground."[7] Lawson had allowed her kids to walk to a nearby playground, but she became worried when she couldn't find them later on (it appears they had gone to a neighbor's house without telling her). When she called the police to help her find them, she became the focus of the investigation. Lawson was furious. "So I walked them across the street, watched them walk up the block to the park and went back inside. When the kids didn't come home I sent somebody up here to bring them home," Lawson explained. "I had no idea that I could get in this much trouble for just walking them up to a playground and play."[8] But how could she have known that she wasn't allowed to let her kids be unsupervised, ever, at all, even for a minute? And was it really a valid use of police resources and good for the family for Lawson to spend the night in jail?

In August 2011, Richard Masoner reported on the *Cyclelicious* blog that police in Elizabethton, Tennessee, threatened to make an arrest and even bring in child services when a 10-year-old girl was observed biking home from Harold McCormick Elementary School. "A driver complained about a girl biking from school on a narrow residential road. The officer 'observed that vehicles had to slow and negotiate around the cyclist' on Cedar Avenue south of the school."

Masoner explained, "To me, this seems like normal and expected traffic movement. The unnamed officer, however, [said that] 'this section of the roadway is not a safe place for a child of her [age] to be riding unsupervised,' so he loaded her and her bike up in the police cruiser, drove her home, and had a chat with the child's mother, Teresa Tryon."

When Tryon disagreed with the officer's assessment, he informed her that he was going to report the incident and that it would be filed with the Department of Child Services. He also lectured Tryon that her daughter would have been safer riding on a sidewalk, given the heavy school traffic on Cedar Avenue, even though there was no sidewalk available.

For Lori Levar Pierce, sidewalks have become her main focus as a Captain Mommy, after her son got in trouble with the police for walking alone.

Pierce lives in a Mississippi town of 25,000. She's a high-school teacher, and she admits that before the incident, she was your average, nervous, overprotective mom. One day her

10-year-old son was ready for soccer practice an hour early, while she was in the middle of cooking dinner. He asked if he could just walk the mile to the field on his own, and even though she was worried about it, she allowed him to go by himself. When Lori got to the practice a little later, she was accosted by a police officer who had picked up her son halfway to the field because (as he absurdly claimed) the station had received "over 100 calls" about a boy walking alone. The officer had stopped Pierce's son, driven him to practice, then circled back to look for Pierce at her home, and, not finding her there, gone back to the field to berate and threaten to arrest her for "reckless endangerment."[9]

Pierce was indignant. There aren't 100 homes between her house and the field, so she remembers wondering to herself what the officer was talking about. She ended up complaining to the police chief, who apologized for his overzealous officer. Meanwhile Pierce became an activist citizen, and another newly minted Captain Mommy, advocating for safer streets and better sidewalks so that kids can walk or bike without fear of being hit by cars—or being hassled by police.

It isn't only mothers who are harassed by police and CPS, either. Fathers feel the weight of the overbearing nanny state as well. A dad in suburban Pittsburgh was charged with two counts of reckless endangerment for leaving his kids playing at the playground while he ran errands. In this case, he had been at the park with them, and it was another "concerned" parent, who actually knew one of the children, who called the police.[10]

In Connecticut, Charles Eisenstein took to his blog, which otherwise concerns his activism on behalf of what he calls "degrowth," to discuss a run-in with police when he was actually with his children. "Last weekend I decided I would get the kids outdoors for a little time in nature. The Susquehanna River was frozen over, with the most remarkable ice formations," he wrote on his blog.[11] Innocent enough, until four police cars and two fire trucks showed up. Eisenstein was yelled at by the police in front of his teenagers, threatened with arrest and cited for disorderly conduct. "This small incident reveals a lot about our society. First is the presumption that legally constituted authority should decide what an acceptable level of safety is for oneself and one's family. I suppose going out onto the ice was more dangerous than staying indoors or on the sidewalk, but I deemed it in my children's best interest to be outdoors in this amazing ice world." Eisenstein writes that what bothered the officers was that he and his sons were engaged in behavior that was a violation of normality. But his point about who should decide the acceptable level of safety or risk in any behavior— the state or the family—is an important one.

It has become standard procedure to apply laws that were once used in child-custody disputes and abandonment cases to parents who want to let their kids do the same things they were allowed to do when they were kids. Is this really the proper use of the penal code? According to one Connecticut law firm, the charges of child endangerment, child neglect, or risk of injury to a minor are usually applied when a child has been put in harm's way by adults. Lawyers explain that examples include outright child abuse, domestic disputes when a child is present in the room, and a drunk-driving accident when a minor is in the vehicle. Apparently, we've all silently and nearly completely acquiesced to fear in the wake of sensational child-abduction and murder cases like those of Etan Patz, Adam Walsh, and Noah Pozner. But the norm, not the shocking exception, should be the basis for governing our lives. When statistics clearly show that our country is safer than it used to be, should parents need to fear the trouble they might reap for letting their kids do things by themselves?

Danielle and Alexander Meitiv were bucking the trend of helicoptering and mindfully allowing their kids some freedom, while the state mindlessly accused them of neglect and put them through the child protective services ringer.[12] "I was kind of horrified," Danielle Meitiv told the *Washington Post*. "You try as a parent to do what's right. Parents try so hard. Even though I know [the State is] wrong, it's a painful judgment."[13]

Meitiv was referring to a finding of "unsubstantiated" child neglect stemming from their decision to allow their 10-year-old son, Rafi, and six-year-old daughter, Dvora, to walk home alone. Someone called 911, and police responded to seeing the children unaccompanied. And even after the kids explained that nothing was wrong, they were still hauled home, where police and child protective services confronted the parents for allowing their kids some freedom of movement.

Slate's Hanna Rosin, who has written about the problems with overprotective parenting, like many others who commented on the case, was upset with the decision by Maryland's Child Protective Services. Rosin has become something of an advocate for letting kids gain experience and deal with risk, and she argues these decisions should be up to parents. Here, the child-welfare authorities had a different idea.

"What they learned from the latest CPS decision," Rosin writes of her discussion with Meitiv, "is that 'teaching independence clearly IS a crime.'" As Meitiv explained it, "the charge means 'something happened but kids were not at substantial risk.' Why then, she reasonably asks, 'find us responsible for neglect?'" Rosin correctly points out that "a charge of 'unsubstantiated' is not quite as definitively closed as 'ruled out.' (The third option is 'indicated,' the equivalent of guilty.)" And leaving that door open is going to put the Meitivs in a difficult position. Rosin rightly demands,

> CPS officials did not say they would keep an eye on the Meitivs. But now they have a charge of child neglect in their file. . . . They believe strongly that children

should be able to roam the neighborhood unsupervised. But they no doubt believe even more strongly that they don't want to be at any risk of having their children taken away from them for a second charge of neglect. Why on earth should the state have any right to put them in that predicament?[14]

Rosin was clearly reading the tea leaves, because there was a second incident in April 2015, when the Meitivs' two children were lured into a police cruiser just a third of a mile from home with promises of returning them to their parents. Instead, the kids were kept in the police car for hours and delivered to CPS while they were denied all requests to call their mother and father. When the Meitivs were finally notified that CPS had their kids and they went to pick them up, officials offered no explanation for why they'd been picked up or why the parents hadn't been informed for five hours. Seems the nanny state doesn't like dissent or challenges to its authority. (We'll see another case of this type of vindictiveness in Chapter 5, "The War on Fun.")

A group called Empower Kids Maryland was formed in response. The idea: To raise awareness among parents about encouraging "children to become independent, confident young adults with sound, non-fear-based judgment about the level of risk that will surround them in today's world," according to their website. Initially the group was focused on changing the laws in Maryland that were used to punish parents like the Meitivs. As cofounder Russell Max Simon explained it to me when we spoke in 2015, his kids play at the same playground as the Meitiv children, and he wants to raise independent children without government oversight or intervention. "Enough is enough," Simon told me. "Our focus is going to be working through the legislative process" to change the rules about children outside unsupervised. "This [issue] should cross political lines. It is a parental-rights issue not a right-left issue. I would think that parents would have more control over their kids. And I would hope that the politicians would agree" that the response to the Meitivs was "a waste of resources."

The case exemplifies the extent of the problem because Maryland authorities felt unrestrained enough to interpret the Meitiv's "crime" from words that aren't part of the applicable law. The rule had stated that children under 8 are prohibited from being unattended in a dwelling or car and that a person must be at least 13 years old to supervise a child under 8. There is no reference to being outside, and in this case there was no "supervising" going on. The 10-year-old was walking with his 6-year-old sister, not babysitting her.

On the bright side, the attention paid to the Meitiv case has been positive for the family; they've heard from CPS that they've been cleared of charges from the initial intervention. But any relief has to be tempered by the realization that it was only through very public and hard-fought resistance of the state authorities that CPS was pushed into doing the right thing. How many parents are going to have the self-confidence to reject state intervention? It is important to recognize that the Meitivs' got more attention than most of these cases. More often than not, CPS isn't forced to defend itself in the media, so reform is often slow or nonexistent. It is also good news that the advocacy group cofounded by Simon has now been re-named Empower Kids America and has broadened its mandate to include the rest of the country. The growth of groups and grass-roots activists in favor of parental discretion is all to the good. And there is other important work being done as well.

In Illinois, an organization called the Family Defense Center researched the issue of "inadequate supervision" child-neglect claims—similar to the charges against the Meitivs—and concluded that the Maryland case was both unique and typical. Unique because of all the media attention, which most families caught in an unnecessary CPS investigation don't receive. And typical because there are so many of this same type of accusation. The Family Defense Center report effectively stated the problem:

> The range of cases that may come to the attention of child welfare authorities is so broad that child abuse reporters, parents, and their advocates, as well as judges and policy makers are unable to clearly and consistently use existing law and policy to distinguish reasonable parenting from child neglect. . . . [P]arents are swept into the system and labeled at fault when they have made reasonable parenting decisions. Child welfare system resources are currently being devoted to the investigations of neglect allegations, such as inadequate supervision, where children are not at risk. This means fewer resources to investigate and indicate the serious cases of neglect or abuse.[15]

When definitions of a problem get too vague, more and more cases will occur; and when the laws are badly written or misapplied, innocent families are the ones who suffer. (We'll discuss problems with CPS lack of transparency more in Chapter 6.)

Back in Maryland, criminalizing parents for using their own discretion seems like something of a sport. A woman named Anna from Rockville wrote to Skenazy about being threatened by her daughter's school principal for letting the 10-year-old ride the city bus to school.[16] As the mom asserted to the busybody administrator, hers was a thoughtful decision. "We did a lot of planning and preparation before we allowed L. to ride the bus. As a parent I feel that it is my job to advocate for her right to practice this new skill, for as long as she wants to do

it and for as long as we her parents continue to feel it is safe."
But that wasn't good enough for the school, and the principal
threatened to consult with local Child Protective Services to
decide if allowing the girl to ride the bus was approved by those
authorities.

As this mother pointed out, the saddest part of this whole
affair was questioning a decision that was important for their
daughter's development and growth. As a result of riding the
bus each day, she'd developed a whole new set of relationships
with adults who rode with her. As the girl explained to her
mom, the adults she was referring to as friends weren't "kid
friends." Instead, she defined them as "people friends." The
mom learned about the Chinese lady, the lady with a baby
that cried a lot, and the grandma who got on at the next stop.
"In a few short weeks," the mom reported, "my daughter had
surrounded herself with a community of people who recognized her, who were happy to see her, and who surely would
step in if someone tried to hurt her." Isn't this exactly the type
of safety that we hope our kids achieve when they leave our
care? And shouldn't we embrace this girl's independence rather
than make her parent feel as if she's done something wrong to
allow it?

CRIMINALIZING PARENTS FOR TEACHING RESPONSIBILITY

In other states, parents have run afoul of the babysitting rules.
One mother in New Canaan, Connecticut, was arrested and
charged with "risk of injury to a minor" for allowing her older
children to babysit for younger ones.[17] Consider that a basic
aspect of families is that members are supposed to care for
one another. Is the law designed to contradict what are natural
bonds? And why is the decision of who is responsible enough
to babysit one that the government makes?

But arrest isn't as bad a losing custody of your kids. *The Atlantic*'s Colin Friedersdorf reported in July 2014 on a mother who had lost custody of her four children because she left them home alone together while taking a class at the local university.[18] She fought for four years—*four years*—to get her kids back, and as she told Friedersdorf, her whole attitude has changed.

> An unexpected knock at the door still makes my heart beat rapidly. I'm more conscious of strangers' stares and comments when I go out with my children. Ultimately, I found this ostensibly well-meaning system of child protection to be an exercise in often baseless finger-pointing, pitting neighbor against neighbor, family member against family member. As people vie for power and victory, it all becomes so much less about kids' best interests and more about adults' selfish interests. In criminalizing previously culturally normal activities, such as an unaccompanied child playing at a public park, we open the door for any unorthodox parental decision to be subjected to similar unfavorable scrutiny.

The *Washington Post*'s Radley Balko notes that from his perch as a chronicler of "the increasing criminalization of just about everything and the use of the criminal justice system to address problems that were once (and better) handled by families, friends, communities and other institutions," he has noticed a growing list of stories highlighting "those themes intersecting with parenthood."[19] Balko was upset by the Harrell case in South Carolina, as well as the arrest of Jeffrey Williamson of Blanchester, Ohio, for "child endangerment" because his son skipped church and went to play with friends instead. As with so many of these cases, nothing had happened to the boy.

Balko's criticism of these types of nanny-state interventions is right on; these problems used to be solved without police or child protective services, whereas today's overreaction is going to cause both parents and their children undue harm.

> You needn't approve of the parents' actions in any of these cases to understand that dumping them into the criminal justice system is a terribly counterproductive way of addressing their mistakes. (And I'm not at all convinced that three of the four stories were even mistakes.) The mere fact that state officials were essentially micromanaging these parents' decisions is creepy enough. That the consequences for the "wrong" decision are criminal is downright scary. It doesn't benefit these kids in the least to give their parents a criminal record, smear their parents' names in their neighborhoods and communities and make it more difficult for their parents to find a job.[20]

In their book *Practical Wisdom: The Right Way to Do the Right Thing*, Barry Schwartz and Kenneth Sharpe raise a similar question about who should decide when a risk is too great and who—if anyone—actually has the power to use their independent judgment to override the system, which has inserted itself into decisions that used to be made by parents and guardians without outside interference.

Schwartz and Sharpe tell the story of a father who took his son to a Detroit Tigers game. The seven-year-old boy asked for lemonade, and the father bought him a Mike's Hard Lemonade because that was all the concession stand had and he didn't know it was an alcoholic beverage (he's an archeology professor at the University of Michigan). A security guard saw the boy sipping the hard lemonade and called the police, who in turn called an ambulance. The boy was rushed to hospital where they found no trace of alcohol in his bloodstream. The story should have ended there as an example of overzealous concern on the part of police and ballpark security. But no. Instead, "police put the child in a Wayne County Child Protective Services foster home," where he stayed for three days. "Next, a judge ruled that the child could go home to his mother, but only if his dad left the house and checked into a hotel. . . . After two weeks the family was finally reunited," Schwartz and Sharpe explain.[21]

The authors note that at every stage the authority figures— the police, the judge, social workers—spoke of how they hated having to follow the rules but insisted that they had no choice; it was procedure. Shouldn't these people have the independent discretion to decide whether in each individual case the rules are actually being applied to protect kids or whether, as with the hard lemonade example, a parent made a mistake that should not be punished by breaking up his family? But commonsense judgments aren't allowed, argue Schwartz and Sharpe. "The policemen, the social workers, and the judge who took [the boy] away from his family, and then forbade his father to see him, were following rigid procedures that assumed that the judgment of these officials could not be trusted. As institutional practices like these become calcified, we lose our bead on the real aims and purposes of our work and fail to develop the moral skills we need to achieve them."[22]

NANNY STATE VS HEALTHY COMMUNITIES

Threatening parents for letting their kids learn independence is not just a waste of precious resources that police and social-service agents really don't have to spare. It harms our understanding of what it means to be part of a healthy and helpful community.

Children's book author Kari Anne Roy was visited by police and child services personnel in Austin, Texas, after her neighbor "returned" Roy's son to his house and informed police about her having allowed her six-year-old son Isaac to be outside unsupervised *down the block* from his house.[23] If a visit from a policewoman, who didn't file any report, it should be noted, wasn't bad enough, Roy then had to deal with a Child Protective Services agent who came to her house, interviewed her kids, and did file a report. When writing about this experience for the *Dallas Morning News*, Roy stipulated that she understood why child services workers have a hard job and even why some of the procedures the agent followed were necessary. But even with that understanding, the impact of this experience is not without a serious cost to her and her children.

> My kids reported that she asked questions about drugs and alcohol, about pornography, about how often they bathe, about fighting in the home. And again, I understand the need for these questions. I understand CPS investigators have an incredibly difficult job. But the conflict I feel is immense. My children were playing outside, within sight of the house, and now my 6-year-old and 8-year-old and 12-year-old have seen their mother spoken to—multiple times—as if she, herself, was a child being reprimanded. They have all been questioned, by a stranger, about whether they've ever been shown movies of other people's private parts. And no matter what I say, I can tell that they think they've done something wrong.[24]

Roy was also bothered, and rightly so, that the woman who originally called police cannot be held responsible for causing trouble. "The neighbor can call CPS as many times as she wants. If she truly feels there's neglect, she can't be prosecuted for making false allegations. We could try to sue her for harassment. We could try to press charges for kidnapping if she approaches our son again and tries to get him to move from where he's playing. But in all reality, when children are involved, the person who makes the complaint gets the benefit of the doubt. For parents, it is guilty until proven innocent."[25]

Tracy Cutchlow, a mom and journalist, wrote for the *Washington Post* identifying the reason there are more and more stories like this one of adults calling the police because they see a child alone—either in a car, at the playground, or walking.[26] "We can't rely on our neighbors to help look out for our kids, and that's why our neighborhoods don't feel safe enough. When you let a 10- and 6-year-old walk home on their own, it feels scary because they're fully responsible for their own safety. What's missing is the sense that we're all responsible for everyone's children," she explained. Everyone has heard the African proverb about bringing up our kids. But the conditions that underlay that folk wisdom are not always readily present. According to Cutchlow, "to reclaim any sense of the village it takes to raise a child, we need to start with knowing our neighbors. I don't know half of the people living in my condo building, let alone on my street. How about you?"

ANOTHER TYPE OF STORY that has become too common is about parents who choose to leave their children in a car unattended in order to run a quick errand and are found guilty of a crime by the nanny state.

Kim Brooks wrote in *Salon* of her ordeal (100 hours of community service, lawyer bills, conviction for contributing to the delinquency of a minor) because police were given a recording of her son sitting alone in a car.[27] Brooks had to run into the store, and her four-year-old son didn't want to tag along. She decided to let him wait for her in the car. How did the police get involved in the first place? Why didn't they tell the busybody recording this nonincident to mind her own business because they have other things to do?

New Yorker Alina Adams made sure that the law couldn't come after her before she admitted in print that she lets her six-year-old daughter stay home alone for short stretches of time. And just like every other time she's loosened the parental leash on her three children, this change came about by necessity. But as a matter of principle, Adams rejects the need for laws defining when children can be on their own. As she explained it to me, "I'm not a fan of arbitrary guidelines. I'm against mandatory minimums for kindergarten or retirement. [I'm] against government making that decision because it is an arbitrary rule without seeing what's going on."

Adams believes that every child is different, making each situation different as well. But that's not good enough for nanny-statists who are convinced they are "saving the kids" by pushing for these laws. The one-size-fits-all solution is the only one government can handle, and so we get rules and regulations that interfere with parents' choices rather than supporting them.

How did we get here? Skenazy is right that raising independent children used to be a value that society embraced. Indeed, television used to depict this independence as part of normal life. Take a look at the first few episodes of *Leave It to Beaver*, for example. The narrative is repeated in several episodes. The Beav goes off alone to walk to school, or into town to get a haircut, and some innocent trouble ensues. The first episode aired in 1957, when the Beav was supposed to be eight years old, and at that time the show's writers took it for granted that a kid that age could and would go places alone. Now, you may be thinking, well, that was the time before crime rates exploded and the cities became dangerous. But standards of childhood independence were normative in the late 1970s as well. As Petula

Dvorak pointed out in the *Washington Post*, the 1979 standards of readiness for first grade (six-year-olds!) included answering the following questions in the affirmative:

- Can your child tell, in such a way that his speech is understood by a school crossing guard or police, where he lives?

- Can he travel alone in the neighborhood (four to eight blocks) to store, school, playground, or to a friend's home?

- Can he be away from you all day without being upset?[28]

Such a checklist would be deemed completely inappropriate today, except for the last one, maybe. But why should standards of self-reliance have changed so dramatically? There are various answers.

For Schwartz and Sharpe, the biggest issue is our society's lost moral will, which they prefer to call practical wisdom, otherwise known as common sense. We need an "antidote to a society gone mad with bureaucracy" they argue, but that kind of personal judgment is simply not something our current culture will tolerate. We have decided we need rules, standards, and regulations to make our children safer, and we are not allowed to ignore those standards and regulations for the sake of our children's development or in favor of our own judgment. Police, judges, and child-welfare workers, meanwhile—those who are supposed to be enforcing the rules—aren't allowed the discretion to decide whether the rules are being correctly applied.

As Scott Simon remarked on *NPR* in regard to the "hard lemonade" case, "[T]he public officials involved . . . needed practical wisdom and the discretion to exercise it."[29] Schwartz and Sharpe believe practical wisdom is a skill that can be nurtured and taught if we were to develop the "institutions to nurture it." But they see our society moving in the opposite direction. "In our ever more corporate, and bureaucratic culture, constant demands for efficiency, accountability and profit have led to an increasing reliance on rules and incentives to control behavior," they argue.[30]

LACK OF FREEDOM COSTS OUR KIDS AND OUR COMMUNITIES

Philippe Petit, tightrope artist and author of *Creativity: The Perfect Crime*, says there is no intuition or creativity without practice, and that requires that parents trust their kids. "[M]y proposal is to not open a door and, you know, propel the kids forward, but to open the door a tiny bit and have the kid use it, moving the door that was ajar. Now it's full. And then they're going to discover; they're going to explore with their own way of thinking, their own intuition and improvisation. And then, yes, the adult is there to make sure there's no accident."[31]

Petit is describing a commonsense approach and the willingness to allow for failure. Trial and error is a basic method of learning, and it demands both halves of that pairing. Without stumbles, failures, and risks (horrifying as the latter word may be to our ears), we cannot inculcate skills important to kids' development and character.

Psychologist Peter Grey talks a lot about creativity and skills that are lost because kids are not allowed to be alone, unsupervised, or spend unstructured time with other kids. When Grey interviewed Danielle Meitiv, he noted that her children appeared self-assured. "When we assume that children are irresponsible, they may behave irresponsibly (partly because they have so little opportunity to practice responsibility), which reinforces our initial assumption. It's a vicious cycle. My own experience has been that children almost desperately want to take responsibility, for as much of their own lives as they can handle, and when allowed and trusted to do so they rise to the occasion and feel proud and happy."[32]

Meitiv seconded Grey's view, explaining that "given the opportunity, kids often prove to be much more capable than we expect. My own kids have done so numerous times." But state institutions are not interested in this essential road to adulthood. Meitiv explained that not only did they have this terrible experience with the local police and child protective services, but that her children's school personnel have also repeatedly undermined her choices to allow her kids their own independence. Their only basis for this interference, she claims, is that "anything can happen." Meitiv told Grey how she'd turned this mania into a game with her elder son. We speculate "about the 'anythings' that could happen. Aliens could abduct him from the hallways! Rampaging wildebeests could trample him! An asteroid could flatten the one classroom where he is doing his homework. Sadly, one thing we don't expect anytime soon is an outbreak of logic or common sense." (We will further discuss stifling creativity by quelling independence and self-reliance in Chapter 5.)

A lack of grit and stick-to-itiveness among children has become a hot topic in education recently as well. As Tough explains in *How Children Succeed*, parents should want to engender traits like conscientiousness, self-control, curiosity, and perseverance in their kids since those are better indicators of success and satisfaction and the kind of future we want for our kids.[33] But as these many examples of government interference show, the teaching of self-reliance and self-control to children is unacceptable to the nanny state when practiced by parents rather than as part of a school's curriculum.

Grit was also the subject of the February 2013 *Harvard Education Letter*, discussing the importance of certain character traits for students' academic success. "We have really good research showing the correlation between perseverance and grit and student success," Boston University assistant professor of education Scott Seider was quoted as saying. "But there is very, very little research that demonstrates that we can take the level of grit or perseverance that a kid has and increase it."[34] This is crucial. Seider is right: Schools can't find a way to increase grit and perseverance in kids because those are character traits, and character traits are effectively taught by parents, not teachers. Yet when parents naturally demand such characteristics from their children, as when Debra Harrell believed her child capable of minding herself while her mother worked, police and child services come along to punish and criminalize parental discretion. So not only aren't we encouraging families to build up our children's positive character traits, the state is actively denouncing and degrading those families that are providing their kids what professionals have decided is a significant advantage to their future success.

Kari Anne Roy knows that her kids and others are going to pay some kind of price for the society in which they are being raised. "What I want to talk about are children who don't feel safe outside—not because of stranger-danger or threat of immediate injury, but because the police will be called if they're just playing like we played when we were young. What will members of the Always on Screens Generation be like when they're adults? When they weren't afforded the ability to play and explore and test limits and problem-solve, when everything was sanitized and supervised, when the crimes committed against them were more likely to happen online than in the park across the street? What will this do? How will society be affected?"[35]

Captain Mommy Roy is coming at the problem of self-assurance from the other side. What will happen to the kids who have developed a fear of police (from being interviewed without their parents about their parents and their home life) and at the same time have been shoved inside their homes because their parents fear allowing them any freedom? Can such children grow up to be the self-assured, independent, entrepreneurial, and fearless adults we so often say we want to ensure that our economy grows and our society improves? And what of these future adults' sense of responsibility for their neighbors and other residents of their communities? Will the experience of having a neighbor call the police on their parents really engender a sense of shared mission with those who live on the same block or in the same apartment complex?

As Michael Brendan Dougherty wrote in *The Week*, the fraying of our communal fabric is not a positive development.

> The decline of neighborhood solidarity isn't universal across America, and it seems far more advanced among upwardly mobile neighborhoods than in working class areas. But it's one of the most obvious and profound changes I've noticed in my own day-to-day life. And it makes me suspect I won't be able to give my children the independence that I know is best for them.[36]

Dougherty is right that he is going to face opposition should he try to give his children the gift of their independence. But there is another concern as well. In her book about resilient cities, president of the Rockefeller Foundation Judith Rodin argues that when neighborhoods lack solidarity, it is harder for neighbors to function effectively as first responders in the face of emergencies and crises. Neighbors who are strangers and who call the police on others' kids, rather than concerning themselves with the fate of an unaccompanied child, are less ready to help out when the inevitable crisis hits the local community. And a crisis will come, says Rodin. She argues in

The Resilience Dividend that since "crisis is the new normal," it is ever more important to develop our resilience, which she defined in the *Huffington Post* as "the capacity for an entity—individual, business, community—to plan for a disaster and rebuild more effectively and adapt and grow in the face of disaster."[37]

"Communities that know one another and trust one another are more resilient in times of disaster because often your neighbor is your first responder no matter how effective the official response network. If you don't know your neighbor and they are not willing to act for you and you for them you are simply less resilient." Even though her book is about responding to emergencies, Rodin has an important lesson to teach parents, police, administrators, and authorities about improving children's lives. Neighbors who get to know one another, meet each other, and connect because of their physical proximity are much less likely to call the police, as one neighbor did to Kari Anne Roy. Instead of needlessly bringing in the authorities, children and parents can learn to trust their community a little more and, hopefully, if necessary, even help one another in an emergency.

TO CHANGE THE CULTURE, CHANGE THE LAW

After nearly a decade of fighting for parents' rights to choose for themselves the level of freedom to allow their offspring, Skenazy believes it is time for laws to reflect that value as well. The current message to kids is harmful, she says. "The world is not perfect—it never was—but we used to trust our children in it, and they learned to be resourceful," Skenazy told the *New York Times*. "The message these anxious parents are giving to their children is 'I love you, but I don't believe in you. I don't believe you're as competent as I am.' "[38]

She's written a kids' and parents' bill of rights that she hopes to get legislated everywhere as soon as possible. The proposed legislation reads in part:

> [T]his legislature decrees that children may walk, cycle, take public transportation and/or play outside by themselves, with the permission of a parent or guardian.
>
> Allowing children to exercise these rights shall not be grounds for civil or criminal charges against their parents or guardians, nor shall it be grounds for investigation by child protective services, removal of the children from their family home, or termination of parental rights.[39]

Skenazy's proposed law also deals with the epidemic of parents accused of neglect for choosing to have their kids wait in the car while they run a quick errand. This parental-rights legislation aims to increase common sense and lessen the regulatory burden as well. "More children die in parking lots than die waiting in parked cars while their caregivers run an errand," it states. "The majority of children who die in parked cars were forgotten there for hours or got into the car unbeknownst to anyone and could not get out," the legislation continues.

> Punishing parents who let their children wait in the car for five minutes will not bring back the children forgotten there for five hours.
>
> Therefore, parents should be allowed to make their own decisions, based on the location, temperature, and duration of their errand, as to whether or not they wish to let their child wait in the car.
>
> Laws against children waiting unsupervised for a short amount of time in a parked car shall be repealed.

There is good reason to hope that Skenazy is successful, even apart from protecting the rights of parents to bring up their own children. Legal reform might ease the way for more of today's children to be allowed to gain the skills necessary for adulthood. Several recent books and articles suggest that, especially among many young people who go to college, adulthood and responsibility are about the last thing they are capable of.

Some of this comes from overprotective parenting, to be sure. And indeed, former Stanford University dean Julie Lythcott-Haims writes in *How to Raise an Adult* about her first-hand experience dealing with college students over the past two decades and how often basic life skills are missing among what is otherwise an accomplished group. What once came naturally is now not happening within the process of maturation at all. Lythcott-Haims claims

> [t]here's a scarcity of information on how one acquires life skills, presumably because children who are otherwise healthy and developing normally used to develop these skills naturally in the normal course of childhood, and we're only just beginning to recognize that these skills are missing in many children and must be affirmatively taught.[40]

In August 2015, well-known social psychologist Jonathan Haidt and noted civil-liberties and free-speech crusader Greg Lukianoff wrote a startling piece for *The Atlantic* chronicling the same desperate problem described by Lythcott-Haims, namely, the trouble with young people and their difficulty dealing with mature responsibilities. "The current movement [on college campuses]," they wrote, "is largely about emotional well-being.... [I]t presumes an extraordinary fragility of the collegiate psyche, and therefore elevates the goal of protecting students from psychological harm."[41] The authors then chronicle the impact this angry protectiveness—that is, punishing those who attempt to interfere with the goal—has on the students themselves.

"Vindictive protectiveness," Haidt and Lukianoff declare, "teaches students to think in a very different way . . . [preparing] them poorly for professional life, which often demands intellectual engagement with people and ideas one might find uncongenial or wrong." Having to engage with people who think and act differently than yourself is supposed to be a function of adult life, not just a job requirement. The authors argue there is a more immediate impact as well: "A campus culture devoted to policing speech and punishing speakers is likely to engender patterns of thought that are surprisingly similar to those long identified by cognitive behavioral therapists as causes of depression and anxiety."[42]

And lo, depression, anxiety, and drug and alcohol abuse are now more prevalent on college campuses than ever before. No one is saying there is a straight-line correlation between how kids are raised and their inability to handle open debate and opinions with which they disagree. But as we've noted throughout this chapter, parents who embrace their role as guides to adulthood, including developing their children's grit, self-reliance, and psychological and physical independence—what Lythcott-Haims calls "affirmatively" teaching life skills—run up against the nanny state.

Sociologist Frank Furedi argues that we are getting the wrong outcomes—the outcomes Haidt, Lukianoff, and Lythcott-Haims decry—because we are misunderstanding what children need to succeed and providing exactly the wrong tools.

> The tragedy is that the best way to protect children is to cultivate their aspiration for independence and autonomy. It is through the experience gained from engaging with the world that children gain the resources to manage risks and develop strategies for dealing with

threats to their personhood. Sadly, in the current cli-
mate of child protection, parents are discouraged from
doing precisely what is likely to provide their kids with
the existential security they need to make their way in
the world.[43]

It may seem like a Sisyphean task to change these laws.
But Skenazy is correctly pushing for legal reform at the local
and state level because these decisions should be debated and
decided locally, and a single federal standard is neither work-
able nor desirable.

It is useful to remember, too, that not long ago a group of
parents had to fight tooth and nail to change the laws so that
they could raise their own kids as they saw fit: what started as
a trickle became a tidal wave of reform for homeschool education. As described by Dana Mack in her book *The Assault on
Parenthood*, the Captain Mommies of the 1970s and '80s were
"home schooling families ... [who] often ran afoul of com-
pulsory school attendance laws, their children labeled 'truants.'
Many of them were forced to battle criminal charges in court,
and there were even cases of children being carted off to foster
homes by welfare workers."[44]

Why did parents in practically every state in the union
have to fight local authorities and ordinances to be allowed to
keep their kids home to learn? Mack quotes homeschooling
advocate Stephen Arons for the answer. According to Arons,
homeschooling "threatened the educational establishment by
implicitly attacking its claims to professional status" (that you
needed to have a teaching certificate in order to educate kids)
"and by challenging the indispensability of school services to
families and children."[45]

Mack argues that the homeschooling fights were part of a
bigger problem. She says the larger issue is "a contest over what

have become two distinct political cultures in our nation: the political culture promoted by extra familial child-rearing institutions versus the political culture promoted by families."[46] It seems that, a generation after the homeschooling fights of the 1970s and '80s, the new battleground between parental authority and the official authority is childhood independence.

CHAPTER 2

Breast Is Best, *or Else*

Advocating for breastfeeding isn't enough —it has to be the law

"YOU ARE TALKING about my body as if it is state property,"
Captain Mommy Suzanne Barston complained when we spoke
by phone. Which part of the body is the activist blogger and author talking about? Barston was referring to all the government
regulations, policies, and requirements when it comes to wom-
en's breasts, or more specifically how a woman's choice whether
or not to breastfeed is a matter of national interest.

Barston is an advocate for what she calls "feeding freedom," and in her book *Bottled Up*[1] and blog *Fearless Formula
Feeder*,[2] she chronicles the personal experiences of those who
feel pressured to breastfeed and the coverage of scientific studies that promote breastfeeding as the best—really, only morally
good—way to feed a baby. She writes that breastfeeding should
be "an empowering personal choice rather than a government-
mandated, fear-induced act." Surely she must exaggerate when
she says the government sees her boobs as state property? As
we shall see, however, she's not exaggerating. Instead, Barston
has her work cut out for her, in part because cities, states, and
most of all the federal government are pulling multiple levers to
promote this particular behavior.

• • •

MICHAEL BLOOMBERG may be the former mayor of New York City, but he'll always be emperor of Nannyville, USA. And he's certainly among those who Barston argues see a mother's breasts as national treasures requiring government protection. During his time as mayor, Bloomberg enacted bans on smoking in public places and trans-fats, and he tried to ban large-sized sodas. But his biggest triumph has got to be the breastfeeding mandate of 2012, which—similar to Iranian law[3]—essentially makes infant formula a controlled substance.

According to recommendations of the Latch On NYC initiative, city hospitals must not only remove the free formula goodie bag that used to be available to mothers in the hospital, but they must also keep formula under lock and key. If a mother requests it, hospital staff administers formula as if it were prescription medication or a narcotic. Moreover, before the mother can get a bottle to feed her kid, she's got to sign a waiver stating that she understands she's making the "less healthy" choice for her baby.[4]

When New York says it wants to "support" breastfeeding, the underlying argument is that only human breast milk is safe for babies. After all, in announcing the program, Thomas Farley, then-commissioner of public health for New York City, claimed that "formula feeding markedly increases serious health risks for infants" and that lower breastfeeding rates "result in excess health care costs and preventable infant illness and death." The millions of mothers who have chosen not to breastfeed would not recognize the characterization of formula as virtually a poison.

Peggy O'Mara, founder of *Mothering* magazine, has certainly internalized the formula-is-poison message. "It is naïve to believe that the formula industry's distribution of formula to you is an innocent gift," she wrote in her magazine about the free diaper swag for new mothers.[5] "A 'gift' of formula is like a 'gift' of a pack of cigarettes when you're trying to quit smoking; it will undermine your resolve," O'Mara wrote.

When the New York City program was announced, it was proudly deemed necessary for public health reasons. "Human breast milk is best for babies and mothers," Latch On claims.[6] The program has four basic elements.

1. Enforce the [New York State] hospital regulation to not supplement breastfeeding infants with formula feeding unless medically indicated and documented on the infant's medical chart;

2. Restrict access to infant formula by hospital staff, tracking infant formula distribution and sharing data on formula distribution with the Health Department;

3. Discontinue the distribution of promotional or free infant formula; and

4. Prohibit the display and distribution of infant formula promotional materials in any hospital location.[7]

"When babies receive supplementary formula in the hospital or mothers receive promotional baby formula on hospital discharge it can impede the establishment of an adequate milk supply and can undermine women's confidence in breastfeeding," Latch On promotional materials declare.

This extreme sort of language about the "need" to breastfeed and the "risk" of formula didn't come as too much of a shock to my sister-in-law, who described how pervasive the lactation dogma was even before the new mandate took effect. When my niece was born in 2010 in New York City, she was delivered early by C-section, and in the 24 hours after her birth, her weight and other measurements had landed her in the NICU.

My sister-in-law was understandably eager to do anything she could to help her child, but it took 24 hours before one nurse quietly suggested that my niece's weight and other "numbers" would go up if my sister-in-law would agree to give the child a bottle of formula. "They'd let her out of here if she gains a little," the commonsense staffer advised.

When my sister-in-law described this scene more than two years later, it was obvious she was still angry, and justifiably so. "Why didn't they just tell me in the first place that formula would help," she fumed. "I was pumping anyways, so what did it matter if I just stored all that milk and they gave the baby a bottle?"

The Latch On mandate did surprise some others, however. Gayle Tzemach Lemmon reacted in *The Atlantic*. "Women who have ... decided—for whatever personal reason—to feed their newborns formula, will now have to justify their reasoning before they are given access to it. When, exactly, exercising a personal right about what to do for your child (and with your own body) became a public statement, open to the city's files and others' judgment, is unclear."[8] As Barston argues, the state seems to be asserting a right over women's bodies that some like Lemmon identify as breathtakingly broad and audacious.

New York City isn't the only metropolitan area taking up this cause, though. Portland, Oregon, banned free formula samples in 2007,[9] and, as of August 2014, all of Philadelphia's birthing hospitals agreed[10] to "ban the bags"[11]—the name for the national campaign to stop mothers' receiving free infant formula at the hospital.

Why the fuss about freebie formula? "What companies have done is co-opted health-care providers into doing their marketing for them," explains Marsha Walker,[12] who is executive director of the National Alliance for Breastfeeding Advocacy. Removing free formula, therefore, means that moms are supposedly only now able to make an unbiased choice between breast and bottle. "It is still the choice of the mom if she breast-feeds or not," but now she is making the decision free of marketing influence, said Katja Pigur, who led the Philadelphia ban-the-bag campaign for the Maternity Care Coalition.[13]

The argument against free formula is that mothers who might otherwise commit to breastfeeding may become "discouraged" or "break down" and give their babies some too-readily-available formula if they are having any complication with nursing, and that in turn will discourage keeping to exclusive breastfeeding going forward. What breastfeeding advocates want to prevent is mothers feeding their kids formula at all, so they want to make getting your hands on it as difficult as possible.

These zealots do have a point about the work required to breastfeed. Mothers' milk does take time to come in after birth, and getting used to breastfeeding and generating an adequate milk supply does require a level of time, energy, and commitment that isn't required when mixing formula. Powdered infant formula gets mixed with water and can then immediately be given to baby. Also, breastfeeding advocates worry aloud about "nipple confusion" if infants are given the breast and then a bottle before they've become accustomed to the harder work of nursing. In addition, the flow through a bottle nipple is quicker than a woman's breast, which critics of bottle feeding say is another reason to stick with exclusive breastfeeding, though it is important to note that even the most ardent breastfeeding advocate will urge mothers to supplement with formula when medically required.

The question is how hard hospitals will make the rational decision to feed babies with formula. Will it be an easily accessible choice, or will new moms have to send their husbands, mothers, grandfathers, friends, or a friendly nurse to Costco or the nearest supermarket to get a can of formula while they are still in the hospital recovering? As new mothers may not be

directly aware but can no doubt sense, there is a web of organizations at the global and local levels that have made it their
agenda to demonize formula and promote breastfeeding as the
only acceptable method of nourishing infants.

PUMPING UP BREASTFEEDING: 1. GLOBAL

The World Health Organization (WHO), which is pushing its
Baby-Friendly Hospital Initiative (BFHI) in the United States
and across the globe, would love for formula to be as difficult
to get as possible. "Launched in 1991, [BFHI] is an effort by
UNICEF and the World Health Organization to ensure that
all maternities, whether free standing or in a hospital, become
centers of breastfeeding support," the UNICEF website declares. And according to their "About Us" statement, breast
milk is really the only correct choice.

> Human milk fed through the mother's own breast is
> the normal way for human infants to be nourished. . . .
> Breastfeeding is the natural biological conclusion to
> pregnancy and an important mechanism for the con-
> tinued normal development of the infant. With the
> correct information and the right supports in place, un-
> der normal circumstances, most women who choose to
> breastfeed are able to successfully achieve their goal.

There is no qualification here. The "normal" and "correct"
choice is mother's milk, and if every mom would just try hard
enough and get enough encouragement from the institution
where she gives birth, the goal of exclusive breastfeeding can
be realized. Of course, the Baby-Friendly designation comes
with strict rules for the institutions that choose to sign up for
certification. These rules include the means for getting most
everyone to breastfeed and include an anti-formula perspective.

For instance, supplementing baby's food at all is discouraged. "Give infants no food or drink other than breast-milk, unless medically indicated," WHO says. Also, since they want staff to "encourage breastfeeding on demand," to be baby-friendly means practicing "rooming in—allow[ing] mothers and infants to remain together 24 hours a day." This is nice in theory but hard on mom in practice. Having just given birth, most moms are in need of rest; but since the breastfeeding police want you to jump at every opportunity to breastfeed, mom is going to spend most of her time listening for baby rather than sleeping. Finally, WHO doesn't want anyone to offer baby pacifiers or "artificial nipples to breastfeeding infants," lest baby develop any attachment other than to mama's milk supply.[14] The fact that babies suck for comfort as well as for food seems to be of no concern to the "experts" at WHO.

Each hospital and maternity ward could and does come up with their own policies about infant feeding, but as one former hospital administrator explained to me, many institutions will take every opportunity to market themselves as the "best" place to give birth. If a globally recognized organization is telling them to institute a few rules to receive a stamp of approval—like baby-friendly—so much the better. Here the standards have been developed and corresponding educational materials created for the sole purpose of getting staff to institute "baby-friendly" procedures. And the whole process is free, almost. There was a study done for the University of Texas' Health Sciences Center to gauge the price of BFHI, but even though results showed that "first year marginal costs will approximate $110 per delivery (birth)" and that "BF hospitals have around a 2% higher cost structure than non-baby-friendly facilities," the researchers believe it is worth it.[15] As my hospital administrator friend put it, "the hospital is thinking of marketing itself to the whole family, not just the baby." She added that when a hospital is focused on gaining the business of every family member and not just performing a single service, like a delivery, then anything that gives them a way to signal they are a leader in quality services, like being baby-friendly, will be deemed worthy.

PUMPING UP BREASTFEEDING: 2. STATE

The hospitals working to earn the World Health Organization–defined label "baby friendly" for banning formula giveaways and the entire cities riding the breast-is-best bandwagon aren't alone in their zeal to promote exclusive breastfeeding.

Five states—California, Illinois, Minnesota, Missouri, and Vermont—and Puerto Rico "have implemented or encouraged the development of a breastfeeding awareness education campaign," reports the National Conference of State Legislators. Twenty-seven states, the District of Columbia, and Puerto Rico have laws related to breastfeeding in the workplace.[16]

Two states—Rhode Island and Massachusetts—have banned distribution of free samples of formula to moms in hospital.[17] And New Jersey is also eager to promote breastfeeding, but at least the state seems to be going about the effort with some humility; while actively promoting breastfeeding to maternity hospitals and staff, State Health Commissioner Mary E. O'Dowd says she doesn't favor banning free formula, à la New York City, since there are moms who may not want to or may not be able to breastfeed.[18]

These city and state breastfeeding encouragement efforts are supported by the enthusiasm and rigid pronouncements of multiple members of the medical profession, which have become more and more rigid in recent years. The American Academy of Pediatrics (AAP), which used to be on the side of all mothers whether they breast or bottle fed, is now squarely in the breast-or-else camp.

As Joan Wolf chronicles, in 1982 the AAP issued a statement reiterating their support for breastfeeding but also criticizing other groups like the World Health Organization for taking a "limited approach to an issue that is complex and involves extensive social, economic, and motivational factors ... particularly evident for the situation in the United States."[19]

Back then, Wolf explains, the AAP argued that significant differences existed between breastfeeding and bottle-feeding mothers and that the actual effects of breastfeeding were "difficult to isolate." AAP concluded that pediatricians should "work to improve the knowledge of all potential expectant and current parents on optimal infant feeding nutrition, emphasizing the positive aspects of breast-feeding and the proper choice and utilization of breast milk substitutes." In short, the AAP argued that breastfeeding was preferable but that formula was an acceptable alternative.

By 2012 that balance was long gone. The AAP's more one-sided policy statement now reads in part:

> Breastfeeding and human milk are the normative standards for infant feeding and nutrition. Given the documented short- and long-term medical and neuro-developmental advantages of breastfeeding, infant nutrition should be considered a public health issue and not only a lifestyle choice. The American Academy of Pediatrics reaffirms its recommendation of exclusive breastfeeding for about 6 months.[20]

The American Medical Association; Association of Maternal and Child Health Programs; Association of Women's Health, Obstetric, and Neonatal Nurses; Center for Male and Family Research and Resources; March of Dimes Birth Defects Foundation; National Association of Pediatric Nurse Practitioners; and American Dietetic Association are on board with the

AAP's message. Meanwhile, the American Congress of Obstetricians and Gynecologists (ACOG) so favors breastfeeding that it doesn't make room for women's free will. "Breastfeeding is the preferred method of feeding for newborns and infants," the ACOG declares. "Nearly every woman can breastfeed her child. Exceptions are few."[21] In the ACOG's mindset, the only decision to be made about infant feeding is what is preferable for the baby. The mother's circumstances, finances, family structure, and preferences seem to have no place in the decision.

Then there is the web of breastfeeding advocates, from La Leche League to local breastfeeding centers to national campaigns to promote breastfeeding awareness and rights. Breastfeeding USA ("empowering you with mother-to-mother support"), Breastmilk Counts ("every ounce counts"), Project Breastfeeding (which is geared toward men with the slogan "If I Could I Would"), the United States Breastfeeding Committee (National Breastfeeding month), and WHO's World Breastfeeding week are just a small sample of the mass of nursing information and propaganda hurled upon new parents.

PUMPING UP BREASTFEEDING: 3. FEDERAL

By far the greatest effort to promote breastfeeding comes from various agencies of the US government. The goal is to raise breastfeeding rates and to lengthen the time mothers nurse. The ideal, upon which much of the breastfeeding research is based, is at least six months of exclusive breastfeeding.

The U.S. Department of Agriculture's Women, Infants, and Children (WIC) program, the Special Supplemental Nutrition Program for Infants and Women, serves the poorest Americans. Piloted in 1972 and aimed at curbing malnutrition among mothers of infants, the program started out serving 88,000 eligible recipients, who received benefits including infant formula.

Infant formula is still among the benefits received by the approximately 9 million women, infants, and children up to age five who are served by WIC today. At a cost of $7 billion a year on average, the USDA (which administers the program) claims that nationwide 53 percent of all infants born in the United States receive WIC benefits. But if the government was providing formula as a way of helping poor mothers 40 years ago, today its attention is focused on breastfeeding.

According to Massachusetts Department of Public Health Commissioner Cheryl Bartlett, who oversees WIC for the Bay State, WIC has changed and evolved over the years. Its focus used to be providing subsidized formula to mothers, whereas today its focus is on nutrition, health, and wellness. Recently, program administrators have emphasized the dangers of obesity and promoted breastfeeding as one way to prevent babies from becoming overweight, Bartlett says.

The USDA WIC website says "mothers are encouraged to breastfeed their infants. WIC has historically promoted breastfeeding to all pregnant women as the optimal infant feeding choice, unless medically contraindicated."[22] Besides the supposed health benefits for mom and baby, WIC beneficiaries who opt to breastfeed get more goodies. Some of the benefits to breastfeeding moms include "a higher level of priority for program certification; a greater quantity and variety of foods than mothers who do not breastfeed; a longer certification period than non-breastfeeding mothers; one-to-one support through peer counselors and breastfeeding experts; and breast pumps and other aids to help support the initiation and continuation of breastfeeding." Got that? The US government promises preferential treatment in the form of an easier time getting certified for benefits, more benefits plus extras like lactation consultants and breast pumps, and a longer eligibility period for those who make the "right" choice regarding how to feed their babies.

If the good folks at WIC really wanted to raise breastfeeding rates among their client base, however, they could opt for a much simpler solution: stop handing out free formula. "If I had to buy formula, with no WIC vouchers, I'd breast-feed," Alia Brooks, a teenage single mom in Baltimore, told the *New York Times* columnist Nicholas Kristof in June 2015.[23] Kristof was writing about health problems among poor Americans and, per the current dogma, reinforced the idea that breastfeeding is the best way to feed an infant. He used his exchange with Brooks to chastise WIC—an otherwise "valuable program," he wrote—for "unintentionally discouraging" breastfeeding by providing free formula. Kristof's complaint would have hit closer to the mark if he'd had his facts straight since, as we know, WIC is promoting breastfeeding.

As a result of breastfeeding promotion efforts like this, the lactation consultant business is booming, and WIC, through many of its 50 state agencies, has devoted resources to create promotional videos about how breastfeeding is the best choice for mom and baby. How a state finds the money for "free" breast pumps is a matter for each individual office's discretion, but the means may include taking money away from the food budget to pay for the pumps.

The allocation of breast pumps for WIC recipients isn't really a problem, though, since even if you aren't on WIC, you can now get a free breast pump through the Affordable Care Act. As the healthcare.gov website states, "Health insurance plans must provide breastfeeding support, counseling, and equipment for the duration of breastfeeding. These services may be provided before and after you have your baby."[24] Just as lactation consultants got a job boost from changes to WIC, breast-pump manufacturers and distributors saw an explosion in demand for pumps since Obamacare mandated their inclusion.

"The law states that we must provide rental pumps," United Healthcare spokesman Matthew Stearns told the *Washington Post*. But since insurers understand consumers want to buy rather than rent a pump, they devised a clever solution, Stearns explained. "We are providing women the option of getting a personal pump in lieu of renting the more-expensive pump."[25] The cost of buying the pumps is reflected in higher premiums because insurers pass on the government-mandated benefit to their customers.

Breast pumps and lactation consultants aren't the only "support" women are getting through the $1 trillion Patient Protection and Affordable Care Act. Thanks to page 1239 of the law, employers are now required to provide "a place, other than a bathroom, that is shielded from view and free from intrusion from co-workers and the public, which may be used by an employee to express breast milk." Only companies with fewer than 50 employees can claim it's an undue hardship to have to find such a space.

The idea for pumping rooms and lactation rights for working mothers didn't originate with Obamacare. The idea was already known around Capitol Hill, especially with the introduction in 2009 of Rep. Carolyn Maloney's Breastfeeding Promotion Act. The Democrat from New York was aiming to create tax incentives for employers to "encourage" female employees to breastfeed by promoting pumping facilities at work. Captain Mommy Suzanne Barston is troubled, though, by the language involved. "Maloney's literature uses the argument that not breastfeeding is a public health threat, listing the requisite statistics about reduction of disease, even though few studies have controlled for whether the babies categorized as 'breastfed' were cared for at home (like the majority of truly exclusively breastfed babies would need to be) or in germ-ridden daycare centers." The other problem with the legislation, according to Barston, is that the case for better pumping rights "leans heavily on the claim that more breastfeeding leads to less employee absenteeism due to sick kids, but this claim rests on shaky ground."[26]

Obamacare took Maloney's legislation and folded it into its mass of health regulations and changed it from an incentive program into a mandate. After all, when it comes to finding ways of changing people's—in this case, women's—behavior, the lever the government knows best is brute force of law. It isn't enough to count on employers to voluntarily encourage their employees to breastfeed by providing them with a place to pump because, according to the authorities, it is a national priority to increase the number of women who breastfeed and the amount of time they nurse.

The Department of Health and Human Services is pushing breastfeeding by others means, however, not just through Obamacare. According to HHS' Healthy People 2020 Objectives for Maternal, Infant, and Child Health,

> The cognitive and physical development of infants and children is influenced by the health, nutrition, and behaviors of their mothers during pregnancy and early childhood. Breast milk is widely acknowledged to be the most complete form of nutrition for most infants, with a range of benefits for their health, growth, immunity, and development. Furthermore, children reared in safe and nurturing families and neighborhoods, free from maltreatment and other social adversities, are more likely to have better outcomes as adults.[27]

At womenshealth.gov (2013 budget: $34 million[28]), which is also a resource of HHS, the rhetoric seems more balanced: "The decision to breastfeed is a personal one. As a new mom, you deserve support no matter how you decide to feed your baby.

You should not be made to feel guilty if you cannot or choose not to breastfeed."[29] But look a little closer at the information provided and the links for further reading, and you see more of a one-sided discussion. The many HHS-run web pages devoted to describing healthy childrearing exclude even a single reference to best practices or healthy outcomes when feeding your baby formula.

There's also a racial aspect to the government-promoted breast-is-best dogma, namely a focus on pressing women in the African American community to breastfeed for as long as possible. *It's Only Natural*, which is a section of the womens health.gov[30] site, has material devoted to "addressing breastfeeding myths," which reads as if government experts are the only trustworthy source of wisdom on the issue.

"Have you been hearing conflicting stories and opinions about breastfeeding from family and friends? Get the real facts and helpful advice here," the site urges. But take a moment to consider that claim, and you realize the point is to usurp the role of tradition and experience with the preferences of the state. Due to the statistics showing that breastfeeding rates are lower among African Americans than among whites (note to feds: there is the nearly the same discrepancy in breastfeeding rates between economic classes as between races), the bureaucrats over at HHS have decided that the only solution is to press black women to breastfeed, instead of, say, seeking improvements to the formula these women are feeding their babies.

First Lady Michelle Obama is also on the breastfeeding bandwagon. She has spent the better part of her husband's two terms championing healthy eating, controlling calorie intake, and encouraging exercise to combat obesity among young Americans. And, as we'll see in Chapter 3, these efforts have included legislation reforming school lunches, aggressive pressure on food retailers and restaurants to improve their "healthy"

offerings, as well as using the power of the First Lady's pul-
pit (which is the traditional mode where First Ladies have had
their greatest impact) to speak to wide swaths of the citizenry
about an issue she deems important.

Michelle Obama has drawn a straight line between breastfeeding and improved health and wellness. "Kids who are
breastfed longer have a lower tendency to be obese," she has
argued. And, like the HHS-directed effort, the First Lady has
also focused much attention on the obesity problem among African Americans. "We're also working to promote breastfeeding, especially in the black community, where 40 per cent of our
babies never get breastfed at all, even in the first weeks of life,
and we know that babies that are breastfed are less likely to be
obese as children," she said in 2011.[31]

The First Lady, the USDA, and HHS, along with the
Surgeon General (with the 2011 Call to Action to Support
Breastfeeding[32]) and the CDC (with the Guide to Breastfeeding Interventions[33]), as well as various other government-run
marketing campaigns, are all part of the federal government's
breastfeeding-is-a-national-priority effort. There are just a few
basic problems with all of this local, state, and federal breast-or-
else campaigning, however.

Not everyone can or wants to breastfeed;

the science behind breast-is-best isn't conclusive; and

the focus on breastfeeding while returning to work,
which means having to use a pump and dedicated lactation room, even where practical, isn't what the scientists,
the doctors, and the activists have in mind when they
argue that breast is best.

But even if all the government's claims were true, the
breast-or-else campaign is actually a myopic solution to what

should be a more robust, inclusive, and necessary discussion about families and raising children.

NOT EVERYONE CAN OR WANTS TO BREASTFEED

The *Washington Post*'s Emily Wax-Thibodeaux is definitely Captain Mommy material since she exposed in October 2014 a very private matter—her own experience with breast cancer—in order to detail the negative judgment, moralizing, and verbal lashings she's received for feeding her son formula instead of nursing. According to her article "Why I Don't Breast-Feed, If You Must Know," she was harassed by overzealous (to put it kindly) lactation experts while in hospital. Instead of reveling in the miracle of new life, her family's peace was repeatedly shattered by "lactivists" who simply refused to take her no to breastfeeding for an answer.

Wax-Thibodeaux's breast surgeon was appalled. "I think that women who have made the difficult decision to have bilateral mastectomies have already grieved the loss of not being able to breast-feed. No group should make a woman feel guilty about the decisions she made . . . or make her feel inadequate about not being able to lactate," Dr. Shawna C. Wiley says.

As Wax-Thibodeaux experienced firsthand, however, the lactation soldiers in the breastfeeding brigade have taken up the message very much as a religious dogma. Indeed, it was nearly impossible for them to face silently a woman who declared her intention to formula feed. Instead, these so-called professionals rejected her choice and pressed her to change her mind. One woman even suggested that if Wax-Thibodeaux tried hard enough, milk might come out of her armpits!

Once out of the hospital, Wax-Thibodeaux has found that she still has to justify her choices to nosy friends and strangers alike. It is shocking that any woman should have to go through this. Millions upon millions of Americans have grown up healthy on formula, as have millions upon millions of breast-fed citizens. In most cases, parents are choosing between two reasonable options—breast or bottle. And let's not forget that parents are still free to choose how they feed their children. We can agree that we haven't yet arrived at the point when this basic decision should be made by someone other than a baby's parent or guardian, right?

Harriet Hall praised the autonomy to decide in a piece questioning the science behind the breast-is-best movement for the website *Science-Based Medicine*.[34] Even as Hall agreed that breastfeeding might produce better outcomes, she raised a valid question: How much better is it really, when compared with a mother's independent judgment and freedom to choose?

> There are a lot of healthy well-fed mothers who have found what they think are valid reasons not to breast-feed. I chose not to breastfeed my babies because it was inconvenient, time-consuming, interfered with my sleep, and was incompatible with my job as a doctor working 24 hour shifts in the emergency room and as a flight surgeon on call. I suppose I could have pumped milk and planned ahead and found a way to do it, but it would have required heroic measures. I can imagine leaking breast milk all over my flight suit when I was on an emergency helicopter mission and simply couldn't stop to pump. Moreover, I tried breastfeeding briefly with my first baby and frankly, I didn't like it. All in all, I thought my babies were better off with a happy mother and a bottle.

I can attest to the pressure to breastfeed faced by anyone who is lucky enough not to have cancer as an excuse for choosing formula. I had a hard time breastfeeding our first child, and when, after six weeks of torturous worrying about our daughter's weight, along with a brutal schedule of nursing, pumping, lactation consultations, weight checks, and doctor visits, we finally switched full time to formula and everything got better, you might have expected that I'd become not only a convert to formula but a proselytizer for its superiority to nursing. Yet, when our second daughter was born 13 months after the first, it still took a while before I came to the rational conclusion that I could not breastfeed a baby while returning to my full-time work-from-home job as a journalist and with her sister running around to boot.

THE SCIENCE IS NOT SETTLED

"The conclusion that breastfeeding confers health benefits is far less certain than its proponents contend," writes Texas A&M professor Joan Wolf of the effort among health and governmental organizations to promote breastfeeding.[35] Reading such a statement can come as quite a shock after what seems like the endless stream of certainty from respected and highly authoritative sources that breastfeeding is superior to formula—period, full stop. And yet, Wolf isn't some formula crusader or breastfeeding basher; she just took a long, hard look at the research and found some disturbing evidence of her own.

> Indeed, an analysis of the epidemiological research on breastfeeding—how studies are designed, carried out, interpreted, and communicated among scientists and between medical professionals and the public—indicates that while breastfed babies, on average, do appear to be slightly healthier, the science does not demonstrate compellingly that breast milk or breastfeeding is responsible.[36]

Wolf reviewed the scientific literature only to find several complications with the conventional wisdom on breastfeeding's superiority. First, she found that many studies had failed to isolate breastfeeding from other possible factors for improved health outcomes in breastfed children. "Breastfeeding cannot be clearly distinguished from the decision to breastfeed," she writes. "The decision to breastfeed could represent an approach to child care that is far more important than breastfeeding itself. When behavior that is associated with breastfeeding has the potential to explain much of the statistical advantage attributed to breast milk, the scientific claim that breastfeeding confers health benefits, or that not breastfeeding increases risk, is precarious."[37]

Another set of researchers, Cynthia G. Colen and David M. Ramey, both of Ohio State University, set out to discover whether all the so-called positive properties of breast milk—"due to superior nutrients unique to breast milk that are absent from infant formula as well as the biochemical reactions triggered by the act of breastfeeding, itself"—delivered as promised.[38] They decided to compare sibling pairs along with "25 years of panel data from the National Longitudinal Survey of Youth (NLSY)." The results were not what the pro-breastfeeding advocates might have hoped. The authors restricted their analyses to siblings and accounted for fix effects within families— effectively testing Wolf's point that choosing to breastfeed is linked to a whole other set of choices that may positively impact child health—and they found "relatively little empirical evidence to support the notion that breastfeeding results in improved health and well-being for children between 4 and 14 years of age." Colen and Ramey argue that their study showed "much of the beneficial long-term effects typically attributed to breastfeeding, per se, may primarily be due to selection pressures into infant feeding practices along [demographic lines] such as race and socioeconomic status."

It might also be useful to look at some anecdotal evidence to compare against the research, namely that so many of those arguing today that breastfeeding is superior were themselves formula-fed as babies. According to a chronicle of historical breastfeeding rates by Anne L. Wright and Richard J. Schanler, "initiation of breastfeeding reached its nadir in 1972, when only 22% of women breastfed."[39] The numbers went up in the 1980s, but simple math tells us that so many of the people who argue for breastfeeding today were themselves the product of formula, and they managed to survive and thrive into adulthood.

The next problem with all the breastfeeding research is that no study has proved any of the individual benefits that "everyone knows" to be true of breastfeeding's superiority over using baby formula. Breastfeeding hasn't been conclusively proven to prevent obesity, asthma, allergies, or eczema, and it hasn't been proven to be a significant contributor to higher IQ, and yet nearly every study focused on one of these breastfeeding benefits ends up asserting that while this study (for whatever it is) didn't show conclusive causation, "we all know" that breastfeeding is still better. "That breastfeeding helps prevent ear infections is assumed by those who judge that it has no impact on asthma, while its protective qualities against asthma are accepted by those who find no connection between breastfeeding and ear infections," Wolf explains.[40]

The one study that looked at random sampling of breastfeeding-promotion efforts based on the baby-friendly initiative supported by WHO and UNICEF returned disappointing results for those who believe breastfeeding is the answer to pediatric obesity. The authors found that among the control group, exclusive breastfeeding went on longer, but "it did not reduce the measures" of obesity in the study group. Moreover, the authors slammed other studies for bias. "Previously reported beneficial effects on these outcomes," they wrote, "may be the result of uncontrolled confounding and selection bias."[41]

None of the research has effectively proven that breastfeeding alone is what makes for healthier outcomes, Wolf argues, but once you have one study after another there is a cascading effect. "Scientists and various other experts produce a constant stream of information about everything from health and relationships to the economy and the environment. . . . The quantity and scope of the information, however inconsistent, create a widespread but false impression that the wisdom to make perfect choices is available to everyone and that all risks, particularly health risks, can be prevented with proper calculation," she declares.[42]

Another issue is that researchers fail to approach the subject with appropriate skepticism when the basic premise—in this case that breastfeeding is better than formula—has already been established. Instead, they move in the same direction as the already established conventional wisdom. "When researchers consistently eliminate the explanatory power of potentially significant variables, including behavior, through inadequate controls, faulty conclusions become operating assumptions," Wolf explains. "Once a variable has been correlated with a positive health outcome, a discourse develops that encourages further investigation of its protective powers."[43]

Finally, the conventional wisdom has become so overpowering that time and money are spent bolstering the original claims and the alternative is deemed not only inferior but also potentially harmful. "That breastfeeding is superior is so widely assumed that studies now try to determine the risk factors for bottle feeding. That is, choosing not to breastfeed has now assumed the status of a disease for which certain mothers are 'at risk,'" concludes Wolf.[44]

Government is just no good at nuance. So when faced with an established crisis, such as childhood obesity, you get very one-sided, black-and-white pronouncements and policies that are supposed to "solve" the problem—in this case, raise breast-feeding rates so that fewer kids will become obese. Suddenly it seems not only important to increase breastfeeding, but also imperative that formula be discouraged. After all, there may be risks associated with it, such as potentially overfeeding babies and thus causing obesity.[45] Again, the premise here is based on a fashionable idea that breast is best, and everything else—including questioning whether formula is even a decent second choice—flows from that first principle.

Emily Oster, writing at fivethirtyeight.com, described the problem succinctly. "The only trouble," she wrote in 2015, with believing that breastfeeding will solve obesity "is [there's] no good reason to think it is correct."[46] The single "high-quality randomized controlled trial of breast-feeding did not show any impacts on childhood obesity," she declared. Oster agreed that there are benefits to breastfeeding; "the trouble is that the evidence they are based on is often biased by the fact that women who breastfeed are typically different from those who do not."[47]

Wolf and Oster pose similar questions—namely, if the science is inconsistent and doesn't actually prove breastfeeding's superiority, then why does everyone agree that it is? Oster says it is a matter of time. "It often takes time for good research to trump bad—many people still think a low-fat diet is a good idea even though randomized trial data has not supported that belief."[48] Oster also thinks the subject matter has something to do with it because we want to believe that the hard work and sacrifice involved in breastfeeding exclusively is actually going to pay off in some tangible way.

Wolf's answer is different and worth considering since it may help to explain why (as we'll see in upcoming chapters) the authorities tend to go overboard, especially when it comes to children. Wolf believes the breast-is-best dogma stems from what she calls the risk culture, which is about managing our overarching anxiety about the future via reducing every conceivable risk for ourselves and our children. "Breastfeeding mandates come from an unrealistic public policy impulse," Wolf says.

> The push to breastfeed is ... part of a larger cultural preoccupation with risk, and especially health risks. We expend tremendous energy trying to stave off illness and disease. And we do this by gathering information and seeking out the opinions of experts so that we can make good, healthy choices. I'm not suggesting that we shouldn't encourage people to behave in healthy ways, but we have a terribly inflated sense of how much we, as individuals, can accomplish.[49]

Consider how much less we base our parenting decisions on what a previous generation of parents did or didn't do, what Jennifer Senior calls folkways. Do we adults have evidence from our own childhoods about the benefits of breastfeeding? In reality, most of us were fed formula because infant formula was mostly thought of as best practice a generation ago. Women were "liberated" to be working outside the home, and if you needed someone else to feed the baby, you also needed something other than breast milk to feed them. It was actually the height of being technologically and politically modern. And yet, we don't now use any of the previous generation's wisdom to raise our own children because of our anxieties and fears.

Wolf explains that "today's grandmothers, who put infants to sleep on their stomachs, left babies and toddlers in playpens, and allowed preschoolers to ride in the front seat, become less credible authorities as their daughters struggle to evaluate risks that their mothers could not have fathomed."[50] We are living at a time when "risk prevention is the moral obligation of individual citizens," Wolf argues. Thus the government telling us how and why to feed our offspring seems natural—except to Captain Mommies, who reject the imposition, of course.

It isn't clear, however, why the government should have an opinion about how mothers nourish their offspring. Worse yet, mandated breastfeeding support means the government is taking sides against women who are clearly not harming their children. As Adam Smith explained it in *The Wealth of Nations*,

> [t]he statesman who should attempt to direct private people in what manner they ought to employ their capitals, would not only load himself with a most unnecessary attention, but assume an authority which could safely be trusted, not only to no single person, but to no council or senate whatever, and which would nowhere be so dangerous as in the hands of a man who had folly and presumption enough to fancy himself fit to exercise it.[51]

There is nothing wrong with formula, and millions of formula-fed, nonobese, highly intelligent, nonasthmatic Americans are the proof. Yet, Smith's statesmen (today's government busybodies) embrace their role of directing "private people" (in this case new mothers) "in what manner they ought to employ their capitals" (breastfeeding over infant formula), and it begins from the first moments of babies' lives, in the hospital, when so much is new, many decisions need to be made, and mothers may actually have difficulty choosing. Similar to other positions taken by the nanny state, the thumb is on the scale for the potentially more difficult choice. Anyone who has been through lactation consulting sessions and pumping regimes could certainly argue that the effort is worth it, but it does take effort, whereas, giving a bottle means anyone can do it—as in fathers, grandparents, friends—which is also a help to moms. But none of these pros and cons, pluses and minuses, can get baked into government policy. The nanny state doesn't do nuance. And this paternalism has a pernicious effect that continues beyond the initial bonding phase well into a new mother's return to work and the rhythms of her previous life.

WHY IS PUMPING AT WORK THE GOAL?

In her 2009 exposé entitled "The Case Against Breast-Feeding," Hanna Rosin discusses the same pressure to breastfeed that Wax-Thibodeaux, Hall, and others have experienced and resent. But Rosin isn't just complaining or questioning the science that informs the dogma. She points out the real-world negative consequences to the myopic insistence that six months of exclusive breastfeeding is "normal" and "important," as WHO and AAP declare. "The debate about breast-feeding takes place without any reference to its actual context in women's lives," Rosin avers.

> Breast-feeding exclusively is not like taking a prenatal vitamin. It is a serious time commitment that pretty much guarantees that you will not work in any meaningful way. Let's say a baby feeds seven times a day and then a couple more times at night. That's nine times for about a half hour each, which adds up to more than half of a working day, every day, for at least six months. This is why, when people say that breast-feeding is 'free,' I want to hit them with a two-by-four. It's only free if a woman's time is worth nothing.[52]

Kudos to Rosin for the blast of cold, hard truth about pumping rooms and mandates requiring employers to twist workplaces into lactation havens. Even if every worksite could accommodate a separate pumping room, it wouldn't make the time and energy required to express milk any less of a challenge for working mothers. Rosin is also correct to question the goal of much of the government-run effort to raise breastfeeding rates. As the rules imposed by the ACA exemplify, women are pressed to return to work *while* they continue to breastfeed. This is not only extremely unrealistic as a goal, it isn't even what the science has supposedly shown will provide for the best outcomes for children.

Feeding-freedom advocate Suzanne Barston says government has not "solve[d] the problem by having a pumping room." Like Rosin, Barston is also critical of the effort to push women back to work full-time while expressing breast milk nearly full-time in order to continue feeding breast milk to their kids. "Exclusive breastfeeding while working full-time is a lot to ask of women," Barston argues, "especially those in the lower-paid, lower-status jobs typical of those in the same demographics that suffer from the highest obesity rates."[53] And the efficacy of pushing all working women to breastfeed is also questionable due to how unrealistic it is for huge swaths of workers.

"We are essentially giving lower-status workers the same lactation rights as higher-status workers—*and higher-status women are still having difficulty pumping at work*," Barston correctly interjects.[54] And yet, given the additional goodies and services to which breastfeeding WIC recipients are entitled, Washington is essentially punishing poor women for choosing formula. Isn't this counter to the goal of food stamps and WIC, to help the poor?

Not only is pushing breastfeeding resulting in harm to mothers, the goal is not based on what science argues would be best for babies. Nearly every study about breastfeeding takes as its model six months of exclusive breastfeeding as a baseline. But if you return to work after 12 weeks and start pumping breast milk to be given to your child in a bottle while you are at your job, then you are not exclusively breastfeeding. Your child is getting breast milk, but not by nursing. As Barston explains, "They do not [have] good research on pumped breast milk."[55] So even if the alleged advantages of breastfeeding were scientifically proven, which isn't the case, the government-imposed solution does not solve the problem by increasing breastfeeding, so it fails to satisfy its own public-health priority.

In *Time* magazine, Amy Tuteur, an OBGYN and the author of *How Your Baby Is Born*, has described the all-or-nothing approach of breast-is-best warriors and how detrimental it is to commonsense public-policy prescriptions. "One of the greatest barriers to breast-feeding in this country is the unreasonable expectations set by breast-feeding advocates," Tuteur declared in 2013.[56]

> They are loathe to admit that many babies may benefit from supplementation [with formula] in the first days after birth, that some babies will require more milk than their mothers produce, and that many mothers must return to work within weeks and simply cannot breast-feed exclusively. Instead of acknowledging those realities, they have alienated new mothers with their all-or-nothing approach, leaving most women to figure out a method of combining breast and formula feeding that works for them on their own.

Leaving it up to the parents and caregivers to decide what's best isn't part of the government playbook for solving public-health issues, however. Instead, a vast array of bureaucrats and officials work hard to promote the flavor-of-the-month salve. "We've turned into a nation of dairy queens," says Barston, "with political support for breastfeeding focusing primarily on achieving pumping rights for working women rather than on fighting for better family leave policies that would allow all parents—both male and female—to spend more time with their infants."[57]

What Barston offers with her blog *Fearless Formula Feeder*, meanwhile, is nothing short of hope and solace to a most-deserving group: parents who want the best for their children but not necessarily through exclusive breastfeeding. The blog offers a forum for what are sometimes harrowing stories of bullying, pressure, and rejection because a parent decides to make an independent choice. For example, after tabulating all the sacrifice, the work, and the ultimate success of both breast- and bottle-feeding, one mother named Lisa says, "I find myself feeling angry when other women are bullied and mistreated as I was by WIC and all the people who lied to me, or weren't educated on biology to know that not every woman can breastfeed."[58] Another mom, Erin, says that feeding her son formula "feels like something for which I must beg forgiveness."[59] While it is true that almost all mothers with infants can be overwrought, it is also true that everyone who posts at Barston's blog are desperate for basic acceptance, and they haven't found it from most nurses, lactation consultants, or service providers.

The other way to improve upon the current breast-or-else dogma would be to encourage discussion about improving the quality of infant formula for those who can't nurse. Indeed, there are actually some people who have given this some thought. Sally Fallon, the author of *Nourishing Traditions: The Cookbook that Challenges Politically Correct Nutrition and the Diet Dictocrats* and a strong advocate for breastfeeding, recognizes that there should be some better alternative to breast milk than processed infant formula. She thinks using raw milk is the right way to go. "Properly produced raw milk does not pose a danger to your baby, in spite of what numerous public health propagandists may assert," she writes. "Raw milk is easier for your baby to digest than pasteurized and less likely to cause cramps, constipation and allergies."[60]

Over at the website *The Healthy Home Economist*, you can find a different homemade infant-formula recipe and helpful video.[61] And a simple internet search can get you any number of suggested replacement formula options from rice milk to goat's milk. The point here is that there could be a wide selection of possible replacements to breast milk or mass-produced infant formula if there weren't such a monopoly on the "right way" to feed your baby.

Stacie Billis became a Captain Mommy the hard way; when she couldn't breastfeed exclusively, she got depressed and felt like a failure. But her turnaround has come with some hard earned wisdom and an important perspective about personal freedom. As she wrote on the *Huffington Post* in 2012,

> Real choice will be available when women can count on hospital staff to provide them not just with breast-feeding skills, but also the tools to make smart decisions about choosing formula. When more than one brand is available in hospitals and health care providers can speak to the health benefits of each chosen brand. When instead of a branded goody bag, new moms walk out of the hospital knowing how to get affordable support for whatever decision they've made, including where to get coupons for their formula of choice.[62]

Well said.

CHAPTER 3

Daycare Nannies

Too few child-care centers that cost too much—the result of too many regulations

"IN TODAY'S ECONOMY, when having both parents in the workforce is an economic necessity for many families, we need affordable, high-quality child care more than ever," President Obama said during his 2015 State of the Union address.[1]

The president is right, of course: We do need a better system for caring for children of working parents. After all, there are some 11 million children younger than five in some form of child care in the United States, according to Child Care Aware. "On average, these children spend 36 hours a week in child care. While parents are children's first and most important teachers, child care programs provide early learning opportunities for millions of young children daily, having a profound impact on their development and readiness for school."[2]

Obama isn't the first president to deal with this issue, though the nature of the problem has changed a lot over the past century. The first White House conference ever, convened in January 1909, was entitled Conference on the Care of Dependent Children. President Theodore Roosevelt explained the gathering's special purpose.

There are few things more vital to the welfare of the nation than accurate and dependable knowledge of the best methods of dealing with children, especially with those who are in one way or another handicapped by misfortune; and in the absence of such knowledge each community is left to work out its own problem without being able to learn of and profit by the success or failure of other communities along the same lines of endeavor.[3]

More than a century later, we are dealing with the same compelling question—how to care for dependent children outside their homes. And today, the reality of modern-day child care is complicated, to say the least. Thirty-five percent of kids "are in center-based care which includes Head Start, preschool and child care centers," reports Child Care Aware of America.[4] Meanwhile, 32 percent are cared for by a grandparent, and 8 percent are at family child-care homes. A further complication: 26 percent are in more than one child-care arrangement during the week.[5] As a parent who had one child in one center and two children at another, I can tell you that even though the daycares were close to one another, my fondest dream the entire time I was in that situation was to have one drop-off and one pick-up per day. I've had the same conversation with so many parents who feel exactly the same way. And all the research on employee productivity and loss of revenue for absences says that when parents have to keep their kids home from daycare because the child is sick or the daycare is closed for a holiday, it hurts an employer's bottom line.

According to Child Care Aware of America, there is a significant impact on the overall economy because of daycare costs: "A 2009 study showed that employees leaving their jobs for child care related reasons represented a potential $6 million loss to employers in downtown Santa Barbara, a community of less than 91,000 residents. Parents in this study ranked cost as their top child care challenge."[6]

There are indeed a lot of varieties of daycare options. Yet the cost of quality daycare is often prohibitive, and in many communities, demand far outstrips supply.

HISTORY OF HIGH DEMAND

The *New York Times* recently covered the problem of supply and cost, even among those parents earning higher salaries. Alissa Quart spoke with Jane Dimyan-Ehrenfeld, a 37-year-old attorney in Washington, DC, and mother of two, who struggled to find quality accessible daycare. "The competition is unbelievable," Dimyan-Ehrenfeld explained.[7] Quart found the same trouble across the country in Kirkland, Washington, when she interviewed Kristin Rowe-Finkbeiner, a 44-year-old "founder of a nonprofit group centered on these issues, MomsRising," who had a "heck of a time" getting off the wait list at her preferred child-care center. "I applied early, and my daughter only got in when she was 3," Rowe-Finkbeiner told Quart. "Access is a problem across the socioeconomic spectrum."[8]

Jeffrey Tucker, distinguished fellow at the Foundation for Economic Education asks a good question: "Why is there a shortage? Why is daycare so expensive? We get tennis shoes, carrots, gasoline, dry cleaning, haircuts, manicures, and most other things with no problem. There are infinite options at a range of prices, and they are all affordable. There is no national crisis, for example, about a shortage of gyms."[9]

He is right, of course; there's no shortage of gyms, but there is a shortage of reasonably priced, safe, and reasonably regulated daycare. The costs have been soaring for years—by as much as 70 percent since the 1980s, in fact. Currently, the average nationally is $1,000 a month for one child, though it can be much higher depending on location. The cost is greater than public college tuition in 31 states and the District of Columbia.

Licensed daycare in American today is too expensive for most working parents. Meanwhile, nationally, and especially in densely populated cities, there's a shortage of spaces. And we've been at this problem for over a century. "It's time we stop treating childcare as a side issue, or a women's issue, and treat it like the national economic priority that it is for all of us," the president said in January 2014. He's right, but why does the landscape look like this at all?

REALITY OF OVERREGULATED DAYCARE

Daycare rules are what turned me into a Captain Mommy in the first place. At the time, I had two small children who were attending a local daycare that boasted of its high-quality rank- ing by the state (five stars!). We had chosen the place because it was conveniently located, the facility and staff were pleasant, and also because there were wait lists for one or another of the children elsewhere. The tuition for two kids would have been eye-popping if we hadn't already experienced sticker shock elsewhere.

We were also comparing apples to oranges. Up to that point, the eldest had been cared for at home by a series of babysitters while I also worked at home. But once there were two children, it was time for either mom or the kids to get out of the house. Plus, the quality of care we could find for a part-time position caring for a toddler and a baby was an issue. We chose to pay more for our kids' daycare because it made it easier for me to earn more money writing from a quiet empty house and the kids were in a warm environment getting all the "enrichment" that President Obama and lots of child-development and edu- cation experts argue is good for our kids' potential.

What I didn't know at the time was how many rules we were going to have to follow and to what degree government regulations control and limit the landscape of available child care.

Food is a big nanny-state bugaboo. Of course, there are no nuts at any daycare because of allergies, and there are long lists of foods you cannot allow your kids to have in school because of choking hazards. But when they started throwing out all the uneaten food, I started to ask questions. You see, I used to know what my toddler ate at daycare every day. I would load up her lunch bag with containers of sandwiches and snacks and get back those same containers with or without the food that had previously filled them. The yogurt was always gone, and the oatmeal, noodles, or sandwich was either eaten or half-eaten, depending on my daughter's appetite.

Then one day, all of the containers came back empty. And not just empty, but rinsed clean as if my girl had licked up every morsel. But it wasn't that she'd eaten everything; it was that Pennsylvania decided to issue a rule for all state-certified day-care centers that no food was to be returned home at the end of the day. Instead of keeping half-eaten fried egg sandwiches, teachers were instructed that they had to throw out any uneaten food into the garbage, period, no exceptions.

Pennsylvania's Department of Public Welfare licensing rules for daycare facilities regulation no. 3270.161 (2008) states, in part, that "food that has been previously served to a person or returned from a table shall be discarded." Why discarded? Because there is *no guarantee* that "potentially hazardous food" might not have gone bad, even though the same rule speci-fies that "food brought from the child's home or provided by the facility shall be refrigerated." In order to avoid a situation where later that day or the next a child might consume said "hazardous" material, the state just deemed it all *potentially* dangerous, forcing teachers and caretakers to toss it all in the trash. I thought there was a mistake. "Don't you mean perishable?" I asked. Why would the state assume that adult parents, teachers, and daycare staff couldn't use their own eyes and nose and mouth to determine whether uneaten food was still good? Because that is the nature of the overarching regulatory state, where the purpose of many rules is to take discretion and judgment out of the hands of those who are supposed to have the authority—in this case parents or daycare workers—and centralize it among bureaucrats far, far away.

In his book *The Rule of Nobody*, Philip K. Howard writes eloquently about this disease. "Dictating decisions in advance has undeniable appeal," he declares.[10] "That's what power is—controlling decisions by other people." And that's just what happens in government-licensed daycare.

It is, as Howard explains, "a rules-based system [that] centralizes decisions even as it rigidifies them. Control is the main mission of all those distant rule writers. They don't trust a thing you do." He then challenges us all to "think for a second about the mind-set of regulators who detail each situation when a daycare worker must wash her hands" or throw out all uneaten food. What else is that about, he asks, than regulators viewing their job as "controlling the minutest details of how people do things"? And he continues, "Over the past few decades, these unknown officials in federal, state, and local government have written millions of words of regulatory dictates, bossing you around for no good reason, and with countless idiotic effects."[11]

The practical impact of rule no. 3270.161 was that, instead of knowing whether my little girl was hungry on Monday or just grazing on Wednesday, I was left with absolutely no concept of how much she ate or didn't eat or even if she liked one thing I'd prepared over another. Pennsylvania regulators decided instead that I can't be trusted to throw out food that has gone bad or that isn't worth keeping. I was supposedly going to make my child sick by giving her the same food she didn't eat at lunch as her dinner or even repackage it for lunch the next day.

Since 2008, the rules have only gotten more onerous and extreme, especially when it comes to the care of infants, who by law can start care as early as six weeks. In 2013, I had my fourth child. As we did with his sisters before him, my husband and I swaddled our son for every nap and at bedtime. So imagine my shock when the daycare administrator politely informed me that they could not honor my request that our baby be swaddled for naps. In the intervening three years since his older sister was a baby, Pennsylvania, along with several other states, has changed its daycare regulations to include a ban on swaddling.

The ban stems straight from *Caring for Our Children: National Health and Safety Performance Standards Guidelines for Early Care and Education Programs* (2011), produced by the HHS-funded National Resource Center for Health and Safety in Child Care and Early Education in conjunction with the American Academy of Pediatrics and the American Public Health Association. "In child care settings," the manual states, "swaddling is not necessary or recommended."

A baby may not be swaddled in a daycare without written authorization from a physician, according to Pennsylvania rules. As regulation no. 3270.119 states, "Infants shall be placed in the sleeping position recommended by the American Academy of Pediatrics [i.e., on their backs] unless there is a medical reason an infant should not sleep in this position. The medical reason shall be documented in a statement signed by a physician, physician's assistant or CRNP and placed in the child's record at the facility." But while swaddling a baby helps them sleep long on their backs (they naturally want to sleep on their tummies), there is no "medical reason" for swaddling. It isn't the same as needing prescription antibiotics when a kid gets an ear infection. So when I tried to get my pediatrician to write the waiver, I got a definite no, along with the official line from the AAP which states that swaddling isn't recommended after two months of age.[12] No swaddling without a waiver, and there's no way to get a waiver, so in effect there's a ban. Similar bans are already in effect in Minnesota, California, and Texas.

The unelected busybodies who write these rules are convinced that swaddling isn't perfectly safe (what is?) because the daycare workers could do a bad job wrapping the baby, the blanket could become loose, the baby might roll over into the loose material, and then the baby might, possibly, die of SIDS (sudden infant death syndrome). Experts also warn that swaddling improperly might also cause hip dysplasia.[13] But there are no known cases of a baby dying at daycare from suffocation by a swaddling blanket. In fact, there has been a 50 percent decrease in SIDS since 1994, and, as Melinda Wenner Moyer reported in *Slate*, a New Zealand study that tried to separate out all possible bedding-related factors that contribute to SIDS concluded that tight swaddling significantly decreases the risk of death.[14]

Dr. Harvey Karp, who wrote the baby bibles on swaddling and sleep, *Happiest Baby on the Block* and *Happiest Baby Guide to Great Sleep*, is furious about the ban. He argues that between two and four months of age is the "absolute worst" time to stop swaddling because that is just the time that SIDS is most likely to occur. Our baby was two months old when he started daycare. "Evidence shows that swaddling may well reduce infant sleep deaths. By reducing crying and boosting sleep, swaddling lessens a parent's temptation to bring the baby into bed with them or to put the baby to sleep on the stomach (both serious SIDS/suffocation risks)," Karp argues.[15]

Until 2011, there were no rules about swaddling in daycare. "Swaddling wasn't part of *Caring for Our Children* before [the 2011 edition]," an employee at the National Resource Council helpfully explained during our phone interview. "The optimal age for children to be in group care settings is three months, and [so we looked at whether babies should] still be swaddled after three months." Never mind that in Pennsylvania, state-licensed daycare facilities can accept children as young as six weeks; the NRC rules apply at every age. And yet the importance of swaddling infants from birth has been proven in study after study. Just as in ancient and aboriginal societies, swaddling reduces crying by promoting feelings of security and safety. Isn't that exactly what we want for babies in daycare, to feel safe and secure even away from mom and dad?

And yet, according to the NRC's conclusions, swaddling isn't necessary. The official line is that they are "worried about monitoring of children in a group care environment. Swaddling can be done differently by different providers, i.e., incorrectly and blankets [can end up] covering faces. We're looking at group care environment for blankets becoming loosened."[16] So all of these neurotic, what-if worries have been collected and codified by the NRC in their safe-sleep standards. As it turned out, my son adopted a nearly no-sleep standard. When I pleaded with the pediatrician that my son wasn't sleeping at his daycare, she advised me to stop swaddling him at home so that he would get used to sleeping unwrapped at school. Long after the conversation, it occurred to me she would never have given me similar advice if we'd been talking about breastfeeding. ("Why don't you stop nursing at home, so that your son can get used to being bottle fed at daycare?")

Karp says there are serious problems with the methodology behind the NRC's no-swaddling standard.

In 2011 the group decided that swaddling (even in gossamer-thin blankets) is unnecessary and risky and should not be used after the first couple of weeks or months. They said swaddling might hurt a baby's hips

(yet no study has found a relationship between modern
swaddling, which leaves room for babies to bend their
legs up and out, and hip dysplasia), might cause babies
to overheat (no study shows overheating from swaddling, unless the head is covered or the room is hot), or
might cause SIDS if loose blankets get wrapped around
a baby's face (studies show that only loose bulky bedding—like a comforter—is a SIDS risk, not light mus-
lin bedding).[17]

Karp isn't alone in his criticism. In her book *Is Breast Best?*,
Joan Wolf discusses the limits of science and official safety recommendations, specifically in regards to putting babies to sleep
on their backs in order to reduce SIDS. The campaign, "sponsored by the AAP, the Consumer Product Safety Commission,
and the National Institute of Child Health and Human Development, took place at the same time as various diagnostic and
behavioral shifts, and the precise impact of having babies sleep
on their backs is difficult to determine," Wolf declares.[18] It is
possible, therefore, that "fewer babies might be dying of SIDS
. . . at least partially because deaths that once were unexplain-
able now fall into other diagnostic categories," Wolf explains.
And it seems the AAP itself acknowledged this possibility in a
little-seen note from the group's report on SIDS.

> [The most recent recommendations] were developed to
> reduce the risk of SIDS in the general population. . . .
> Scientifically identified associations between risk fac-
> tors (e.g., socioeconomic characteristics, behaviors, or
> environmental exposures) and outcomes such as SIDS
> do not necessarily denote causality . . . [and] it is fun-
> damentally misguided to focus on a single risk factor
> or to attempt to quantify risk for an individual infant.[19]

The science is not settled, and yet when rules are written, they leave no room for individual judgment or experience. The predictable outcome removes one potentially effective means of comforting a crying baby from a caregiver's quiver.

Listen to the tale of woe from one daycare worker in Texas, where they were swaddling infants until the new regulations came out and the state effectively banned the practice. "Young babies that were sleeping an hour [or] an hour and a half are now sleeping 20 minutes," she told the *Huffington Post*.[20] "I have some babies who are not sleeping at all." Speaking for others at her facility, the employee complained that [teachers] "feel ... they are not able to meet the needs of the infants they are caring for.... They are not allowed to do what they feel is needed."

As a parent, I feel the same way. Why should the decision to wrap or not wrap my baby be up to an unaccountable stranger? It makes much more sense and would be more efficient for me to have a conversation with the daycare workers watching my son, and together we could decide how best to care for him. If swaddling is so important to me, why couldn't I look around to find a daycare that would accommodate my needs?

And remember also that, as the NRC admits, they are making policy based on what *might* happen. They are not basing their recommendations on reported cases of babies in daycare who were swaddled and then died from SIDS. The NRC doesn't even want to claim they are anti-swaddling. When I asked why they'd enacted a ban, the woman on the phone sounded positively Orwellian. NRC standards, she explained, are based on the recommendations of Dr. Rachel Moon at the American Academy of Pediatrics. And Dr. Moon, she continued, isn't anti-swaddling; she's just against any blankets in cribs in daycare. But you have to have a blanket to swaddle the baby, I spluttered. "We aren't anti-swaddling," the woman replied. "We're just against blankets in cribs."

The AAP, for its part, is backing up the no-wrapping standard. "If the infant kicks the blankets off, or the swaddling blankets are not applied correctly, loose bedcovers would be in the crib, which is against AAP policy," a spokesperson told the *Huffington Post*.[21] "The AAP understands why NRC has implemented this standard."

And the NRC also denies it is making law, which is in theory true. They come up with the standards and guidelines, but state legislators decide whether to adopt the rules as law.

Once the law is in place, however, punishment has followed. Two sisters in California were put on probation for "abusing" babies by swaddling.[22] They are barred from ever taking care of children even though nothing happened to any child in their care due to swaddling.

A similar ban was enacted in Washington, DC, recently and with predictable results: Parents and daycare workers are upset.[23] "You get these little babies in daycare who can't sleep and are extremely fussy," explained Rachel Turow, a 33-year-old attorney whose eight-month-old goes to a local daycare. "It's really bad for the baby, it's really bad for the teachers, and therefore, it's really bad for all of the kids," she complains. She worries that the teachers will now have to spend an "inordinate" amount of time soothing the youngest babies, hurting her son's experience. "Our teachers are very committed to what they do, and they're feeling very frustrated that they can't do what they know helps the baby," echoed one daycare provider. "There's more crying. The babies are not as happy or content when they're awake. It makes everything a lot more stressful."[24]

Beyond extreme safety measures over blankets and food, daycare rules extend to hilarious-if-they-weren't-so-maddening standards of hygiene as well. Massachusetts enacted a requirement on teeth-brushing for all children in care, whether or not they have teeth. Some states require parents to provide up to four sippy cups a day because providers are not allowed to offer a cup more than once. And then recently I got the following note from the director of my children's daycare: "Please refrain from sending items to school in a plastic bag. Lunches need to be sent in a brown paper lunch bag or lunch box.... Our center is required to keep plastic out of children's reach when they are in our care." It was followed by this: "All fruits (especially grapes), vegetables and general food (fish, meats, hard cheeses) must be pre-cut and peeled at home. For infants, all foods available to them need to be ¼" or smaller and for Teeny Tiny Tots, Tiny Tots and Toddlers all foods must be pre-cut ½" or smaller. Staff is not allowed to pre-cut ANY food items. We are required by the Department of Health and Safety to follow these guidelines."

Next, I'm expecting to get a note alerting me to new organic, non-GMO, natural-fiber-only clothing requirements. Or perhaps the state will adopt a cloth-diaper standard in order to lessen waste to landfills.

A more serious consideration is why the talented, committed, and responsible staff at my son's daycare has to spend its time enforcing someone else's rules in this way.

If your kid's daycare is run by the federal government, such as Head Start, the Obama administration decided in early 2015 that the Department of Agriculture would take care of the food rules to bring them into alignment with the federal rules for school lunches. (See Chapter 3 for discussion of Michelle's Meals.) As reported by the *Wall Street Journal*'s Tennille Tracy, the news didn't go over so well with some daycare providers.[25] "Despite the department's assurances, April Manning, owner of Doodle Bug Family Childcare in White Marsh, Md., said she's concerned the new requirements would increase her grocery bill," Tracy wrote. And "Stacie Wrage, owner of Cribs to Crayons Daycare in Grundy Center, Iowa, doesn't anticipate having to make major changes to her menu, but said 'the more rules you put on [providers], the less people are going to want to be a part of it,'" which goes for parents as well as providers.

These types of rules are onerous—the USDA is banning certain types of cooking methods—with the added dubious distinction of being inflexible, impractical, and unreasonable.

For proof of how onerous, scan the legislation governing licensed daycare in almost any state to begin to grasp the dimensions of the problem. Arizona has 45 pages of rules and regulations[26] and another 69 pages for child-care facilities.[27] Michigan has 329 pages of rules.[28] In New York you get pedantry such as "coat hooks must be spaced so that coats and other outer garments do not touch each other."[29] It is hard to understand the need for this type of rule-writing and how this relates to giving children a safe, nurturing place to spend their days while their parents are at work.

Talk to many daycare employees, and you'll hear stories about useless and ill-defined regulations that are nevertheless the focus for inspectors. "When it's 100 degrees for a month, there's going to be flies. Licensing doesn't want any flies," said Debera Nielsen, who has owned and run her preschool for 40 years, with animals present on the grounds all that time. She complains that in recent years, licensing regulators have become more judgmental and less friendly and helpful. She has found the process for appealing violations frustrating and opaque. "A fly is different from somebody breaking their neck," she said.[30]

Talk to parents, and you hear about how tough it is to find a place that offers the flexibility that they would prefer. In some cases, the rules mandating certain procedures are as disturbing as those banning other procedures. When I interviewed Sara Burrows, she had just left her job as a journalist to take care of her daughter full-time at home. The reason was that she didn't want the provider to offer her 18-month-old cow's milk to drink, "but licensed daycare has to show proof of nutritional requirements," including cow's milk, Burrows explained. There is a "long list of food groups that have to be served at daycare," she added. And because she didn't want her kid to be offered certain foods, and the rules offered the provider very little flexibility, Burrows chose to stop working so she could care for her daughter at home the way she wanted.

She's not the only person who made that decision. But the exasperation of inflexible procedures and lockstep thinking is only one element forcing parents out of what should be an invaluably helpful system. For many, the reason is economic. A 2014 PEW study reported that, for the first time in 20 years, more women were leaving the workforce to stay home with their kids because of the high cost of daycare.[31]

> The economic ups and downs of the past decade likely influenced mothers' decisions on whether to stay home or go to work. The share of mothers staying home with their children rose from 2000 to 2004, but the rise stopped in 2005, amid economic uncertainty that foreshadowed the official start of the Great Recession in 2007. The increase in both number and share eventually resumed: From 2010 to 2012, the share of stay-at-home mothers (29%) was three percentage points higher than in 2008 (26%), at the height of the recession.[32]

We may imagine that it is the women with rich husbands who stay home to care for kids, because they don't need to work, but the current reality is exactly the opposite, says researcher Paula England, a sociology professor at New York University. "Women who can't get good jobs anyhow—maybe not enough to cover their child-care costs or maybe not worth it in meaning—are the ones who are more likely to, if they have a husband, make the calculation (to stay home)," England said.[33]

In a slowing economy, with mostly lower-wage job openings, many parents have been compelled to abandon the workforce and stay home with children. The increase in cost due to regulatory excesses has been a huge contributing factor in the abandonment of daycare facilities—to the dismay not only of parents but also the centers' operators.

"The problem comes in when the rules and regulations become so one-size-fits-all, focused on quality rather than health and safety," said Sandy Bright, who operates three child-care centers in Weld County, Colorado, and had serious criticisms when in 2011 the state's Department of Human Services proposed rules to raise the bar on quality for licensed daycare facilities.[34] Some of the proposed rules included the following: "Toddler and infant classrooms must have a minimum of 10 pieces of each art material, such as 10 paints, 10 paint brushes and 10 crayons," and "Each classroom shall have a minimum of 12 books and one additional book for each child in the room." Then there were rules that were more, shall we say, political in nature. Classrooms were to have "at least 10 visual displays—not in one place—with two 'representing nature realistically' and two 'presenting diversity in a positive way,'" and "All doll collections shall have three races represented." The new rules were put aside after a major outcry, but the existing 37 pages of regulations (e.g., "cots or pads must be spaced at least 2 feet apart on all sides during rest time" and "the light must be dim at nap time to promote an atmosphere conducive to sleep") are still in effect.[35]

A short three years later, the excesses of the regulatory burden were exposed. As Madeline Novey reported in the *Coloradoan*, by August 2014, the cost of care across the state had skyrocketed. "Tuition and fees for in-state students attending Colorado State University on a full-time basis total $9,807 per year. Larimer County parents pay an average of $14,798 for infant care," she explained.[36]

When I spoke to Hindy, a daycare operator in Denver, she expressed similar frustrations. Her facility has a wait list in some age groups, which makes one wonder why she can't just expand her facility to accommodate the additional children. When I asked about whether she's seen rules growing in number or moving the other way, she was clear: "Yes, there has been a recent new change of an increase in regulation," Hindy explained. "It is optional for the schools to do, though. Standard licensing is a 1 grade but you can get up to a 5. . . . Plus, they are requiring more schooling for the teachers." She explained that Colorado requires daycare facilities to follow the Infant/Toddlers Environment Rating Scale (ITERS) and Early Childhood Environment Rating Scale (ECERS) in order to get a higher grade. Together these rule books include hundreds of pages of directives on how to run a daycare. If you don't follow the rules, you get a bad grade. (No five stars for you!) And what happened to tuition because of these new rules? Well, the state decided to offset the cost of implementation by offering grants. But that just means that taxpayers are footing the bill, and those who are paying tuition are paying twice. When asked whether she could ever lower tuition for families if the rules were maybe not quite so stringent, she replied with a smiley face emoticon and this: I "love the thought of being able to decrease tuition for the families." The thought, mind you, not the actual possibility.

The story in Colorado isn't exceptional, as Child Care Aware America's 2014 report entitled *Parents and the High Cost of Child Care* amply detailed.[37] According to the report, the difficulty of affording quality, licensed child care was shared across the socio-economic spectrum and family structure. "Across all 50 states," the Child Care Aware report states, "the cost of center-based infant care averaged over 40 percent of the state median income for single mothers."[38] Married parents with two children in child care—say a baby and a four-year-old—

are paying an average of 21 percent of the state median income for couples. Too bad that's double the benchmark for what the U.S. Department of Health and Human Services considers affordable child care.[39] It is nice that the government provides the ideal benchmark, but the data show that few people are able to manage that trick. Instead, parents in many states are paying more for child care than they would for in-state college tuition.

In Pennsylvania the cost of full-time child care for one kid averages more than $10,000 per child.[40] And, as Duquesne University economist Anthony Davies explained during our interview, "states that impose more regulations, on average, have higher child-care costs. By comparison, one year of tuition and fees at the average four-year public university (in-state rate) is $6,900." So put Pennsylvania in the same column as Colorado. And they have plenty of company.

Massachusetts has a unique daycare requirement: Teeth brushing, even if the child in question doesn't have teeth. Now take a guess at the most expensive place to have a baby in full-time daycare. Why, Massachusetts, at a whopping $16,000 a year. There are many complicated reasons why the birthrate in the United States is as low as it is. But as Jonathan Last pointed out in his excellent examination of population called *What to Expect When No One's Expecting*, the cost of raising a child, including child-care expense, is certainly a deterrent.

When the Child Care Aware report was published, the *Washington Post*'s Christopher Ingraham helpfully pointed out the big difference between paying for college and paying for daycare.

> While parents have years to prepare for college costs, there is literally no time to save for child care—a baby is born, and parents typically have to go back to work in just a few weeks' time. We accept that it typically takes

18 years to sock away a sizeable-enough college nest egg. Considering that child care is an equivalent, if not greater, expense and that the average maternal age at first child birth is 26, this suggests that we should similarly start putting money away for day-care expenses when we're roughly 8 years old. Sorry, kids: Your allowance money is going to the day-care fund now.[41]

All kidding aside, the cost of regulated child care is at a level that makes it unaffordable for middle-income and especially for low-income parents. And as Jonathan Cohn noted in a piece on daycare woes in the *New Republic*, the opposite condition is extremely important for the economy as a whole. "When parents can find safe, affordable child care, they are more likely to realize their full economic potential," he wrote.[42]

Some advocates for the current status quo are undeterred by unaffordability, arguing that you get what you pay for. Diane Barber, the director of the Pennsylvania Child Care Association, says there's a good reason why it costs Keystone State families so much for daycare. "It costs more to do quality," she says. Perhaps her idea of quality is the growing pile of regulations that govern every aspect of licensed daycare, sending the cost skyward.

REGULATIONS RAISE PRICES

A Rand Corporation–sponsored study in 2004 reinforces this paradigm. "Our evidence indicates that state regulations influence parents' childcare decisions primarily through a price effect, which lowers use of regulated childcare and discourages labor force participation. We find no evidence for a quality-assurance effect."[43] Parents either decide to forgo a second income and have one partner stay home with the kids because the price of licensed care is so high, or they forgo regulated daycare and opt for child care that doesn't cost as much. And not every parent can decide between these options since single parents don't have the option of a second paycheck they can forgo in lieu of paying for child care.

The argument justifying greater oversight and control of daycare isn't unique. It is nearly the same argument that is made for teeth-whitening, hair-braiding, and ride-sharing: We—the regulators, the advocates, the bureaucrats—have to make sure that consumers—or parents in the case of daycare—don't get defrauded. Researchers M. Rebecca Kilburn of Rand Corporation and V. Joseph Hotz of the University of Chicago helpfully summarized the position of these government nannies: "The lack of perfect information faced by consumers in the child care market has . . . been cited as a justification for legislating minimum quality standards and the licensing of day care providers. Parents may be imperfectly informed about the quality of available care because the multidimensional attributes of these services are difficult to evaluate and/or monitor."[44]

The reality is, however, that every imposition of rules and standards means additional costs for the daycare provider to comply with those rules, and those costs are then passed along to the consumers of the service—the parents. As Jordan Weissmann detailed in *The Atlantic*,

> If a center is required by law to have 25 square feet of space for every kid in a program, it can't ever downsize its building when rents rise. If it has to hire a care giver for every two children, it can't really achieve any economies of scale on labor to save money when other expenses go up. A comparative case in point: in Massachusetts, where child care centers must hire one teacher for every three infants, the price of care averaged more

than $16,000 per year. In Mississippi, where centers must hire one teacher for every five infants, the price of care averaged less than $5,000.[45]

Another problem is that very few states, if any, are satisfied with "minimum quality standards." The opposite is most often the case. Take the current argument that child-care providers should have more training. This issue is pressed onto daycare because of the current failure of the general K–12 system to properly educate millions of children. Instead of focusing on that problem, politicians, academics, and advocates now argue that children, and most especially low-income, at-risk kids, have to be "prepared" for school by having them get the support they need at daycare. As a result, there's been a growing move to standardize daycare into more of a preschool model.

As Katharine Stevens detailed in the *Wall Street Journal*, federal government money for improving standards of care come with strings. "The devil is in the details," Stevens writes. "Child-care providers who receive the new funding will be subject to federal monitoring and required to comply with the 2,400 Head Start 'Performance Standards' stipulating everything from staff qualifications to cot placement to how to clean potties."[46]

Jeffrey Tucker has a pretty good explanation for why and how we've gotten to this point. He says that the "regulatory structures began in 1962 with legislation that required child care facilities to be state-licensed in order to get federal funding grants. As one might expect, 40 percent of the money allocated toward this purpose was spent on establishing licensing procedures rather than funding the actual care, with the result that child care services actually declined after the legislation."[47] Child-care supply has fallen short of demand ever since. The federal government is still imposing standards through Head

Start programs using the argument that if you want our money then you have to follow our rules. And the increased demands for "quality" only make it more expensive to open and operate licensed facilities.

Another recent additional requirement is that providers have more education. Stevens makes a good argument for why such a requirement is problematic: It doesn't ensure the kids are better cared for. "The requirement that all preschool teachers have bachelor's degrees (in any field) to ensure 'a qualified workforce' in early childhood education is particularly detrimental. Young children don't need a qualified workforce. They need an effective workforce. There's no evidence that bachelor's degrees make preschool teachers more effective."[48]

Moreover, there is research showing that it is the relationship between kids and their teachers that matters most, not whether the daycare worker or preschool teacher has an undergraduate degree. University of Virginia professors Bridget K. Hamre and Robert C. Pianta found that "[c]hildren who form close relationships with teachers enjoy school more and get along better with peers. Positive relationships with teachers can also serve as a secure base for young children; they are better able to play and work on their own because they know that if things get difficult or if they are upset, they can count on their teacher to recognize and respond to these problems."[49]

This really isn't rocket science; it is common sense. Most children who spend their days in a warm, loving, clean, and safe environment are going to thrive in that environment, and you don't need a university degree to give love to toddlers. The insistence on such rules hurts the very parents and kids that it is meant to help.

Creating higher hurdles for staffing daycare means that you have to pay more to that staff and then raise tuition to help offset those costs. That pushes "high-quality" daycare out of reach of middle- and low-income parents and especially high-risk poor kids. Hotz and Kilburn put it this way: "More stringent educational requirements on child care providers may reduce the uncertainty parents have about the quality of child care services they are likely to receive in the market. As a result of this greater certainty, parents may be more willing to use nonparental child care."[50]

Jonathan Cohn weighed in on the virtues of licensed daycare exactly for the population that Hotz and Kilburn say are lost if costs go up.[51] Even as he agreed that regulations cost money ("daycare is a bruising financial burden for many families—more expensive than rent in 22 states"), Cohn explained how good daycare—what the experts call "high quality"—is imperative given studies showing that

> [k]ids who grow up in nurturing, interactive environments tend to develop the skills they need to thrive as adults—like learning how to calm down after a setback or how to focus on a problem long enough to solve it. Kids who grow up without that kind of attention tend to lack impulse control and have more emotional outbursts. Later on, they are more likely to struggle in school or with the law. They also have more physical health problems.[52]

The trouble is that this mandate, while it may tempt parents with the thought of supposedly more expert child care, may put the entire experience out of reach. Hotz and Kilburn explain that "imposing more stringent regulations on child care services—such as requiring child care providers to have greater formal training—will result in an increase in the price charged for such services which will cause parents to shift *out of* regulated care into cheaper lower quality care."[53] They conclude that regulations raise the cost of licensed daycare to the point where it isn't used by those children—poor kids of single moms—who could benefit the most. "State regulations both increase the cost of child care as well as have direct (non-price) effects on utilization but ... their total effect tends to reduce the utilization of market-based child care, especially among households with non-working mothers," they explained.[54]

Ten years later, when David Blau of the University of North Carolina at Chapel Hill examined the impact of regulations on child-care regulations in 2006, he found that imposing "quality" standards depressed the salaries for child-care workers. "Tougher regulations," he writes, have been imposed by "many states ... in recent years." But Blau's results "raise the question about why states impose such regulations. They appear to be ineffective at improving the average quality of child care, and the higher costs they create are absorbed largely by the staff of day care centers."[55]

As part of an exposé of unregulated daycare in Virginia in 2014, *Washington Post* reporters David Fallis and Amy Brittain admitted that daycare regulations are what make licensed child care so expensive. "For regulated child care [in Virginia], costs can exceed $300 a week per child. That cost reflects the background checks; mandatory training and certifications; mandatory staffing ratios; and child-proof facilities that meet state standards for square footage and safety," wrote Fallis and Brittain.[56]

Increased regulations result in lower wages for child-care providers and/or higher costs to the parents. And who is most hurt by those higher costs? Why, the very people who were supposed to benefit most from the improvements: the parents with kids who need more help (via daycare and preschool) to prepare for starting regular school. "Since economically disadvantaged and black women are disproportionately represented in [this] group, it appears that one of the consequences of regulations is to deter the utilization of child care by households with children for whom the purported developmental benefits of organized day care might be most beneficial," Hotz and Kilburn explain.[57] What good are daycare centers that meet bureaucratic standards for space per child and staff educational attainment if no one can afford to send her kids there?

NANNY STATE WANTS MORE CONTROL, BUT LESS IS BETTER

President Obama was correct to call child care in America a "must-have" and not a "nice-to-have" because of another must-have: labor-force participation by women as well as men. We are no longer living in a world where most couples can afford to have one person stay home to raise the kids, and since so many parents aren't married or living with a partner, working outside the home is the reality of most people's lives. Given those circumstances, reasonable options for safe and affordable daycare are another must-have. The variable in this equation are the options for safe, affordable daycare. As we've seen, those options are limited by overly aggressive regulation. And the current adherence to long lists of safety and hygiene rules about coat-hook placement, hand-washing standards, food preparation, and educational certification are what prevent the marketplace for child care from blooming.

Happily, there is nothing that says we have to stick with these types of costly, ineffective, inefficient, and (sometimes) irrational rules! "Modern government is designed to be a kind of legal machine. But it is badly designed. Indeed, it may be one of the worst machines ever invented. Its core flaw is that it aspires to make choices without human judgment at the moment of action," writes Philip Howard.[58]

Howard's analysis will resonate with any parent who has had a kid in regulated daycare. As I explained, there are notes sent home all the time about no plastic bags and reminders about what size foods are allowed at school. And these aren't driven by the child-care providers. We are often reminded that the "rules" that govern the daycare require that we be informed of, made aware of, and updated about every policy handed down from the state. As Howard says, the daycare isn't being allowed to use independent human judgment (does every grape need to be cut and into how many pieces) at the "moment of action" (when they are actually feeding the kids).

Howard does have a suggestion:

> Nothing will get fixed until we give back to officials the authority that goes along with their responsibility. This requires more than reform. It requires remaking our structure of government—toward radically simplified structures with room for humans in charge to accomplish public goals. That's what other countries are doing—replacing thick rule books with a few dozen goals and principles, liberating citizens and regulators alike to use their judgment and better accomplish public goals without getting paralyzed by red tape.[59]

For parents and child-care workers, there is no greater source of paralysis than the red tape that rules daycare regulations. So why not change the way we think about the rules governing child care. Instead of preemptively making lists of dos and don'ts, how about making much more general principles of value within which every provider can operate.

Research on daycare regulations and quality would seem to reinforce Howard's point. "The overall effect of increased regulation might be counter to their advocates' intentions.... Relatively modest changes in regulations would have large and economically important consequences," Randal Heeb and Rebecca Kilburn wrote in their 2004 study.[60]

For a model of what is possible, Howard offers examples of "new governance standards" that are principles-based and values-based rather than rules-based. In Germany, for example, "a Bavarian statute requires that the [school] principal 'work together in trust' with teachers and parents. Instead of rigid 'zero tolerance' rules, the regulations at one high school state simply that 'dangerous objects may not be brought to school,' leaving it to the principal to decide what's dangerous," Howard writes.[61]

Howard argues that "the best approach, for many areas of government oversight, is to invert the current legal structure—where the general principles are binding but the explanatory rules are generally not."[62] Replace the rules about how small to cut the apples and cucumber with general rules about the well-being of every child in daycare. This would lead to what Howard calls "a radically simplified structure focused on public goals," and you could then "make officials take responsibility to meet those goals."[63] When I interviewed Howard, he explained the problem with the "1,000-page rule book" for daycare providers. "What one wants in daycare is human accountability to meet certain values and goals that can be overseen, but to do so with originality and a sense of humor. Instead, we make everyone go brain dead."

In his book *The Rule of Nobody*, Howard explains that Australia radically changed their regulatory scheme of nursing homes in 1988.

> It abandoned hundreds of input-oriented regulations (for example, requiring floor area of "at least 80 feet per resident") and replaced them with thirty-one outcome-oriented standards (such as providing a "homelike environment" and honoring residents' "privacy and dignity"). Australia also transformed nursing home enforcement, focusing on overall quality, not

hard metrics or paperwork compliance. Instead of slapping nursing homes with fines whenever something was amiss, the regulators required meetings among all interested parties, including families, consumer advocates and nurses, to discuss how to improve things. The state preserved its authority to sanction or close nursing homes, but kept it in reserve.[64]

The effect, report John and Valerie Braithwaite of Australian National University, was staggering, especially considering that the researchers had started out perfectly sure the reforms would fail miserably. Instead, it turned out that values-based, outcome-oriented standards were much more effective than an input-based rule book. As the Braithwaites concluded,

> Our research findings provided quite strong grounds for believing that the broad, unrefined Australian standards are not just more reliable than US standards but more reliable by a wide margin. Furthermore, observations of 59 nursing-home inspections in Australia and 44 in the USA between 1988 and 1993 suggest that the reason Australian ratings are more reliable is precisely because they are more (a) broad, (b) subjective, (c) undefined with regard to protocols, (d) resident-centered and (e) devoid of random sampling.[65]

Does anyone think that caring for the elderly in nursing homes is somehow radically different than caring for babies and toddlers? To be sure, nursing homes are more complicated since babies don't live at daycare as seniors at nursing homes do. But the principles are the same. And indeed, there seems to be progress in the US in terms of freeing nursing homes from an oppressive regulatory burden.

As Anthony L. Fisher wrote at *Reason*, greater autonomy

at nursing homes, instead of burdensome regulations, makes for happier residents and better living conditions.[66] And that is just what has happened among some senior homes in America. Fisher spoke to Christopher Perna, CEO of The Eden Alternative, which has spent 20 years working "with nursing homes to venture as far they can into the 'grey areas' of regulations" to help "reinstitute a degree of autonomy" for both the residents and the staff at the homes.[67]

Perna explained that "if residents want to sleep in in the morning, let them sleep in. If they want to be an early riser, let them wake up early. If they go to bed early, let them go to bed early. If they like to be a night owl, let them be a night owl. And adapt the organization and staffing approaches to the needs of the elders."[68] What a concept, to let the staff adapt to the needs of individuals in their care. It would have helped my son's transition to daycare if his caretakers, in consultation with me, could have decided together on what he might need to thrive. The problem for daycare operators who might want to adopt this more flexible model is the seeming lack of regulatory "grey areas" in which to try and maneuver.

Yet there is precedent for regulatory reform. In 2011, the state of Idaho eased rules about teacher-child ratios and who is considered capable of taking care of kids.[69] The point was to make it easier for operators to function and maintain a minimal safety standard. The reforms still focus on inputs rather than outcomes and values, but at least there is a model for lowering the bar rather than raising it. There hasn't been some explosion of accidents or trouble in Idaho as a result of the reforms, either.

Whether you take care of your kids yourself or send them to daycare of whatever variety, parents are the ones responsible for making an educated decision about where and how their kids spend their days. Given that responsibility, it doesn't help when regulations enforce a standard that many parents can't afford or might not even want. The best-case scenario would be regulatory reform that allows for a broader market of child-care options, all of which provide a minimally safe, reasonably clean place for kids to spend their days. If I want to spend $16,000 to have my infant's gums "brushed" like teeth, great. But why can't I have the choice of spending a whole lot less and brush his gums myself at home?

CHAPTER 4

School Statists

Obsessed with health and fat shaming

IN NOVEMBER 2014, a group of parents and children in Florida rallied, picketed, and protested to earn their kids the right to a healthier school day. In a nod to Disney's *Frozen*, some kids dressed in costume hoisting protest signs that read "Recess: Don't let it go." Ultimately the Lake County school district agreed to require that all elementary-school students receive an hour of free play time per week, though what the parents originally demanded was 30 minutes of recess a day, every day.

The timing of these protests is ironic since, in other ways, children's health has become such an obsessive focus of governmental nannies that nearly all public and private schools have been touched by the effort. But instead of concentrating on the simplest and cheapest remedy to the stated problem—too much obesity and a sedentary culture—by increasing physical activity at school, other prescriptions have been imposed, such as weight information and especially food mandates. Of course, eating well at school is important, but when debatable science is coupled with the force of government dictates, the result is inefficient, expensive, ineffective policy while children and parents lose. In this chapter we will explore the imbalance between ignoring, even eroding the physical-activity needs of school kids—and obsessing, often counterproductively, over food intake when it should not be a government concern.

Michelle Obama is the patron saint of the nanny-state diet. She gets the honor not only for initiating her Let's Move campaign and revamping the school-lunch program in 2010, but also for expanding access to her dietary mandates in 2014. Now if a school district has at least 40 percent of students eligible for free lunch, she is throwing in free breakfast too.

The government's logic does seem reasonable. "Many children consume at least half of their meals at school, and for many children, food served at school may be the only food they regularly eat," the Let's Move campaign website declares.[1] But what started out as a positive effort to promote good habits in American children has morphed into yet more government overreach rather than effective problem solving.

Consider for a moment the basis of the effort to change school lunch. Let's Move argues that since some percentage of kids eat some percentage of their meals at school, then all school meals ought to be designed for the exceptional cases of kids who are either at risk of being overweight or obese or who may not get food anywhere else but school. This is an amazing claim. It means applying the contours of an outlier case to a huge pool that is normal. There are some 50 million K–12 public-school students in America, according to the Department of Education. In the 2013–14 school year, 31 million students received five billion meals at a cost of some $16 billion.[2]

How many of those 50 million kids are in situations that require the restricted diet that is currently in use? Good luck finding the answer. Of course everyone should have healthy meals at school. But over the past several years, things have gotten out of hand, with nutrition mandates for all public schools in the form of legislation included in the Healthy Hunger-Free Kids Act and the National School Lunch Program, absurd rules for healthy snacks at private schools, and invasive letters home to parents warning that their child's body mass index may be unhealthy. All these new rules have inspired some new Captain Mommies who just don't like government-defined healthy living.

MICHELLE'S MEALS ARE ONE-SIZE, ONE-DIET FITS ALL

Give the folks who really don't like the revised federal school-lunch program some credit. Many have been creative and funny in their criticisms of the standards set out by the 2010 law. There's the YouTube video covering the hit song "We Are Young," by the band Fun, replacing the chorus with the lyrics "we are hungry" and "set this policy on fire." The video has been viewed over a million times. For a good laugh, check out the Twitter hashtag #ThanksMichelleObama and #brownbaggingit, where you can see pictures of lunch trays exhibiting the low-calorie and equally unappetizing offerings at various public schools across the country. There are even a couple of top-ten lists cataloguing the best of the worst among the hashtags.

When the new reduced-calorie lunches were introduced in 2012, Twitter, parent blogs, and advice sites blew up with complaints about how kids were coming home hungry and how the school lunches were just too small. Whether the meals are too small for every student is debatable. But parents were right about the restrictiveness of the new rules, which institute more limited calories and define what sort and how many of each type of calorie are allowed.

According to the USDA, which administers the National School Lunch Program, students in grades K–5 are to receive no more than 650 calories per lunch; middle schoolers are allowed a maximum of 700 calories; and for grades 9–12, the limit is 850 calories. There are also fine-tuned limits on fruits, vegetables, meat, milk, and grains allowed per week, with vegetables broken down among dark green, red/orange, beans and peas, and starchy. The total calories are also broken down with strict limits on salt and saturated fat.[3]

This uniformity is to be expected since government mandates are by necessity one-size-fits-all, and when the USDA announced the new menus, the point was to reduce fat and sodium along with calories. Health was the reason the USDA decided that lunch standards needed to be updated. "The nation faces an obesity epidemic with nearly one in three children at risk for preventable diseases like diabetes and heart disease due to overweight and obesity. Left unaddressed, health experts tell us that our current generation of children may well have a shorter lifespan than their parents. Since kids may consume as many as half their meals in schools, school meals play a critical role in helping children learn how to lead healthy lifestyles."[4]

It is quite a lot of work to get past all those ifs and maybes. *Nearly* a third of kids are *at risk* for diseases that *may* be due to being overweight and obese, and *if* these possible health risks are left unaddressed—though the USDA doesn't say why or whether it is likely that such risks would be completely ignored—it *might* shorten their lifespan. So if *some* of these kids eat *nearly* half their meals at school, we'd better make sure *all* of those meals conform to a restricted diet for those who are overweight and obese. That's big-government logic for you.

Putting aside these wildly expansive assumptions, the USDA goes on to explain the science behind the menus. "[T]he new standards reflect the latest knowledge base about health and nutrition. The standards are based on the Dietary Guidelines for Americans (DGA)—the Federal government's benchmark for nutrition—as well as the recommendations of the nutrition experts at the Institute of Medicine (IOM)—a gold standard for scientific analysis."[5]

At first glance, the key findings from the DGA make sense

as the basis for school lunch menus. The first two items on the list read as follows:

> Control total calorie intake to manage body weight. For people who are overweight or obese, this will mean consuming fewer calories from foods and beverages.

> Increase physical activity and reduce time spent in sedentary behaviors.[6]

The DGA goes into detail as well about what kinds of calories people at risk for overweight and obesity should be careful to avoid and which to try to increase in their diet. The DGA is anti-fat, anti-sugar, and anti-salt, and pro–whole grains. "A healthy eating pattern limits intake of sodium, solid fats, added sugars, and refined grains and emphasizes nutrient-dense foods and beverages—vegetables, fruits, whole grains, fat-free or low-fat milk and milk products, seafood, lean meats and poultry, eggs, beans and peas, and nuts and seeds," declares the 2010 DGA.[7]

For the purposes of controlling calories, the DGA recommends that school meals "increase intake of fat-free or low-fat milk and milk products, such as milk, yogurt" and replace "protein foods that are higher in solid fats with choices that are lower in solid fats and calories and/or are sources of oils." The DGA also recommends replacing solid fats "where possible" and choosing foods "that provide more potassium, dietary fiber, calcium, and vitamin D, which are nutrients of concern in American diets. These foods include vegetables, fruits, whole grains, and milk and milk products."[8]

Now, the anti-fat position is debatable, especially when strict limits have been adopted as the basis for children's lunches. The point here is not to argue that deep-frying everything is healthy, of course. But it is equally useful to remember that chil-

dren do need fat for healthy development—physical and intellectual—and that the DGA is recommending modifying your
diet based on being at risk for being overweight or obese. The
researchers' initial consideration, therefore, is not how to live a
healthy life. Rather, they assume that everyone should restrict
their diet because everyone is considered to be on the verge of
being overweight or morbidly obese.

The folks who write these reports are also obviously so
caught up in inoffensive bureaucrat-speak that the DGA reads
at times like it was written in jest. Take this pronouncement for
example: "A basic premise of the Dietary Guidelines is that nutrient needs should be met primarily through consuming foods.
Foods provide an array of nutrients and other components that
are thought to have beneficial effects on health."[9]

Did it really take a team of more than 40 experts to discover
that food has "a beneficial effect on health"? Or that achieving
basic "nutrient needs" should be "met primarily through consuming food"? What else were these "experts" thinking Americans should consume for their sustenance instead of food?
Perhaps they considered the efficacy of recommending a liquid
diet. God help us if they did.

Beyond the absurd language, though, the real problem with
offering all American school kids a restricted-calorie diet at
lunch is that it turns out not to guarantee healthier eating. First,
the problem is that lots of students have rejected being forced
to eat what's being offered. "When lunch ends, I feel that the
trash cans are more full than my stomach," student Lindsey
Russell told her local newspaper in Fort Mill, South Carolina.[10]

This observation is borne out by various news reports about
wasted lunch and about school lunch ladies begging Congress
to change the rules so they can get out from under severe,
ineffective mandates. Students are throwing out pounds and

pounds of food that ends up costing millions of dollars. And meanwhile, schools and their administrators are telling the federal government that one size doesn't fit all.

In December 2014, the School Nutrition Association (SNA) published a survey of trends that found multiple challenges for school districts.[11] "More than half of school meal program operators surveyed anticipate that their program expenses will exceed revenue this school year," reports the SNA. And indeed, since the new national school-lunch regulations were introduced, many schools and even several school districts have decided to opt out of the new restricted-calorie meals. The complaint is that kids hate the new menus—a fact borne out by a 2014 Government Accountability Office audit showing that more than one million students aren't buying lunch anymore.

It is worth remembering that the SNA lobbied hard in support of the reformed school-lunch program.[12] It seems, however, that the reality of trying to run a successful (read: profitable) food-service program within the new regime isn't what the "lunch ladies" thought it would be. Turns out that the food costs more, and they are getting reimbursed by the USDA at a lower level than they expected. "Some of the new regulations have just been so restrictive, and the costs involved in implementing them have been unexpectedly high," explained Diane Pratt-Heavner, a spokesperson for the SNA.[13] She estimates that while the cost of preparing lunch has gone up by 10 cents a meal, the government is reimbursing at a rate of six cents a meal.

One response to this new reality is that wealthier schools have hired chefs to improve the school lunches. Chef Brittany Young was hired in Valencia, California,[14] and Scott Hudak was hired as a regional chef for The Nutrition Group.[15] Their task is to make the new meals more palatable to more students, and as they tell it, following the rules isn't easy. "Whatever it is," Hudak explained, "it has to fall into a category. To make a simple sandwich like a turkey Reuben, you have to go through the requirements with the bread for the grains, the meat, the cheese, the protein. It takes more than just 'Hey, let me slap this together.'"[16] If we agree that food in school should be healthy, can we also agree that trained chefs and multiple miniscule calorie calculations should not be necessary to accomplish the goal of a good meal?

Another important question to address is whether targeting school lunch in this manner—through one-menu-fits-all directives from the USDA—is actually the most effective way to reduce obesity among our kids. What if there are other, more dangerous contributing factors to childhood obesity, like whether the parents are on food stamps? It turns out that of the 46 million Americans receiving benefits from the USDA's Supplemental Nutrition Assistance Program (SNAP), 40 percent are more likely to be obese than even the poor who don't take SNAP benefits but who could qualify.[17] And children in families participating in SNAP were also more likely to be obese than children in families not accepting the benefit.[18]

The USDA claims to have a handle on solving this crisis, however. A 2015 report explains that "[w]hile most Americans need to improve their diets substantially to conform to the [government's dietary guidelines], this analysis revealed a number of patterns that can inform nutrition promotion efforts specifically among SNAP participants."[19] The USDA is sure that education programs will "encourage participants to replace whole and reduced-fat milk with low-fat or nonfat milk" as well as "encourage participants to increase consumption of fruits and vegetables" and "encourage participants to reduce consumption of regular sodas."[20] No strict menus or calorie counting for food-stamp recipients and their families, mind you.

THE POLITICS OF GREEK YOGURT

One aspect of the school-lunch program that is important to recall for the purposes of our discussion is that it was originally constructed to take care of two problems at once: providing free food to school kids and supporting the nation's agricultural sector. Challenges arise when these two interests conflict rather than coalesce, however.

In its earliest incarnation, free-food programs at school were about combating real deprivation. "To reduce the incidence of crime, vagrancy and prostitution, Children's Aid opened its first industrial school for poor children and initiated the first free school lunch program in the United States" in 1853, according to the Children's Aid Society website.[21] Eighty years later, during the Great Depression, the federal government served "one million undernourished children ... 80,000,000 hot well-balanced meals ... at the rate of 500,000 daily in 10,000 schools throughout the country," according to the Works Progress Administration.[22]

By the middle of the 20th century, Congress passed the National School Lunch Act, which clearly defined its policy purpose "as a measure of national security, to safeguard the health and well-being of the Nation's children and to encourage the domestic consumption of nutritious agricultural commodities and other food, by assisting the States, through grants-in-aid and other means, in providing an adequate supply of food and other facilities for the establishment, maintenance, operation and expansion of nonprofit school lunch programs."[23] The law served two purposes, striving to feed school kids while simultaneously balancing their dietary needs with those of the "food supply," which meant agricultural output. Hence, it was and has remained under the control of the Department of Agriculture ever since.

In 2012, the USDA announced it was buying hundreds of

millions of dollars in meat, poultry, and fish from farmers and ranchers to help them through a terrible drought. The food was then to be distributed to the national school-lunch program, along with various other food-assistance programs. As Agriculture Secretary Tom Vilsack announced at the time, help was needed for "producers who are currently struggling due to the challenging market conditions and the high cost of feed resulting from the widespread drought." The USDA bought "$100 million in pork products; $10 million in catfish; $50 million in chicken; and $10 million in lamb products" and distributed those products to America's school children and others who receive government food assistance.[24]

Is catfish the healthiest seafood the USDA could provide to school kids? Not really, but there was an urgent need to help American producers out of a crisis. This balance between helping farmers by buying up their commodity and then passing that product along to kids for school lunches has been part of the lunch program from the beginning.

These days, however, there are various interest groups that oppose how that balance is struck. For example, in 2012, a group called the Physicians Committee for Responsible Medicine (PCRM) petitioned the USDA to "stop the dairy industry from milking school lunches for profit."[25]

"Milk doesn't make children grow taller and stronger, but it can make them heavier," says PCRM nutrition education director Susan Levin, M.S., R.D. Yet the federal government spends more money on dairy products than any other food item in the school-lunch program. "We are asking Congress and the USDA to put children's interests above the interests of the dairy industry. Focusing on milk as the single most important source of calcium in children's diets distracts schools and parents from foods that can actually build bones, like beans and leafy greens," Levin explained. The PCRM petitioners also claim that "abundant research shows milk does not improve bone health and is the biggest source of saturated ('bad') fat in the diet—the very fat that Dietary Guidelines push us to avoid." On this basis, they want the USDA to stop requiring milk in school lunches.[26]

There was also a political scrum over the salt restrictions in the new lunches that got so heated it became part of the 2014 budget battle. In the end, Mrs. Obama might not have been too happy that her husband signed the $1.1 trillion budget bill since it relaxed rules on salt limits until they are "supported by additional scientific studies."[27]

Sometimes it works the other way, as political cronyism actually trumps what's most efficient and nutritious. An example came to light in the summer of 2013 when the USDA announced it would pilot a new menu item in four states. The product was Greek-style yogurt, and not only is it more expensive than comparably nutritious dairy products, but Greek-style yogurt specifically serves to help one state's economy—that of New York. Indeed, it was only after one company—Chobani—and one Senator—New York's Chuck Schumer—lobbied the USDA that this new product was announced. And the pilot program had to be limited because this sort of yogurt is actually so much more perishable that the USDA could only guarantee it could get it to schools that were close enough to the distribution centers. Seems that where expedient the USDA will choose to benefit those few who have the influence over the many parents who might not want their tax dollars spent in this way for school lunches their kids hate.

PARENTS VS SCHOOL LUNCH

Now that the USDA has decided there is only one way to eat "properly," parents have been hearing complaints from schools about the home-packed lunches they prepare.

On January 20, 2015, Justin Puckett got a letter from his daughter's substitute teacher at Kirksville Primary School in Kirksville, Missouri, critiquing his lunch choices (based on inaccurate information as it turned out) and asking him to pack her a "proper" lunch next time. To her credit, the school principal apologized for the overzealous teacher, but Puckett's real complaint is not going to be fixed with an apology. "The issue isn't what happened at the Primary School and with my daughter because she is very independent and going to be completely unaffected by this. But what does bother me is that it just seems that we are constantly being inundated with the inability to be parents of our children," Puckett told reporters.[28]

It isn't really a question of what parents pack or don't pack for their children's lunch, however. Where do teachers get the idea that they have been given the authority to critique lunch?

In Aurora, Colorado, a mom complained to reporters in April 2015 when her daughter's teacher wouldn't allow the girl to finish her homemade lunch because it was deemed insufficiently nutritious.[29] In Richmond, Virginia, one elementary school has been sending notes home telling parents that if they wanted to send in home-packed lunch, a doctor's note would be required.[30] At Chicago's Little Village Academy, the principal decided to ban homemade lunch because she just didn't like the choices parents were making. "Nutrition wise, it is better for the children to eat at the school," Principal Elsa Carmona said. "It's about the nutrition and the excellent quality food that they are able to serve (in the lunchroom). It's milk versus a Coke."[31] This explanation makes it sound as if the principal is certain parents won't make good choices for their kids. Is that really true in all cases? And is it really her business to police this area of their lives? Apparently, not, because when this story was reported widely, the principal quickly retracted the policy. So let's hear it for shining a light on a bad idea.

After the nanny state crashed into Heather Parker's life and turned her into a new Captain Mommy, she complained to her state representative and a couple of congressional legislators who got equally bent out of shape about what had happened to her four-year-old daughter. In February 2012, as widely reported by local and national news outlets, Parker sent her kid to school at West Hoke Elementary in North Carolina with a lunch consisting of a turkey and cheese sandwich, apple juice, a banana, and potato chips. But that seemingly inoffensive collection of food was an alarm bell to the food inspector who confiscated the child's lunch for failing to meet federal nutrition standards.

Instead of being allowed to eat her home-packed lunch, Parker's daughter was given a school-prepared lunch because it supposedly met the proper dietary requirements. She was given chicken nuggets. And according to state law, the food inspector was just doing his job. "When children bring their own food for meals and snacks to the center, if the food does not meet the specified nutritional requirements, the center must provide additional food necessary to meet those requirements."[32] But doesn't it seem a bit nutty that a turkey and cheese sandwich was replaced with chicken nuggets as the healthier option?

Parker wrote a letter to her state representative, Republican G. L. Pridgen of Robeson County, to complain about the inspection regime. "I don't feel that I should pay for a cafeteria lunch when I provide lunch for her from home," Parker wrote.[33] Pridgen took up the challenge and began investigating why a food inspector was confiscating a perfectly good homemade lunch. Then Capitol Hill got in on the action when two North Carolina congressional representatives decided that Secretary of Agriculture Tom Vilsack should answer for the incident as well. "This unfortunate and absolutely unnecessary event exemplifies the very definition of 'government overreach' and further perpetuates a growing reason of why the American people continue to hold less and less faith in our government," wrote US Reps. Larry Kissell (D-NC) and Renee Ellmers (R-NC).[34] More recently, Rep. Steve King (R-IA) has reintroduced legislation called the No Hungry Kids Act (it was originally introduced in 2012) to repeal USDA "calorie rationing" rules and protect "the rights of parents to send their children to school with the foods of their choice."[35]

We are at a point when food choice has been severely restricted for society's own protection. Cities and other government authorities have decided that adults cannot choose for themselves how much soda to drink, whether to eat foods fried in oils high in trans-fats, or whether consuming goose liver is OK. When the farm bill came up for reauthorization last time, there was a terrible fight over the regulation of small organic farms, with bigger agribusiness demanding rules for smaller growers that would stifle competition. There are significant regulations regarding open-air green markets and homemade food because elected officials and appointed bureaucrats have decided that responsible individuals can't decide for themselves what to eat and drink; instead, the government has to do it for them, to protect them. These efforts at safe, healthy eating are also about calculating the economic impact on the whole of society when individuals eat badly. It is supposed to benefit all of society to curtail food choice, because if some of us overindulge, we will get fat; we might contract diabetes or liver disease or a heart condition that will mean we will cost the health-care system more than if we had made better choices in the first place.

When it comes to kids, however, this overzealousness almost knows no bounds, because when speaking of children, we assume that it is the role of adults (not just parents, but the community, the village, the authorities) to protect and provide. How does this attitude square up with families and the role of parents to protect and provide for their own kin though? We have gone past the point of trusting parents to care for their kids. Instead, we have government programs staffed by unaccountable bureaucrats making questionable decisions. What is done supposedly in the name of nutrition and health doesn't necessarily result in healthier kids, but more anxious, disempowered parents.

When I discussed this phenomenon with one father I know, he countered that food in school used to be junk that wasn't healthy and that schools should be offering nutritious food to children. That's a great and logical premise, but I replied that the result of current meddling costs too much and wasn't actually solving the problem. His response was to shake his head and say that "the government is always inefficient and expensive," but there's still a public-policy problem that needs to be addressed. In other words, he accepted the paradigm that doing anything was better than doing something actually effective. As a Captain Mommy, I reject this thinking, and as a parent, I demand and deserve better. So does everyone else.

HEALTH SCREENING AT SCHOOL CREATES PROBLEMS

"Why not just be honest and admit that this isn't about helping people; it's about what 'nanny schooling' is always about: power and control," demanded Reuben Navarette Jr. at CNN .com, when he wrote about a letter sent home from school to parents regarding their kids' weight.[36] Navarette's is a legitimate critique about another aspect of the current efforts to prescribe from on high what will "solve" the crisis of children's weight.

The federal government and some 21 states have instituted rules that public-school kids get health screenings during

school hours. In our data-driven times, collecting health information about individual children outside the family or medical
context is deemed useful and even necessary because of the risk
to society as a whole when too many of us are unhealthily overweight or obese.

The measurement used in these screening programs is the
body mass index. BMI is the ratio of weight to height squared,
and it is often used by doctors as part of routine medical assess-
ments to determine whether someone is of normal weight, un-
derweight, overweight, or clinically obese. As useful as it can be
as a health guideline, BMI is not without problems, including
the fact that the result does not differentiate between weight
from fat and weight from muscle. Professional athletes, for example, can have high BMI but are not categorized as overweight or obese because of their muscle mass.

The trouble with such screenings begins with the fact that
some schools have failed to properly collect the information.
At times, high-school students have been entrusted with the
task of weighing and measuring each other, or due to a lack of
health staff, teachers and administrators are trained to take the
information in lieu of a school nurse. At other schools, the data
is collected as part of the physical-education curriculum.

The headline-grabbing issue with all this is that, after collecting this data, some schools have chosen to alert parents
with a letter home "warning" parents that their children may be
overweight, at-risk, or even obese.

Laura Cacdac's daughter Charley asked her mom if the letter she brought home meant she was fat. "Is there something
wrong with me?" she asked her mom.[37] The six-year-old was
referring to the form letter from her school about her BMI,
which read in part, "From the results of this test, it is suggested
that your child's health be examined by a physician, particularly
as it relates to the problem suggested by the screening. A prob-

lem such as this that goes uncorrected or untreated can severely affect both the health and academic performance of your child." This sort of letter has been upsetting parents nearly everywhere it is in use.

"Why are we doing this?" asked Tracy Watson after her son Cam brought home a letter reporting he was obese. "These letters were doing more harm than good to kids out there."[38] Parents from Florida to California to New York have spoken out against these letters for a variety of reasons, including the intrusiveness of their schools shaming their kids about their bodies.

In New York City, approximately 870,000 students each year take what are called "Fitnessgrams." The problem recently has been that kids have been opening the letters and getting a very nasty shock. One mom told Fox News it was "awful to see" her four-foot-one, 66-pound, eight-year-old daughter's reaction. "My daughter is thin; she knows she doesn't have a weight problem, but that night, I caught her grabbing the skin near her waist, and she asked me, 'is this what they were talking about?'" Laura Bruiji Williams explained.[39] "With body image such an issue, it's amazing to me that these letters weren't mailed to parents," she said.

For Laura's daughter Gwendolyn, the "Fitnessgrams" are just dumb. "I know that I'm not overweight, so why should I believe the New York Department of Education?" she told the *New York Post*.[40] At age eight, Gwendolyn has now become a young Captain Mommy, as she has realized that what "officials" say isn't always to be believed or accepted.

Sometimes when parents find out about this stuff, they fight to keep hold of their authority. "In 2011, parents complained when Hawthorne Elementary School in Elmhurst [IL] planned to include BMI results as part of a physical fitness grade. The school hastily dropped the idea," reported the *Chicago Tribune*'s Julie Dierdorff.[41] But then schools don't decide not to collect the information; they just opt to share it with the state instead of sharing with parents as well.

The problem of these letters goes beyond hurt feelings or privacy, however. "Dieting, especially for kids, is the gateway drug for eating disorders, and so is the public shaming that can come with this," Chevese Turner of the Binge Eating Disorder Association explained of these sort of fitness letters. "My organization and others believe that BMI report cards have no place coming from schools and can be more harmful than helpful," she told the *New York Post*.[42]

Kathleen MacDonald is Policy Director of the Eating Disorders Coalition, and her group says that schools just aren't the right place for BMI testing. "The American Academy of Pediatrics offers guidelines to practicing pediatricians that they track BMIs as part of their routine health care. The standard practice for pediatricians is to measure a child's body weight upon yearly examinations. Pediatricians are trained [professionals and can] advise parents and children if BMI rates rise significantly. The doctor's office is the appropriate environment for measuring weight not the schools."[43] MacDonald worries along with her colleagues that, while reporting BMI through school has not been proven to have any beneficial effects on weight and health, the negative consequences could be severe. "Individuals simply told they are too fat can be at risk for using dangerous weight loss strategies such as the use of amphetamines, intestinal bypass, fasting, very low calorie diets, laxatives, purging, etc. Such dangerous weight loss strategies are associated with negative health outcomes including death."[44]

In Massachusetts, parental opposition to schools reporting on their kids' BMI was so intense it led to the state revoking the policy of sending out the letters. The Massachusetts Department of Health reported in 2013 that there'd been "reports of incidence where student confidentiality concerning height and weight measurements was not appropriately safeguarded, leading to alarm, confusion or embarrassment."[45]

Clinical psychologist Michael Friedman argues that the eight other states that send similar letters should follow suit. He says that "fat letters," as they've been called, "can result in increased poor self-concept and unhealthy dieting behaviors. The result is a cycle of negative body image, rigid dieting and unhealthy eating that can last a lifetime, with devastating consequences" for children.[46]

Ending the practice of reporting individual BMI directly to the parents and students doesn't, however, reverse the policy of collecting the information in the first place. The next logical question, therefore, is what problem the states are trying to solve with these screenings. If it is the priority of every public school to ensure that students are healthy, where does that effort cross the line into the private matters of families? And what impact does this form of government health nannying have on education? As Reuben Navarette Jr. eloquently put it at CNN.com, "Schools can't afford foreign language courses, sports programs or music classes. But they found funds for dieticians?"[47] Good question.

Even as it admits that there is little evidence proving the "utility" or effectiveness of BMI surveillance programs in schools, the Centers for Disease Control advises that "schools that initiate BMI measurement programs should have . . . a comprehensive set of science-based strategies to promote physical activity and healthy eating."[48] But all schools should incorporate physical activity and healthy food because that's just common sense. Why waste time on taking measurements when the schools could be spending more time having the children engage in the behaviors that we already know are good for them, like running around and eating well?

"Schools have a changing role in wellness because that's

where kids spend most of their waking time," said pediatrician Lynn Gettleman Chehab, who runs the school clinic obesity program at Evanston Township High School. "It's a crucial time for prevention, but many kids aren't going to the doctor unless they're sick."[49] This is a common argument for those who support government intervention. The basic premise is that, since we can't trust everyone to do the right thing, especially in this terrifically important realm of children's health, the state has got to take its opportunity where it can. It is a question of access. Most American kids are in school, so when the government wants to modify behavior among children (and their parents in this case), it decides that where it has access it should act.

Using this same logic, schools have added various issues to the more traditional list of academic subjects. Comprehensive sex education was vigorously debated in the 1980s because many parents rejected the notion that school was the best place to discuss pregnancy, condoms, and AIDS. School administrators and government health bureaucrats have similarly argued that distributing condoms and educating children about oral versus penetrative sex is important for the health and well-being of the students and to prevent pregnancy. Is school really the best place for all this useful information to be disseminated?

Those who support efforts like collecting BMI data do it from a place of honest concern. Even as Chehab acknowledged that the BMI is flawed, the pediatrician argues that access is too important to ignore. "If it's done in the right way," she told the *Chicago Tribune*, "where privacy is protected and the child is not subject to embarrassment, it's useful information."[50]

This argument about BMI screenings providing useful information, even when done correctly, is seriously flawed, however. According to three researchers from the University of California at Berkeley, "schools may falsely mislabel ... children as overweight based on BMI screening," because the measure is just one piece of information.

> In order to assess a child's weight, health professionals examine the child's growth history, taking into consideration the heights and weights of the child's biological parents. They also ask questions about the child's eating and activity patterns. Armed with this information the health professional is in a position to determine if the child is "at risk of overweight or underweight" or is "overweight."[51]

Many experts express skepticism that BMI serves as a good measure of health at all. Kristine Madsen, an assistant professor at the University of California at Berkeley's School of Public Health told the *Chicago Tribune*'s Julie Dierdorff that "about half of children whose BMI labels them as overweight (but not obese) are healthy and have no increased risk of diabetes or other conditions."[52]

Schools have access to a lot of kids and so can easily collect medical information like height and weight, but as we've seen, there's no proof that reporting BMI as separate from a general health evaluation by a pediatrician or primary-care doctor is actually an effective way to prevent obesity, and it may result in other health and social problems. All this demands that we ask ourselves: Why not just find a better way to deal with what officials always call an epidemic?

It is too hard to change course, apparently, because rather than reassess the efficacy of such BMI-data-collection programs, the USDA has announced that it plans to weigh and measure children in federally funded daycare as part of Mrs. Obama's expansion of the Healthy Hunger-Free Kids Act.

The USDA's rationale is classic bureaucratic thinking: We have access to these kids, and we are helping to pay for their daycare through subsidies, so why shouldn't we be allowed to study what they do all day.

Good nutrition is a key to proper childhood development, but not enough is known about the food children are eating in child-care and related programs. In 2011, 32.7 million children were in a regular child-care arrangement while their parents worked or pursued other activities outside of the home, according to the U.S. Census Bureau. The USDA has tasked Abt Associates, a research firm, to document the quality of meals and snacks offered in child-care facilities, describe the child-care providers' "nutrition and wellness policies and practices," what the children eat both in and out of child care, the cost of meals, and the amount of wasted food.[53] The study will also provide insights into how nutritional quality and physical activity in child care might be improved.[54]

SIMPLER SOLUTIONS

It's a good thing that the USDA wants to understand how physical activities in daycare "might be improved," but does answering the question really require a study?

One mom in Washington, DC, understood the problem as soon as she saw her third-grader's school schedule in August 2013. "It makes me wonder whether anyone making these schedules has met any actual children," said Laura Marks, who added that her son "is going to be chewing on the rug" if he did not get more than the scheduled 15 minutes per day to run around.[55]

Parents in DC and Florida know the solution. But whereas overly intrusive USDA bureaucrats pray at the altar of detailed rules, requirements, and mandates when it comes to food in schools, there is no such reflex regarding gym and free play at school.

The reality is that over time gym periods and recess have been reduced or eliminated. And yet, increasing the number of hours in a given week that kids are moving around and allowed to make their own fun is of proven value when it comes both to children's overall health and to better learning. So while all government bodies dealing with children's health and educa- tion—Department of Education, Centers for Disease Control, and USDA—agree that physical activity and exercise is benefi- cial, none has done as much to get more play time for kids as those protesting parents in Lake County or the nation's capital.

Indeed, parents across the country understand what's go- ing on and are worried. According to a September 2013 survey by NPR, Harvard's School of Public Health, and the Robert Wood Johnson Foundation, most parents give their kids' school failing grades for daily physical activity. Nearly half of the par- ents surveyed said their child got physical education twice a week or less. A third of parents said that the gym period was 30 minutes or less. And less than a quarter reported that their kids got what the CDC recommends, which is daily physical exercise.[56]

Parents aren't the only ones who've noticed the problem of disappearing recess and gym, mind you. At the University of Michigan, Kathy Speregen has tracked the state of physi- cal education in American public schools and found it sorely lacking.

Despite the wealth of knowledge concerning the ben- efits of physical education and physical activity, only 8% of elementary schools, 6.4% of middle schools, and 5.8% of high schools provide daily physical education to all of its students. . . . In addition, 20 percent of all elemen- tary schools in the U.S. have abolished recess in favor of increased classroom time under pressure to improve

student achievement.... Less than 25% of children are
engaged in 30 minutes of any type of daily physical activity.... Even when physical education programs are
in place, most students are not engaged in vigorous
physical activity for the majority of their class time....
It is estimated that boys only spend about 18 minutes
engaged in moderate and vigorous activity and girls
spend about 16 minutes.[57]

Speregen is upset by these results because she knows the
consequences. "These statistics are disappointing and are resulting in negative outcomes in health and school performance
for America's children. Many parents and educators are probably wondering: Why are we neglecting the health needs of our
children?"[58]

As Speregen notes, too little physical activity is harming
both the health and academic performance of school children.
Rebecca Spencer speaks both as a parent and as neuroscientist
at the University of Massachusetts, and she argues that recess
isn't necessarily the best solution since there is no guarantee
that kids are engaging in vigorous physical activity. "Exercise—
any exercise—is great for brain development," she says. "Most
of the studies that have been done that show how the brain
develops through exercise actually don't use any special form of
exercise," she says. "They typically use just treadmill walking."[59]
But she'd prefer some kind of structured gym period. "The
physical education is giving them some of the motor skills that
they need," she says. But, she also told NPR that she understands her kids' school might not necessarily have the resources
to provide more P.E. classes.[60]

Spencer is a lot more understanding than I am since there
is nothing complicated or expensive about jump rope, for example. Just ask, Captain Mommy Irene Trello and her hus-

band, Patsy, about their son Jeremy, who changed his life for the better by jumping rope. Jeremy was always big, but when he weighed in at 200 pounds as a 13-year-old, his parents drew the line. He's been training like a boxer by jumping rope, as well as doing other exercises, ever since. Jeremy made the newspaper when he started a clinic for other teens at his local YMCA to show his peers what a little sweat equity can do for your physique and overall health. And his dad had a word for anyone who might argue that you need expensive equipment or special certification as an instructor to get in shape. "You can go into the city and give any kid a jump rope for a dollar. You don't need a $12,000 elliptical. We're trying to get back to the basics."[61]

Some educators claim prioritizing gym isn't easy. "We all want healthy kids. It's a great goal, but a difficult one. You have to look at the unintended consequences of things like this. They are well-meaning, and they are good for kids, but you have to alter the amount of time you have for other subjects," says Mark Terry, president of the National Association of Elementary School Principals and a principal at Eubanks Intermediate School in Southlake, Texas.[62]

Terry isn't just mouthing excuses, either. There's evidence that No Child Left Behind legislation did, among other things, push administrators and teachers toward prioritizing standardized-test prep over other subjects. The situation is so bad that the National PTA has addressed the issue by trying to enlist support for more P.E. and recess, as has the Institute of Medicine.[63] "This is a whole-of-school approach. It's not just physical education. It's everything that occurs during school as well as around the school day," explained Harold Kohl III, professor of epidemiology and kinesiology at the University of Texas School of Public Health and chair of the committee that did the Institute of Medicine report.[64] The recommendation is that the Department of Education designate physical education as a core subject like math and reading. "It is as important because it affects kids' health, cognitive function and overall development," Kohl says. "The report urges state legislatures and departments of education to adopt and/or strengthen physical education and recess policies, as well as before- and after-school policies."[65]

Kohl and his colleagues got one thing right with their report: They suggest the solution to improving health outcomes for school students should be addressed at the state and, better yet, the local level. The same is true of food and nutrition. When solutions to problems are devised at such a remove from those who are its intended beneficiaries, the tendency is to generalize to a degree that may create more problems than it solves.

CHAPTER 5

The War on Fun

Banning play, toys, and games

YOU'VE NO DOUBT heard of the war on poverty and the war on women, but what about the war on fun? As unhappy as it sounds, there has been a decades-long march by government-empowered bureaucrats, school administrators, regulators, and health professionals against nearly every aspect of childhood fun, both indoors and out.

Toys, games, playground equipment, and general free play have all been banned, recalled, curtailed, or removed. And often the decision is taken without consultation with or even informing parents and the local community. The reasons are both legal and cultural; they include safety concerns that get blown out of proportion and well-founded fears of liability and litigation.

Toys that have caused no permanent or even serious harm are recalled and even banned. Games have been outlawed and schools have cut recess down and out. And playgrounds have been redesigned, with concrete replaced by shock-absorbing rubber or mulch just so kids won't experience falling on a hard surface. Kids tend not to experience much fun at these "playgrounds," either. Independent play is practically extinct.

Popular toys have been banned because they've been incorrectly played with and some kids have gotten hurt, even though the vast majority has enjoyed the same products without incident. But what the majority does without incident is not persuasive to the regulatory state. Instead, arbitrary and probably impossible-to-achieve safety standards, combined with our collective and ever-growing fear of risk, have replaced a commonsense approach to assessing what is dangerous, harmful, or hazardous.

The nanny state is incapable of agreeing to disagree about standards of care. The nature of government oversight is to create a single universal standard and apply it equally everywhere. Therefore, the decision of what is safe is removed from parents and put into the hands (most often) of bureaucrats. The consequences are easy to spot. Do a quick Internet search, and you'll come upon multiple top-ten lists of childhood activities, toys, and school fun that are today completely unacceptable.

When Frank Furedi published his 2001 book *Paranoid Parenting*, he found a "growing tendency to extend adult supervision into every aspect of children's lives. It was apparent that the outdoors had become a no-go area for many youngsters," he explained in his regular newspaper column.[1] "During the past decade or so, the banning of a variety of activities associated with children's life has acquired a relentless dynamic," Furedi continued. "[I]n February 2007 after a group of children were suspended from school for throwing snowballs, an angry mother [wrote] to me to ask: 'What will they think of next?' Regrettably, the obsessive impulse to regulate children's life ensures that the next target of child protection is already on the horizon."

Tim Gill agrees. In his book *No Fear*, Gill argues "childhood is becoming undermined by risk aversion. Activities and experiences that previous generations of children enjoyed without a second thought have been relabeled as troubling or dangerous, while the adults who still permit them are branded as irresponsible. At the extreme . . . society appears to have become unable to cope with any adverse outcomes whatsoever, no matter how trivial or improbable."[2]

Lest you think it is just experts spouting off about this trend, children know their lives are being systematically *de-fun-ded* too. Gill quotes Hannan, a teenager from Newcastle, whose assessment of the state of risk anxiety sounds exactly like a child-development expert.

> To be honest, adults can be very stupid at times. They ban everything, for health and safety reasons. If they're going to ban very simple stuff like [the game of tag], they might as well lock all kids in empty rooms to keep them safe. Kids should be allowed to experiment and try things. Otherwise when they grow up they'll make very stupid mistakes from not getting enough experience at childhood.[3]

But is there really a government entity banning fun and taking toys out of the hands of children? Why, yes—it's called the Consumer Product Safety Commission. Though, as we will see, CPSC isn't alone. There are state-government nannies, otherwise known as legislators, who are working hard to make life less fun for children and adults.

CPSC JUMPS THE SHARK

When the government bureaucrats at CPSC decide that a product must not be sold to adult consumers because it has the potential to harm a child, even though it hasn't done anything of the kind, you know the nanny state has jumped the shark—that is, declined in quality, efficiency, purpose, and mission to the point of absurdity.

In 2014, CPSC recalled all 191,000 Go Gaga Squeeze & Teethe Coco the Monkey teething toys (which had been sold exclusively at Target) because Infantino, the company that makes the toy, "received seven reports of infants choking or

gagging on the monkey's tail. No injuries have been reported."
So a product that, as I wrote at the time, causes gagging in babies the same as spoons or fingers is deemed too dangerous for
parents to purchase to relieve their kids' aching gums.[4]

Part of the trouble is that in our current moment, there
is supposed to be some result/solution/recompense for every
trouble/problem/mistake, especially when it comes to children.
We have become more risk averse and less tolerant of the inherent trade-offs between safety and utility when it comes to adult
products. But when it comes to children, we are conditioned
to accept nothing less than perfect safety. And yet, as former
Obama regulations czar Cass Sunstein explains, we are misunderstanding a basic principle of life: "People seem to think that
products and activities are either 'safe' or 'unsafe' ... without
seeing that the real questions involve probabilities."[5]

Indeed, such trade-offs and probabilities should be the entire raison d'être of the Consumer Product Safety Commission.
Instead, more and more often, it is losing perspective and going
to extremes.

CPSC was established in 1972 as part of the congressional
Consumer Product Safety Act with the mandate to "protect the
public against unreasonable risks of injuries and deaths associated with consumer products."[6] Notice the word *unreasonable*.
It is the most important word because there is a legal definition
behind it. An unreasonable danger is one that is hidden from
the public. According to the commission's website,

> The U.S. Consumer Product Safety Commission is
> charged with protecting the public from unreasonable
> risks of injury or death associated with the use of thou-
> sands of types of consumer products under the agency's
> jurisdiction. Deaths, injuries, and property damage from
> consumer product incidents cost the nation more than

$1 trillion annually. CPSC is committed to protecting consumers and families from products that pose a fire, electrical, chemical or mechanical hazard. CPSC's work to help ensure the safety of consumer products—such as toys, cribs, power tools, cigarette lighters and household chemicals—contributed to a decline in the rate of deaths and injuries associated with consumer products over the past 40 years.[7]

From this limited and eminently reasonable mandate, the CPSC has expanded its definition of what is an unreasonable danger. This expansion has been followed by an exponential growth in its reach and its interests. What was a $34 million budget in 1972 is today a $125 million budget.

It isn't that CPSC isn't useful, because the agency can do its job well and effectively. For instance, in January 2015, a huge shipment of toys—a child's backhoe in this case—was seized by U.S. Customs and Border Protection agents and sent for testing by CPSC for high concentrations of lead paint. The toys were confiscated, and consumers, especially kids, were protected from ingesting potentially dangerous toxins.[8]

A look at CPSC's weekly recall announcement on February 13, 2015, however, offered a perfect example of the current too-expansive definition of duties. On that day CPSC announced the recall of the "Marin 2014 model MBX 50 and Tiny Trail bicycles with 16-inch knobby tires," which are kids' bicycles. The CPSC put out the recall because "the handlebars can loosen or separate during use. This can cause the rider to lose control and crash." The problem here is that no one has been injured from this alleged danger, and the number of bicycles sold is practically microscopic—"about 400 in the U.S. and 50 in Canada," says the CPSC.[9] There were 16 million bicycles sold in the US in 2013, and no one was actually injured because of these tiny trail bikes. Why is there time and taxpayer money being spent on this? A quick review of the CPSC weekly updates for children's products reveals a steady stream of warnings, recalls, and advocacy against products that have not actually harmed anyone. And when the CPSC does focus on a product that has caused harm, the punishment simply doesn't fit the crime.

Take, for example, the Bumbo "Baby Sitter" seat. In 2007, the South African company announced a voluntary recall of over one million seats because of data from the Consumer Product Safety Commission showing 28 reports of infants falling out of the seats after the molded-rubber chairs, which allow infants to sit upright before they are physically strong enough to do it themselves, were placed on tables. The Bumbo was a highly popular product, with more than four million sold from the time it hit the American market in 2003. The company issued a new warning label, "WARNING—Prevent Falls; Never use on any elevated surface," but that wasn't enough for nanny-state regulators at the Consumer Product Safety Commission. Four years later it issued an unusual post-recall warning (for up to 4 million seats) because another 45 incidents had been reported by then. The fact that nearly half of those reports were cases of the seats being used improperly (still putting them up on tables in spite of the warning label) seems not to have mattered to the nannies at CPSC. Instead, the company was forced to offer a new safety strap that Bumbo owners could use to make the seats "safer." Needless to say, the second recall and the required modifications to the Bumbo have hurt its US sales.[10] But looking at the numbers, were the recalls really necessary?

Kids do get hurt in various ways throughout their childhood, so was the Bumbo an especially "dangerous" infant seat? The final count of reported incidents of trouble with the Bumbo: 123. There were 4 million seats sold in the US. That means that a grand total of 0.00307 percent of Bumbo users had trouble with the seats. That's not 1 percent of users, not 0.5 percent of users—it isn't even one-hundredth of a percent of users. Is this really a meaningful "danger"?

There are economic implications to this type of over-regulation, and there are cultural implications as well. Unnecessary bans and recalls hurt legitimate businesses and do nothing to blunt our current age of anxiety. The opposite is more likely the case as the risks of injury are blown out of proportion. According to libertarian journalist David Harsanyi, who wrote in detail about this case in his 2007 book *Nanny State*,[11] the decision by CPSC to attack baby bath seats was so intense that it seemed as if sowing anxiety was considered part of CPSC's mission. Harsanyi's book is a terrific chronicle of the many excesses of do-gooder policy makers.

"Imagine a parent holding a soapy, squiggling baby," railed then–CPSC commissioner Ann Brown in December 2004. "A parent would never leave that baby alone for a second. But even the best parent can be seduced into bad behavior if they see a child sitting upright in a little seat. But it takes only a couple of minutes for a baby to drown, and it's a silent death that can happen in three inches of water."[12]

Brown took it upon herself to battle a deadly scourge of complacent parents lulled into a false sense of security by evil, silent, killer baby seats. Yet, the reality was very different. The agency decided to go after a product that was selling at a clip of 800,000 annually. One hundred twenty deaths over 15 years were "linked" to the seats, which, Harsanyi explains, actually means "an accident had befallen a child when the seat was present."[13] That is, the deaths were not necessarily *caused* by the seats—Brown was warning that they were present at the time of the tragic deaths. As any statistician will tell you, correlation and causation are very different.

There were 12 million baby seats sold during the same

15-year period, which means that the likelihood of death "linked" to baby seats was 0.00001 percent. But such a miniscule probability of death by bath seat was inconsequential to Brown, who took the tragic death of a nine-month-old baby girl in Baltimore as the starting point for her crusade. "Bath seats and rings may make caregivers believe that a baby is in a relatively safe environment. Any such belief can have devastating consequences because these products—regardless of how sturdy they look—will not prevent drowning. And babies can drown very quickly if they are left alone in a bathtub, with or without a bath seat or ring."[14] Dispensing with the original limited mission of CPSC—"*unreasonable* risks of injuries and deaths associated with consumer products"—Brown became more like a desperate helicopter parent.

Lawyer and reasonable-regulation crusader Philip K. Howard argues that losing a commonsense appreciation for acceptable risk leads CPSC to take a more expansive and expensive approach to problem solving. He worries that the cure can be worse than the disease. Howard writes,

> There's a compulsion to move heaven and earth to eliminate a risk even if in the clear light of day, everyone agrees that the effect is a grotesque misallocation of resources. There was a panic to require flame-resistant pajamas for children in the early 1970s—at a cost seven times greater than the cost of smoke alarms that would save the same number of lives. Then it turned out that the flame retardant was carcinogenic, and it had to be banned.[15]

Former CPSC commissioner Nancy Nord agrees. Current regulations, she told me, "seem to address speculative risks, allow no tolerance for risk, and show little concern for burdens that may be imposed."

This is not to say there aren't reasonable people who want to serve the public on the CPSC. The trouble is that those who see the mission of the agency in more limited terms—as the original mandate of the organization specifies—have been punished, whereas those who promote a more expansive mission have been embraced and encouraged. After CPSC Commissioner Mary Sheila Gall criticized her own agency in 1999 for acting as a parental coach rather than as regulator, she was attacked, vilified, and denied the appointment to replace Brown when President George W. Bush nominated her. During much of the Obama administration, the CPSC has been led by Inez Tenenbaum, who not only has put the agency mission on steroids, but also has destroyed a successful adult-desk-toy manufacturer and then has taken the unprecedented step of trying to financially ruin a single individual—Craig Zucker, one of the company's co-founders—in a vindictive and chilling prosecution.

Craig Zucker is a Captain Daddy for taking on the CPSC in defense of his product and the right to sell a fun and frivolous toy. "As a former CPSC chairman, I believe in regulations and rigorous industry standards. But there is a line between safety regulation and overreach. That line has been crossed in the government's action against Buckyballs and their creator, Craig Zucker," wrote Nancy Nord in 2013.[16] When I interviewed Nord in 2015, she expressed concern that, as the Buckyballs case had shown, "the government rather than the marketplace [was] determining the merits and value of a product."

Nord was attacking the lawsuit aimed at Zucker in the amount of $57 million, the estimated cost of paying back everyone who ever bought Zucker's adult desk toy Buckyballs—a set of small, strong magnetic balls to play with at work. The government's initial problem with Buckyballs was the potential danger if the magnets were misused and accidentally swallowed

by children. At first Zucker's company and CPSC worked together to develop a safety plan, and the company complied
with every request for warning labels. (The final tally was half a
dozen on a package just a bit bigger than an eight-ounce tub of
cream cheese.) At some point, however, CPSC decided that the
warnings weren't enough, and a full-scale war against Buckyballs to ban and recall the product ensued.

Tenenbaum and CPSC were overstating the risks since, as
Jim Epstein explained in *Reason*, "there were 22 reported incidents of ingested Buckyballs from March 2009 through October 2011, or one for every 100,000 sets sold. That makes the
product orders of magnitude less risky than dogs, tennis, skate-
boarding, and poisonous household chemicals."[17] And as Zucker
pointed out during his ultimately unsuccessful PR campaign to
save Buckyballs, there are many more cases of kids swallow-
ing balloons and laundry-detergent pods than Buckyballs, yet
CPSC wasn't banning those. "Compared to other products in
the marketplace, it is an extremely low rate of injury," Zucker
told *CBS This Morning*.[18]

The lawsuit was ultimately settled for much less than $57
million, but the precedent of selective enforcement and vindictive bureaucratic legal maneuvering stands. And the legal community took notice. "For the first time, the CPSC is pursuing
individual and personal liability against an executive for a company's alleged violations of the Consumer Product Safety Act.
Although it remains to be seen whether the CPSC will adopt
this approach in other cases, at minimum, this demonstrates
just how far the CPSC is willing to push the envelope," warned
the law firm Gibson Dunn.[19]

As a former CPSC commissioner herself, Nord knows
how the agency operates, and her view is troubling, to say the
least. As she explained it to me, the regulators here decided
they would go after a product and a company they could better

control rather than face off against more powerful or ubiquitous products CPSC had no real hope of banning. The following worries Nord:

> Contrast the agency's approach to button batteries— which present the same risk of injuries, i.e. small children swallowing them. However many more children have been injured, and a number have died, from swallowing button batteries than from magnets. Yet the agency has agreed to a voluntary program with industry to increase warnings, make the packaging stronger and educate the public. Obviously the agency understands it cannot ban button batteries, but it also realized that it could do so with respect to magnets.[20]

The feds aren't the only ones on the overprotective bandwagon, however. To cite just one example, in 2005, then–Illinois governor Rod Blagojevich signed legislation outlawing sales of yo-yo water balls—a toy made of a liquid-filled ball and elastic cord. "If we know a toy like the yo-yo water ball is dangerous to young kids, then the responsible thing to do is take it off the market," Blagojevich claimed.[21]

What was the danger that required the ban on sales? Perhaps Blagojevich was reacting after a child was severely injured or swallowed some part of the toy they shouldn't have and got sick? Was the danger so great that a child died because of playing with a yo-yo water ball? Thankfully, none of these things happened; no one got even seriously hurt. Yes, there were kids who when playing with the toy *inappropriately* did get sick from drinking the liquid inside the yo-yo or got the rubber band caught around their neck. But none of these injuries were more than superficial and temporary. And, of course, following such incidents, children or their parents could obviously throw out the toy.

Simple common sense would have worked in this case, but
that wasn't good enough for Lisa Lipin, a mother from Skokie
who yelled about a ban for two years before Illinois legislators
and the governor capitulated. "I lobbied for this ban because I
saw what this toy can do to a child, and children continue to
keep getting injured," said Lipin.[22]

NO FUN IN PUBLIC

If overreacting to the potential hazards of certain toys is de
rigueur for the federal government, constraining and limiting
outside play is dealt with at the state and local level.

The winter of 2014 saw the expansion of the latest front
in the war on fun when it was reported that the list of public
hills where sledding was prohibited had grown. Yes, sledding.
Dubuque, Iowa; Hamilton, Ontario, Canada; Montville, New
Jersey; Lincoln, Nebraska; and Columbia City, Indiana have all
banned tobogganing. And Paxton, Illinois, went one step beyond when it actually removed the sledding hill—which was a
mound of dirt people had taken to sledding on in winter. Now
it's a dog park, which is nice for the pets but less fun for the
human children. In some of these cases, the actions were pro-
phylactic, and in other instances, elected officials were reacting
to lawsuits that had already cost thousands of dollars to settle.

Winter is not the only season for burdensome rules against
recreational activities. For summer non-fun, day camps in New
York State were urged to stop games like red rover, wiffle ball,
kickball, and freeze tag because these may pose a "significant
risk of injury," argued the state's Health Department.[23]

But a closer look at the rules shows that what the state
was interested in promoting wasn't safety but rather more revenue and more control. As reported by the *New York Daily
News*, "The law sought to close a loophole that legislators said

allowed too many indoor camp programs to operate without oversight."[24] Instead, the new rules mandate that "any program that offers two or more organized recreational activities—with at least one of them on the risky list—is deemed a summer camp and subject to state regulation," which includes a fee of $200 to register as a summer camp and requires that the organization provide medical staff. The fact that these costs might be burdensome to small programs doesn't seem to have concerned the regulators. Better no day camp than unsafe play, it seems. In this instance, happily, after a significant uproar by several state legislators (representing some angry kids and parents), the health department backed off.

On the whole, sadly, public play spaces have become less fun over time. Structures have been designed for safety and to ensure fewer accidents rather than for fun, and many playgrounds are "surfaced" with rubber or wood chips instead of concrete. The hazard of scraping a knee on pavement has been removed, but with the pavement has gone the notion that children can actually learn to avoid falling on a hard surface. Unfortunately, this has introduced a different danger. Some municipalities and schools have had to erect tarps and string up awnings because the rubber tiles get so hot in the sun that burning the bottoms of the feet of barefoot kids has become the new playground danger.

"Safety, as it turns out, is only half an idea. The right question is what we are giving up to achieve safety. A playground may be designed to be accident-free, but so boring that children don't use it," Philip K. Howard cogently explains. "Conversely, a playground may serve its purpose perfectly, but there will be a certainty that every once in a while, a child will be hurt. Safety and risk always involve trade-offs—of resources, of efficiency, and especially in the case of children, of learning to manage risk."[25]

There are some newer, innovative playgrounds that harken

back to the time of rougher play, however. They just don't exist in America. *The Atlantic*'s Hanna Rosin had to fly her son all the way to North Wales in order to play at a really fun public play space. Why more fun than American playgrounds you ask? Well, listen to Rosin describe her son's experience. At first he doesn't know what to make of the playground known as the Land.

> The ground is muddy in spots and, at one end, slopes down steeply to a creek where a big, faded plastic boat that most people would have thrown away is wedged into the bank. The center of the playground is dominated by a high pile of tires that is growing ever smaller as a redheaded girl and her friend roll them down the hill and into the creek. "Why are you rolling tires into the water?" my son asks. "Because we are," the girl replies.[26]

Soon enough, the boy is hurtling through space directly into that water, and it is Rosin who is left to explain about the strange transformation that has occurred over seven hours, as her five-year-old enjoys unadulterated, unchaperoned, childish fun.

> I hadn't seen much of my son that day. Kids, unparented, take on pack habits, so as the youngest and newest player, he'd been taken care of by the veterans of the Land. I inched close enough to hear the exchange.
> "You might fall in the creek," said Christian.
> "I know," said Gideon.
> Christian had already taught Gideon how to climb up to the highest slide and manage the rope swing. At this point, he'd earned some trust. "I'll push you gently, okay?" "Ready, steady, go!," Gideon said in response.

Down he went, and landed in the creek.

In my experience, Gideon is very finicky about water. He hates to have even a drop land on his sleeve
while he's brushing his teeth. I hadn't rented a car on
this trip, and the woman who'd been driving us around
had left for a while. I started scheming how to get him
new clothes. Could I knock on one of the neighbors'
doors? Ask Christian to get his father? Or, failing that,
persuade Gideon to sit a while with the big boys by
the fire?

"I'm wet," Gideon said to Christian, and then they
raced over to claim some hammers to build a new fort.[27]

The Land is what's called an "adventure" playground, and
it also has fire and sticks and wood pallets and mud. What it
doesn't have are parents. Rosin reports that mostly the kids
came to play on their own. There is a facilitator at this playground, but that person does not engage in organizing anything. The children are left to their own devices to figure out
how to have fun. Such adventure playgrounds have one other
unique element: surprise.

The reality of most American playgrounds is that consumer
and child-protection advocates, along with the government's
anti-fun agency, the Consumer Product Safety Commission,
have defined all the fun, surprise, and risk out of publicly funded
playgrounds.

In 1981, the CPSC published the first "Handbook for Public
Playground Safety," which was modest compared with what it's
become. The 2010 version is 60 pages of general guidelines, and
CPSC recommends that it be coupled with the American Society for Testing and Materials handbook of standards for public
playgrounds, which is another 132 pages of technical standards.
And CPSC is proud to tout the fact that 16 states have adopted

its guidelines as requirements.[28] Just as we saw with Chapter 3's "daycare nannies," a government-empowered entity makes up a long list of official-sounding recommendations that are then adopted as law by states looking for an easy way to "guarantee" that daycare centers, or in this case playgrounds, are made safe. The result is much more red tape and expense, and the playgrounds are less fun to boot.

Lest you worry that the CPSC ignores home playground equipment, rest assured, there is another 15-page book of safety standards in order to mitigate those particular risks.

"More and more, the standards are set by engineers and technical experts and lawyers," with little meaningful input from "people who know anything about children's play," says William Weisz, a design consultant who has sat on several committees overseeing changes to the guidelines.[29] "The handbook includes specific prescriptions for the exact heights, slopes, and other angles of nearly every piece of equipment. Rubber flooring or wood chips are virtually required," while "grass and dirt are not considered protective surfacing because wear and environmental factors can reduce their shock absorbing effectiveness," reports Rosin.[30]

The situation with fun-numbing regulations has gotten so bad that even a former safety crusader has become an outspoken proponent of kids' free play. University of Texas at Austin professor Joe Frost used to side with those who wanted to ensure playgrounds were more safe than anything else. Today he acknowledges the error of his ways. "I travel the nation and abroad consulting on play and child development, playground design, and play equipment safety," says Frost, "speaking about the value of play and emphasizing the importance of appropriate play opportunities to a healthy child. What we've seen over the past three or so decades is what could be termed the demise of play. This is largely due to a frenzy of litigation over playground injuries and a misunderstanding of the educational and developmental value of play—the consequence has been complete removal of playgrounds and recess." But those removals, argues Frost, aren't good for kids. "If the children don't play, they won't get hurt and if they don't get hurt, we won't get sued. It's an extreme stance, and it's detrimental to the children ... much more so than a scratched knee or bruised elbow."[31]

There are some places, such as New York, that have decided some overbearing guidelines aren't useful, so they don't adopt them. But of course there's a price tag—$20 million over ten years, according to a news report in the *New York Post*. When asked about the astronomical sum of taxpayer funds going to pay off the families of injured kids, New York City Comptroller Scott Stringer tried to thread the needle. "We need to not only reduce claims against the city, but to protect our children," he added.[32] But reducing the number of claims versus "protecting" children may just turn out to be mutually exclusive. To lessen lawsuits, the city would have to adhere to a set of safety standards that ultimately may not even reduce claims, since rubber matting, which is softer than concrete, gets so hot that lawsuits have been filed for burnt little feet. But taking away playground apparatuses that are actually fun and have a measure of risk means reducing children's opportunities to grow and develop and have fun.

There are at least some government employees who seem to understand the problem. "You want them to have fun, to experiment, take some risks," Liam Kavanagh, first deputy parks commissioner of New York City said of the city's decision to forgo federal standards. "Part of the allure of a playground is to climb to the top and swing as high as you can," said Kavanagh. "You don't want to ... make it too antiseptic of an experience."[33]

Too many states—17 and counting—go the overregulation route, however. Lou Pellegrini, who heads the Hoboken, New

Jersey, parks department, recently oversaw a $3.7 million reno-
vation of its playgrounds following CPSC safety guidelines,
including all new play surfaces. "It replaces asphalt and rubber
mats because it has no give," Pellegrini said. "It kinda bounces
so when you fall you're not going to have an impact."[34] No one
wants kids to get seriously hurt, but wouldn't it be useful to learn
that when you fall on something hard you can get a boo-boo?

In response, the vast majority of municipal playgrounds in
the US have become so standardized as to be boring, which is
exactly what David Harsanyi rejects as an ineffective and extreme response to a limited problem. "According to the U.S.
Public Interest Research Groups, approximately 17 American
children die every year from injuries on playgrounds. And
170,000 kids are hurt badly enough to hasten a visit to the
emergency room," Harsanyi writes. "These numbers would be
bone-chilling were it not for the fact that tens of millions of
children use playgrounds every day."[35]

In his book *Nanny State*, Harsanyi argues against the
lengths that officials have gone to "protect" children from potential harm in public parks. For example, he correctly ridicules
a "painfully detailed, fun-nullifying" warning sign at a public
park in Broward County, Florida, that reads in part, "Do not
use equipment when wet; No bare feet, wear proper footwear;
Do not use equipment unless designed for your age; No bike
riding or skate boarding; No running."[36]

It's a public playground, and there's no running? How have
we gotten to this point? The answer lies, once again, in the expansion of what was once a reasonable definition of risk. As
Philip K. Howard explains, "In any social dealings, whether
selling products, managing employees, running a classroom or
building a playground, there's a chance that someone might be
offended. And in modern America that carries with it the risk
of being sued."[37]

In the realm of children's play, the definition of reasonable risk has been so eviscerated by either actual or threatened lawsuits that local officials believe the risk of such suits is much greater than the risk of making a playground that no one wants to play at. The proof is exemplified by that sign in Broward County, whose officials "decided to ban running in playgrounds after [the county] got a report showing that it had settled 189 playground lawsuits in the prior five years."[38] As a member of the Broward County School Board explained, "To say 'no running' on the playground seems crazy ... but your feelings change when you're in a closed-door meeting with lawyers."[39]

Perhaps all those warning labels the CPSC is so fond of could be put to better use with every public playground, sledding hill, and park in America outfitted with a simple, 5-word lawsuit-prevention sign: Play At Your Own Risk. Inviting, right?

FIRST THEY CAME FOR DODGEBALL

In Loveland, Colorado, seven-year-old Alex Evans was suspended from school for pretending to save the world. He had devised an imaginary game in which he was the protector of the world, but when he launched an *imaginary* grenade into an *imaginary* box to kill the *imaginary* evil forces inside, school administrators told his mother he'd have to stay home from school for real. The no-fun-kins at Mary Blair Elementary have a list of absolutes that include zero-tolerance for play fighting or play weapons.[40]

Kermit Elementary school officials in Texas suspended nine-year-old Aiden Steward for "threatening" a classmate with his ring from J. R. R. Tolkien's Middle Earth. Steward told his friend he could make him disappear, but school officials fulfilled the promise by making Aiden stay home.[41]

Restricting imaginative play is just the latest in a series

of attacks on fun in schoolyards. Fear of only negative consequences has meant curbs or bans of nearly every variety
of play at schools across the country. As a recent list at the
CafeMom blog pointed out, what was normal in schools in the
1980s—tetherball, dodgeball, playing Cowboys and Indians—
would never be tolerated now.[42] "It's fun stuff," said Azia Orum,
a Rio Linda, California, sixth-grader. "We just can't do it. People get hurt."[43] Orum is referring to her school's policy banning running games like tag and the dreaded dodgeball, which
was first to be banned and has been banned consistently across
the country.

You can't really blame school administrators for viewing
dodgeball as Enemy Number One in the war on fun. They've
had trouble with it not only for reasons of safety but also due to
litigation. In 2005 a schoolyard game of dodgeball led to a legal
ordeal for a 12-year-old and her family. Complaints by parents
of an injured student at a California school prompted authorities to charge Brittney Schneiders with battery. Five other students plea-bargained down to probation, but Brittney refused.
"I don't think I did [commit a crime]," she explained. "I thought
I was just playing a dodgeball game. I never thought it would
come up to this level."[44]

If you don't agree that dodgeball is a crime, many might
agree that it is a violent, exclusionary, and anxiety-provoking
game that should be eliminated because generations of kids
have hated playing it. Or, then again, maybe not, since there is
a case to be made for its positive attributes. "Dodgeball teaches
students eye-hand coordination and gross motor skills. Getting
singled out and eliminated from competition is part of life,"
said Tom Reed, professor of early childhood education at the
University of South Carolina Upstate in Spartanburg. "Life is
not always fair," said Reed, also a member of the Association
for the Study of Play. "You don't get what you want. Things like
this are learned on the playground."[45] But learning life lessons

is nearly the last thing school administrators want to deal with at recess.

Charlotte Avenue Elementary School in Nashua, New Hampshire, has banned tag because, as the principal told a reporter, kids said they'd been "pushed aggressively" while playing tag.[46] Parents were of course not consulted and many did not support the decision.

Recess is "a time when accidents can happen," says Willett Elementary School principal Gaylene Heppe, so she and other school administrators in the Boston area approve of the ban on tag, touch football, and other chase games during recess.[47] And again, the policy was enacted without consulting parents. "I think that it's unfortunate that kids' lives are micromanaged and there are social skills they'll never develop on their own," said Debbie Laferriere, a parent at the school. "Playing tag is just part of being a kid."[48]

Schools in Cheyenne and Spokane, Washington, and Charleston, South Carolina, have also dropped contact sports at recess. These policies are enacted without consulting parents and are critiqued by some childhood-development experts, who argue that play is essential and physical activity is important at a time when obesity is so common.[49]

In Grand Rapids, Michigan, at Zeeland Elementary School, tag and any chasing games have been banned. And at New Groening kindergarten, the school sent parents a letter about their policy, describing the problem as children "running in packs, pushing, knocking other children over, and making the game dangerous."[50] That means in effect that running around is frowned upon or outright not allowed.

In New York a ban on certain play at school was even more extreme. As *CBS News* reported in October 2013, "The ban at Weber Middle School in Port Washington, N.Y. will apply to footballs, baseballs, soccer balls, lacrosse balls or any other equipment that might harm a child or school friends. Students will be allowed to play with softer Nerf balls."[51] The fact that you cannot play football or lacrosse with a Nerf ball doesn't seem to matter to the administration.

During lunch recess at Natomas Elementary School in Sacramento, California, yard supervisor Janice Hudson spotted a first-grader pushing a girl on the swing. "Do not push," Hudson told the student. "Let her push herself, please." If her reasoning had been about encouraging independent play and building skills, Hudson should have been commended for taking good advantage of the teachable moment. But it was not to be. As she explained her reasoning, "One person can be a little stronger than the other."[52]

Harsanyi makes the point that too often these changes and new rules are done without consulting parents. "One morning," he writes, parents and children in Plano, Texas, "woke up to find that the swing sets at all 40 elementary schools had vanished—ripped out by officials over 'safety concerns.'" He reports that one "exasperated" father tried to fight back by lodging a complaint with the local district on the grounds that residents, as in other parents, agreed with him that the swings decision was absurd. "His attempts to bring back swings were to no avail," says Harsanyi, and adds that similar scenes have played out elsewhere, like in Portland, Oregon.[53]

Mike Lanza became a Captain Daddy around the issues of recess, free play, and children's independence and transformed from a Silicon Valley entrepreneur to the author of a play manifesto called *Playborhood: Turn Your Neighborhood into a Place for Play*. A father in Menlo Park, California, Lanza says recess in school has been sacrificed on the altar of safety. "A lot of schools limit recess because of safety and don't want kids to be competitive," he told me. There is even a school nearby with a "no touch policy and one kid nearly got suspended because [he] high-fived another kid."

Lanza also points out that, instead of allowing free and un-supervised play, there is a growing move to "facilitate" recess through government-supported programs like PlayWorks in California. The group has a contract with AmeriCorps, through which they send facilitators to improve recess. Lanza doesn't think much of the idea. "They try to get kids to do things to-gether but through a smiling militaristic play," Lanza explained to me. Of course to hear PlayWorks tell it, their mission is a bit more utopian. "On our playgrounds, everyone plays, everyone belongs, everyone contributes to the game. Coaches encourage kids to bring out the best in themselves and each other, and kids learn the value of fair play, compassion and respect."[54] Of course, there's nothing wrong with these goals except that now schools are aiming for behavior modification rather than allow-ing free play.

Tim Cushing over at Techdirt.com complains that the problem with all this overzealous rulemaking is that while school administrators and staff are promising the impossible, parents are holding unreasonable expectations.

> No one involved knows what they're doing, blindly thrashing around towards unachievable goals while hamstrung by misguided "security" efforts. I bash school administrations frequently, but [school game bans, for example] is not *solely* the fault of blundering, overreach-ing institutions. There are plenty of parents who should share in the blame. If schools have set themselves up as paragons of child safety, it has as much to do with par-ents' ridiculous expectations as it does with bureaucratic striving for complete control.[55]

Cushing is right when he argues that school leaders have allowed parents' unreasonable demands to guide their policy making. And the results are predictably silly. "This leads to ridiculous policy changes like eliminating 'hard' objects (with no sharp corners or heavy materials) from everyday play. This leads to kids being suspended for bogus weapons policy 'violations.'"[56]

It is true that some parents are shocked and upset when games and playground equipment are banned. But it is also true that when one's own child gets hurt, many parents lose all sense of reason, just like the mom in Skokie who demanded a ban on the water yo-yo because her kid nearly got injured. "Parents may express disbelief that tag is no longer allowed at their school, but many of those protesting need to take a long look at their own expectations. . . . I think most parents realize this, but when something happens to their kid, all rationality flies out the window as the psyche indulges the very common human urge to attribute blame and hold someone—anyone— responsible for this 'crime' against their flesh and blood," Cushing explains.[57]

This irrationality about safety and ameliorating risk isn't strictly an American phenomenon either. Across the pond in the UK, there have been bans on leapfrog and a traditional children's game called conkers, which is played with horse chestnuts. "Almost one-in-six teachers said their schools now outlawed conkers in case children are hit in the face by a stray horse chestnut. One claimed the ban had been imposed to protect pupils with nut allergies," reported the *Telegraph* in 2011. The news report also stated that "research by the Association of Teachers and Lecturers found evidence of schools stopping pupils from playing leapfrog, marbles, tag and even skipping."[58]

Banning conkers and the silent acceptance of the policy, according to sociologist Furedi, is a mark of how far along the path of irrational child safety standards society has traversed. The game is really innocent fun, where two players, each with a conker (horse chestnut) threaded onto a piece of string, take turns striking each other's conker until one breaks.

More than any of the bans introduced in recent years, the attempt to discourage children from playing with horse chestnuts symbolised the irrationality of the crusading spirit driving child protection. In 2001, no one imagined that English children would be prevented from pursuing the age-old custom of conkering. At first, many adults were shocked when they discovered that a few local authorities had introduced a new policy of "tree management," a euphemism for preventing children from climbing on horse-chestnut trees or playing with conkers. Today, that shock has turned into a sense of resignation. The refrain "we live in a different world" signals this uneasy acquiescence to the new reality.[59]

Having defined the problem, however, doesn't mean that a solution is easily achievable. Indeed, the answer is much more complicated than a simple ban. "Schools need to stop over-promising (and reacting badly when they inevitably under-deliver). Parents need to realize the only way they can protect their kids from bad things is to keep them locked up at home. Both need to cede control, especially over eventualities they can't possibly hope to have any input in," says Cushing.[60] Guaranteeing perfect safety and a perfect play environment where every child is safe and included and perfectly happy every day is why such endeavors like PlayWorks are bound to fail. The expectations are of another world, and the remedy may require more than simplifying the rules and lowering expectations, or there may not be any reasonable remedy at all.

Simplicity could work, and there is even an example from New Zealand to prove its effectiveness. After agreeing to be part of a university study on encouraging active play, Swanson School in Auckland decided to go whole hog and did away with all of their playground rules. "We want kids to be safe and to look after them, but we end up wrapping them in cotton wool when in fact they should be able to fall over," explained school principal Bruce McLachlan.[61] Throwing out what had been an extensive health and safety rule book was a shock to teachers, but the results have been stunning, with more active play, less bullying, less violence, and less graffiti. "When you look at our playground it looks chaotic. From an adult's perspective, it looks like kids might get hurt, but they don't."[62] The kids are now allowed to climb trees, skateboard, and mudslide. There is also a "loose parts pit" (à la Wales' the Land adventure playground), where kids play with pieces of wood, tires, and an old fire hose.

The professor who worked on the research says the study and the children's response to greater freedom should serve as a lesson. There are benefits to risk taking, like learning about consequences. "You can't teach them that. They have to learn risk on their own terms. It doesn't develop by watching TV, they have to get out there," explained one of the researchers, public-health professor Grant Schofield. "The great paradox of cotton-woolling children is it's more dangerous in the long run."[63]

PLAY FOR PLAY'S SAKE

There was a tremendous response to the news of Schofield's research at the Swanson school. Coverage shot around the world to news outlets, parenting blogs, and social media. Clearly the experiment rang a bell because it concerned a simple truth that lots of parents and even teachers know about how risk and learning consequences is so important when children are young. As Schofield explains it, "the right time to learn how to manage risk and manage emotions is when you are eight years old, up a tree or in a fight with the kid next door. Rather than when you are in a Subaru WRC at 18 with the cops after you and a few beers on board."[64]

Closer to home, a growing number of psychologists, education experts, sociologists, and child advocates argue on the same side.

"Pairing recess with quality instruction provides an essential feature of the school day that promotes learning across domains," explains Early Childhood and Education professor Judith Kieff.[65]

Evolutionary psychologist Peter Grey has looked at how unsupervised kids operate during play and makes a convincing case that a deficit of play is having severe negative consequences on today's young people, including a lack of empathy, limited socialization skills, and greater anxiety and depression.

> Today's children have less opportunity to play than their parents had and far less opportunity than their grandparents had, and we are seeing the consequences. Rates of childhood anxiety, depression, and suicide are at all-time highs; creativity is declining, and so is empathy. . . . [T]here is strong reason to attribute these sad effects to the loss of play. School is part of the problem. With every passing decade, school and homework have occupied increasingly large portions of children's lives. And school itself, with its focus on high-stakes testing and its sacrificing of recess, has become a less playful place.[66]

Grey's understanding of the importance of play is deep and persuasive because it is based on actually studying what happens when kids play together without adult organization or supervision. As a mother of four, I actually took time to watch my own kids playing outside together and witnessed exactly the dynamics he describes.

The reason why play is such a powerful way to impart social skills is that it is voluntary. Players are always free to quit, and if they are unhappy they will quit. Every player knows that, and so the goal, for every player who wants to keep the game going, is to satisfy his or her own needs and desires while also satisfying those of the other players, so they don't quit. . . .

[W]atch an age-mixed group of children playing a "pickup" game of baseball . . . directed by the players themselves. . . . They have to co-operate not just with the players on their team, but also with those on the other team, and they have to be sensitive to the needs and abilities of all the players. Big Billy might be the best pitcher, but if others want a turn at pitching he'd better let them have it, so they don't quit. And when he pitches to tiny Timmy, who is just learning the game, he'd better toss the ball gently, right toward Timmy's bat, or even his own teammates will call him mean. When he pitches to walloping Wally, however, he'd better throw his best stuff, because Wally would feel insulted by anything less. In the pickup game, keeping the game going and fun for everyone is far more important than winning.[67]

Christina Hoff Sommers, author of *The War against Boys*, says the play-deficit problem is especially acute for the male of the species. She isn't arguing that anyone purposefully sets out to hurt boys, but she says that the current, underlying presumptions of our education system is bad for our sons.

As a group, boys are noisy, rowdy, and hard to manage. Many are messy and disorganized, and won't sit still. They tend to like action, risk, and competition. . . . [Yet], today's classrooms tend to be feelings-centered, risk-

averse, competition-free, and sedentary. As early as preschool and kindergarten, boys can be punished for be-
having like boys. The characteristic play of young males
is "rough-and-tumble" play. There is no known society
where little boys fail to evince this behavior (girls do it
too, but far less). In many schools, rough-and-tumble
play is no longer tolerated. Well-meaning but intoler-
ant adults are insisting "tug of war" be changed to "tug
of peace"; games such as tag are being replaced with
"circle of friends"—in which no one is ever out. Boys as
young as five or six can be suspended for playing cops
and robbers. Our schools have become hostile environ-
ments for most boys.[68]

Why is some risk so important to kids? Because "children's
brains do not fully develop without the excitement and challenge of risk.... All these activities—merry-go-rounds, tag,
climbing trees, wandering around on their own—involve risk.
That's what's appealing," says Philip Howard. The other piece
of risk is that it serves children both physically—by challenging their bodies to perform—and mentally. "That's how kids
stay healthy. That's what fires their neurons, leading to better
brain development. That's how kids learn to smell danger, and
to deal with difficult people. That's how kids learn confidence,"
Howard avers.[69]

In his best-seller, *Last Child in the Woods*, Richard Louv describes what independent play was like when he was a boy.

I spent hours exploring the woods and farmland at the
suburban edge.... We climbed fifty, sixty feet off the
ground, far above the Osage windbreak, and from that
vantage looked out upon the old blue ridges of Missouri
... often I climbed alone. Sometime lost in wonder-
ment, I'd go deep into the woods, and imagine myself

as Rudyard Kipling's Mowgli, the boy raised by wolves, and strip off most of my clothes for the ascent. . . . Now my tree-climbing days long behind me, I often think about the lasting value of those early, deliciously idle days. I have come to appreciate the long view afforded by those treetops. The woods were my Ritalin. Nature calmed me, focused me, and yet excited my senses.[70]

Louv believes his relationship with nature, along with the time he was able to be left alone or with peers rather than adults, was what was most critical to his development. He argues that all children need to have a connection to nature and that through the system of schools and scheduled, supervised activities, we are denuding our kids of their biological birthright.

Philippe Petit thinks about the problem of child development a bit differently, though it seems that he would agree about the importance of creativity and play. He's the only man in the world who ever has or ever will have crossed between the two World Trade Center buildings on a tightrope. Petit is lionized for his independence, his grit, and his imagination in Robert Zemeckis' 2015 movie *The Walk*, and rightly so. Petit did the impossible, and he considers parents the best source for trusting and building up their children.

I think the best way to open the door to intuition for a child is to put them in front of a creative problem . . . a little origami or building something. And then first let them do what they feel and then rely on their intuition. And then if they go in a completely wrong direction, they . . . will stop and turn to an adult for help. . . . [I]t's a very delicate thing to teach—to bring intuition to a child. . . . They're so sensitive about being forced to do and to think a certain way. So my proposal is . . . to open the door a tiny bit and have the kid use it, moving the door that was ajar. Now it's full. And then they're going to discover; they're going to explore with their own way of thinking, their own intuition and improvisation. And then, yes, the adult is there to make sure there's no accident.[71]

Opening the door for kids but letting them walk through themselves is very close to Captain Daddy Mike Lanza's modus operandi. He developed his passion for play by seeing how far and how often it and children's independence has been curtailed. The serial entrepreneur decided not only to change his family's way of life, but also to study what other neighborhoods and communities have done to change the sedentary, atomized, dependent, inside culture into more of an outside, independent, social, and active one. He was a dad raising his family; now he's a full-blown activist for inculcating the values of self-reliance and community, play and nature, freedom and family.

When I interviewed him about his book, *Playborhood: Turn Your Neighborhood into a Place for Play*, Lanza explained that he went about creating a play space at his house that could serve his own children as well as his community. He and his wife did a lot of research before choosing a house on a street with other families with young children. Then they decided to improve their outdoor spaces—what Lanza calls the front yard family room—while ignoring indoor spaces. He opened his front yard to any local kids who want to come and hang out, and in the summer he runs a week-long "neighborhood camp" at his house for any kids who want to come and play without parental interruption or organization. As a result of his efforts and his book, there are other parents who have taken lessons and ideas to improve the play lives of their own kids and neighborhoods.

Lanza has run into problems as well. Like Louv, he also

spent time outside in nature as a kid and wants to share that
with his own children. He's lucky enough to live near a creek
and woods, and he's practical enough to know that he should
be with his boys when they go exploring. Trouble is that, even
so, he's been harassed by police. He told me that when they
were approached, the police officer seemed more concerned
that the city might get sued if something happened to the children, rather than sincerely worried that they were engaged in
dangerous behavior. Lanza asked the officer (politely), "Under
what grounds are you telling me to stop doing what I'm doing?" since the wooded watering hole wasn't even public property. The response was that local police "are instructed to warn
people not to do certain things at the creek." So often it seems
that even when parents are trying to create a connection with
the outside world, there is often an authority figure that comes
to say, "Stop it."

There is reason of course to be pessimistic that any
Auckland-style, throw-out-the-playground-rule-book, widespread, or sweeping change will happen quickly. The cotton-
wooling—*bubble-wrapping*, in our parlance—of our kids is not
likely to go away without a fight. "No school administrator
wants to roll back policies only to deal with the wrath of parents who still expect schools to provide a protective bubble for
their children. Very few parents (other than the realists) want
to accept the fact that their children cannot be protected from
every eventuality. Because of this impasse, ridiculous policies
and overreactions will continue to be the rule, rather than the
exception," Cushing argues.[72] Entrenched norms and practices
aren't easily displaced, not to mention that lawyers who make
a living off of other people's pain don't support reform efforts.

On the good-news side, there is evidence that changes
are happening in individual communities and neighborhoods,
among well-meaning and energetic parents who are deter-

mined to give their kids a different kind of childhood than the one defined by the safety-obsessed majority culture. There are local parent organizations working toward making their communities more hospitable to kids roaming independently and unsupervised. There are also private, nonprofit organizations— for example, Kaboom!—that encourage play through redesigning playgrounds and pushing local conversations about the importance of play for kids.[73]

CHAPTER 6

Obesity Police

Kids taken into state custody because they're fat and other child-welfare woes

"I AM HORRIFIED," says Walter Olson, father and senior fellow at the Cato Institute's Center for Constitutional Studies.

"People like to punish parents. They don't like to look into the system that causes this," says Yodit Betru, assistant professor at the University of Pittsburgh's School of Social Work.[1]

These experts are railing against the now well-established practice of taking children away from their parents for the "crime" of obesity. When this transgression was originally conceived and defined as "medical neglect," advocates of such state action agreed that it should only be contemplated in extremely rare cases of imminent harm. The fact that in practice the state removes children from their parents and then subsequent to the removal goes through the process of defining and proving its case, means that parents face the disruption of their family life, whether or not there was anything imminent about their children's health condition. Understandably, therefore, few parents accept the logic that it should ever happen at all.

Stormy Bradley is an Atlanta mother with an overweight daughter who was participating in a Georgia advocacy group's "Stop Childhood Obesity" campaign when interviewed in 2012. She personally struggles with the problem, and yet she was upset by the possibility that the government could remove her child from her care. Taking youngsters away from their parents "definitely seems too extreme," Bradley said.[2]

It is true that removals for obesity may happen less often than for other forms of neglect, suggesting that it is as rare as advocates had hoped. Except that one removal would have been too many, given the repercussions of this policy, and there have been many more than that.

It is troubling to note how much of the legal literature sides with the pro-removal camp, as if the discussion has been settled on whether such removals are (a) constitutional and (b) an efficient use of public resources to effectively solve a serious issue. The reality of removals is quite different from the theory: more complicated, more negative, and much less clearly useful. And this is where some context can help to illuminate a troubling landscape and history of parents' rights versus child-welfare policy. A close look at these cases underscores how the child-welfare apparatus views families—essentially as battlegrounds pitting children against parents rather than homogeneous single units that at times may be in need of support services.

Taking custody of an obese child may be a relatively recent development in response to a severe crisis. But it also appears that parents have lost custody of their children for so many varied—justifiable or not—definitions of violence, abuse, and neglect that the "medical neglect" diagnosis, as pediatric-obesity removals have been categorized, is the current crisis to which child-protective and child-welfare services have focused attention. This would not be the first time, after all, that a scare or fad has focused the public's attention on child-welfare issues. The string of daycare sex-abuse cases in the late 1980s and early '90s is just one example.

Child welfare has long struggled with what Betru calls the "fundamental dilemma" of child welfare, balancing social policy with parental independence. "Save children but preserve the family," as she says.[3] NYU historian Linda Gordon offers a good explanation in her history of child welfare.

> Agencies devoted to the problem of family violence are in many ways typical of the entire welfare state. They have faced great difficulties in maintaining a balance between social order and privacy, between protecting and rights of some individuals and preserving the autonomy of others, and they have often been the means of imposing dominant values on subordinate groups.[4]

This has certainly been the case with obesity. Over the past two decades there has been a growing concern for "solving" the problem of obesity, especially as it relates to children. In Chapter 4, we learned about the push to put all public-school kids on a restricted diet because of the minority segment of the school-aged population that is at risk for developing weight issues. And given all that we have learned thus far about the near hysteria and terrific pressure that can surround a problem relating to children's health, the appearance of the obesity "epidemic" is no surprise.

Let's begin with some case histories of obesity removals.

Forty-nine-year-old Jerri Gray of Travelers Rest, South Carolina, was arrested in June 2009 and charged with criminal neglect. Her crime was her obese son, Alexander, who by age 14 tipped the scale at 555 pounds.[5] According to the arrest warrant, Alexander's weight was "serious and threatening to his health," and his mom was charged with placing him "at an unreasonable risk of harm." All of this caused a media firestorm; after all, this was the first time a parent was accused of being criminally responsible for a child's obesity. Two years later, by August 2011, charges against Gray were still pending, and Alexander continued to live away from his mother.[6]

In 2011, outside Cleveland, Ohio, a third-grader was taken

from his mother because he was obese. At the time, Cuyahoga County did not have a specific obesity policy, and yet the local authorities "removed the boy because case workers considered this mother's inability to get her son's weight down a form of medical neglect," said Mary Louise Madigan, a spokeswoman for the Department of Children and Family Services.[7] The state argued that the mother wasn't following doctor's orders, though the mother disagreed and said his weight gain was due to his environment. "This child's problem was so severe that we had to take custody," Madigan said.

The agency argued that they had to take this step because, despite repeated warnings from CPS and after working with the mother for a year, the boy's weight had reached 200 pounds instead of going down. But the mother expressed the pain of separation and rejected the state's theory that pulling him away from her was going to improve his life. "They are trying to make it seem like I am unfit, like I don't love my child," the mother told the Cleveland *Plain Dealer*. "Of course I love him. Of course I want him to lose weight. It's a lifestyle change, and they are trying to make it seem like I am not embracing that. It is very hard, but I am trying."[8]

In 2000, in New Mexico, three-year-old Anamarie Regino was taken from her parents and placed in foster care for two and half months; she weighed 124 pounds and was nearly 4 feet tall. "Literally, it was two months of hell. It seemed like the longest two months of my life," mother Adela Martinez said. As it turned out, it was two unnecessary months of hell. Anamarie didn't improve at all in foster care, and she was returned to her parents. The young girl was later diagnosed with a genetic predisposition. "They say it's for the well-being of the child, but it did more damage that any money or therapy could ever to do to fix it," Martinez said.[9]

Anamarie agreed when years later she was asked her opinion of the controversial opinion piece "State Intervention in Life-Threatening Childhood Obesity," by Dr. David Ludwig and Lindsey Murtagh of Harvard's School of Public Health, published in the *Journal of the American Medical Association*. The commentary was the first big endorsement of obesity removals. "It's not right, what [Dr. Ludwig] is doing, because to get better you need to be with your family, instead of being surrounded by doctors," Anamarie said.[10]

Ludwig and Murtagh might take issue with Anamarie's characterization of their solution to morbid childhood obesity, but she is right that they set the terms legitimizing pediatric obesity removals by defining the term *medical neglect* to justify their recommendation. "In severe instances of childhood obesity," they wrote in the 2011 essay, "removal from the home may be justifiable, from a legal standpoint because of imminent health risks and the parents' chronic failure to address medical problems."[11] The doctor and lawyer, together, laid out the combined conditions under which removal should be considered: imminent health risk and parental failure. We'll examine each in turn.

Let's first consider their definition of *imminent health risk*, words which were carefully chosen to mirror the federal standard for action. "Obesity of this magnitude can cause immediate and potentially irreversible consequences, most notably Type 2 diabetes. . . . Without major weight loss, Type 2 diabetes usually becomes permanent several years after onset . . . which decreases life expectancy significantly," they wrote.[12] Does shorter life expectancy really meet the standard of "imminent risk," though?

Ludwig and Murtagh were trying to deal constructively and responsibly with a significant challenge. As they wrote, other solutions had been ineffective or were discounted because of risk factors. "Because of the poor outcome of conventional treatment for pediatric obesity," they explained, "bariatric surgery has become increasingly considered for adolescents with Type 2 diabetes. However, the long-term safety and effectiveness of this invasive procedure in adolescents remains unknown."[13] Ludwig and Murtagh also dismissed other methods of weight loss for young people because they didn't find that any had proven effective enough.

Not everyone agrees that gastric surgery is as risky as Ludwig and Murtagh make out, however. Clinical psychologist Martin Binks asserted in 2011 that "review of data show that surgical approaches (some of which are considered reversible such as Laparoscopic Gastric Banding) have been effective in reducing weight and comorbidities in severely obese adolescents."[14]

Given these limitations—excessive risks associated with surgery and the ineffective weight-loss programs that were then available—Ludwig and Murtagh opted for what in their view was the next logical step in reducing childhood obesity, by suggesting that in extreme cases removing children from their parents could work. "As an alternative therapeutic approach, placement of the severely obese child under protective custody warrants discussion."[15]

To recap their argument, traditional weight loss hadn't worked in extreme cases of morbid obesity—defined as a body mass index higher than the 99th percentile for children of the same sex and age—and surgery to control weight was dismissed as invasive and risky. Conclusion: Take some kids away from their parents to fix their weight. Ludwig and Murtagh even admit the limitations of their solution. "Despite the discomfort posed by state intervention, it may sometimes be necessary to protect a child," they wrote. And they included a rather rosy prediction of how removals should happen, too. State intervention "ideally will support not just the child but the whole family, with the goal of reuniting child and family as soon as possible," they explained.[16]

Ludwig and Murtagh's commentary was innovative for combining the medical and legal justification and conditions for removal. In their medical reasoning, however, they were following in the footsteps of other activist health professionals, like the overbearing nannies at the American Academy of Pediatrics, representatives of which published a pro-removal paper in the AAP journal *Pediatrics* in 2009.[17] "In our opinion," wrote doctors Todd Varness, David B. Allen, Aaron L. Carrel, and Norman Fost, "removal of a child from the home is justified when all three of the following conditions are present: (1) a high likelihood that serious imminent harm will occur; (2) a reasonable likelihood that coercive state intervention will result in effective treatment; and (3) the absence of alternative options for addressing the problem."[18] At the time, the authors did not address how primary-care physicians encountering extreme pediatric obesity cases could possibly determine whether all these conditions were met before engaging the child-welfare authorities.

The piece caused a huge stir and was followed by numerous supporting and critical responses. From the legal realm, there was, for the most part, positive, reinforcing argumentation.

Writing in the *Yale Journal of Health Policy, Law, and Ethics*, Shauneen M. Garrahan and Andrew W. Eichner supported removals, arguing that "morbid childhood obesity is a modern phenomenon that justifies greater state intervention."[19] They did admit to a significant problem with defining morbid pediatric obesity as medical neglect, however, given that most states didn't have such a standard in their legal codes and even those states with a definition of medical neglect didn't necessarily include obesity as part of the definition. But this is semantics, surely, since state legal codes can be changed and have changed over time.

Melissa Mitgang argued in the *Columbia Journal of Law*

and Social Problems for taking a closer look at the risks of setting too lenient a standard for removals versus setting one that
is too stringent.

> Applying a lower standard of harm or an analysis less
> focused upon the actual effects of obesity upon a child's
> health in considering whether intervention is war-
> ranted would unjustifiably impinge upon parental au-
> tonomy and would potentially inflict more harm than
> benefit upon the affected child. Applying a more strin-
> gent standard, such as allowing intervention only when
> death is imminent, would prevent the state from pro-
> tecting children seriously in need of help whose best
> interests, both short- and long-term, would be well-
> served by intervention.[20]

In response to Ludwig and Murtagh, Dr. Lainie Ross, a
medical ethicist at the University of Chicago, admitted that
"there's a stigma with state intervention." She didn't reject the
idea, however. "We just have to do it with caution and humility
and make sure we really can say that our interventions are going to do more good than harm."[21] Does Ross really believe that
intentions are all that matter? The parents and children ripped
apart by the obesity police likely disagree that *intending* to "do
more good than harm" is an adequate standard.

Arguing for removals in Massachusetts, Kristen E. Brierley
in the *Western New England Law Review* explained how courts
should consider the parents' health in cases of pediatric morbid
obesity in order to prove they are guilty of neglect and abuse.

> If Massachusetts's courts do not include parents' overall
> health and well-being in their analyses of parental fit-
> ness in cases involving morbidly obese children, it is the

child who will ultimately suffer. It is not surprising that morbidly obese children who have experienced weight loss success in foster care often revert back to their poor diet and exercise habits when returned to unfit parents. Such a problem could be prevented in Massachusetts if the courts' consideration of parental fitness and ability to care for the child took into account the parents' own health and well-being, including their physical limitations due to morbid obesity.[22]

Basically her argument is this: If you are an obese parent, you should absolutely lose custody of your child because, after all, even if your kid loses weight in temporary care, that won't continue after returning home. In essence, obese parents can't possibly "properly" care for their children, so they shouldn't get to keep them.

It is worth noting that a glance through previous cases reveals that removing obese children from their parents preceded academic legitimization. For decades, obesity has been considered along with other issues when deliberating removal.

THE FIRST CASE is from 1992, when a 10-year-old girl in Iowa was removed from her parents' custody due to her obesity as well as other psychological problems.[23] At the time the court based the girl's removal after finding her to be "a child in need of assistance."

A California case decided in 1998 involved a 13-year-old girl named Christina Ann Corrigan who weighed more than 680 pounds. When the child died before the case was heard, the court responded by charging her mother with misdemeanor child abuse through inaction.[24]

An Indiana case decided in the late 1990s involved a four-year-old boy named Cory Andis who weighed 111 pounds.

Cory's parents pled guilty to criminal child neglect. The court ordered Cory's mother to serve one-and-a-half years of probation and perform 100 hours of community service for endangering Cory's health, and Cory's father was placed on probation for three years.[25]

According to court records, there were discussions with Cory's parents about why they were not following recommended dietary guidelines to bring down the boy's weight. Details offer a glimpse at the difficulty of fulfilling the mandate to "exhaust" all other options and work with parents before taking the "last resort" step of removal. Writing about the case, Abigail Darwin says the parents complained in court that "they did not understand the suggested diets [which] were too hard to follow." There is also some evidence, Darwin suggests, that the court lost patience with the parents after they seemed to be flouting the rules by bringing fast food to their boy while he was in hospital.[26]

Writing for a publication of the Child Welfare League of America, Darwin claims that under different circumstances families could benefit from services provided by other state actors, rather than the courts or child protection. "Courts should look at whether the state has provided the family with intensive, family-oriented services including: family counseling, education regarding proper nutrition and exercise, income supports, menu planning, a visiting nurse, and a visiting homemaker. These components are necessary to form the basis of a comprehensive 'reasonable efforts' protocol to help families with morbidly obese children overcome all the challenges associated with helping their children lose weight."[27]

In Texas, a case decided in 2002 involved a four-year-old boy identified as G.C. who weighed more than 136 pounds. In that instance parental rights were terminated.[28] And in another 2002 case, Pennsylvania removed a 451-pound 16-year-old identified as D.K. from his single mother (his father was deceased), who was herself so obese that she was homebound. The government intervention in this case was complicated by a parent who initially had sought help from the state, followed by an unsympathetic judicial system that refused to prioritize family unity.

"D.K.'s mother voluntarily entrusted his care to the state, and he was placed on strict dietary and physical regimens in foster care," writes Elizabeth Ralston in her law review study "KinderLARDen Cop: Why States Must Stop Policing Parents of Obese Children." In this instance, the state got involved only after the boy's school had initially taken the initiative to evaluate him.[29]

The court then found reasons why Pennsylvania could remove the child. "The court noted that it would not intervene solely because the child was overweight or was not engaging in a 'healthy and fit lifestyle,'" explain the authors of the legal newsletter "Courts Struggle with the Growing Problem of Child Obesity." They describe how, in this case, the court-ordered removal was justified only because obesity had reached "the life-threatening or morbid state, which [had] also manifested itself in physical problems."[30]

Three months later and 50 pounds lighter, the teenager told the court he wanted to go home. He said he understood the way to live a healthier life, his mother could help him succeed, and he was able to shop and prepare healthy meals for himself (and his mother, presumably). He also expressed how much he missed his mother and wanted to be back with her and nearer his friends, school, and community. The court was unmoved and blamed his mom for failing to give the boy "a minimum standard of care for [his] physical, intellectual and moral well-being" due to her own obesity. As a result, the child would not be returned home.[31]

This is confusing. If the standard for removing a kid is imminent harm, why suddenly is the court concerned with how good a mother this woman was to her son? His moral well-being wasn't the basis for removal, so why should it be part of the consideration for his return? Beyond this inconsistency, there's the question of whether there was anything else child protection or the courts could have done before removing D.K. "Without citing any examples of when or how, the court held that the state had made reasonable efforts to preserve and reunify the family. In reality, the state made no attempt to provide [the boy]'s mother with the assistance she needed to maintain custody of her child," Ralston argues.[32]

In New York, the first rulings in this area show courts disregarding the parents and the child. In 2006, the Empire State removed an obese girl from her parents seven different times in under two years because the court said the parents were failing to "address her obesity and to ensure she went to school."[33] The family court's finding of neglect and its attempt at revoking parental rights were overturned, however, by the appellate court. "[T]he appellate division painted a different picture—one of parents who joined a gym they could not afford and who voluntarily gave up custody of their daughter as a last resort to try to help her," Ralston explains.[34]

The fact that two different courts came to opposing conclusions about the behavior of these parents toward their obese daughter highlights another significant problem with legitimizing removals. Let's say one accepts the argument that state custody is a last resort and that before removal parents must be given the option of working with child-welfare and legal authorities to help reduce their child's weight. There is still no system available to parents to try and work out the problem voluntarily, and there is no agreed upon standard of assessment for how successful parents have been at following the state's directions.

These severe limitations haven't stopped some analysts from imagining rosy scenarios for why removals aren't really so terrible. At *Slate*, KJ Antonia defended obesity removals by explaining that advocates were in reality threatening removal more often than they actually intended to carry it out. "It's not the parents who haven't found a way to help their child that these advocates are targeting. It's the parents who can't or won't take the help that's being offered."[35] Except that removals have already happened even when parents were *complying* with state recommendations and action plans, as the case in New York shows. Government isn't terrifically patient, and often child-protection and family courts have their own schedule for adjudicating matters.

A further complication is that the federal definitions of neglect and abuse don't meet a reasonable threshold for removing obese kids. "Whatever power government has to seize kids from their parents ought to be restricted to, at most, objectively dangerous situations that are well outside the range ordinarily expected of parents in that community, usually with an element of immediate peril. Making calories readily available to kids on demand may be unwise parenting, but it is not far outside the range of what any normal parent would do," legal expert Walter Olson explained in our interview.

Olson's argument makes perfect sense, except for the fact that we are talking about very unhealthy kids who are going to die young without some form of intervention. As a mother of four who spends a lot of time (and probably too much) focused on making sure our kids are safe and healthy, these stories of obese three- and four-year-olds tear at my heart. But it is precisely at such moments that a recommitment to first principles is most important because, as we shall see, a government response—and especially the nanny state's version of a response—is neither right on the law, nor right on the merits.

Children and parents, even those who have made poor choices, deserve to have their liberties protected from overzealous, interfering government.

THE CHILD ABUSE Prevention and Treatment Act (CAPTA) of 1973 was the first federal legislation enacted to combat child abuse and neglect and to establish a uniform national standard. All fifty states have since enacted statutory definitions of child abuse and neglect that conform to CAPTA, which defines child neglect as "any recent act or failure to act on the part of a parent or caretaker, which results in death, serious physical or emotional harm, sexual abuse or exploitation, or an act or failure to act which presents an imminent risk of serious harm."[36]

Dana Mack, author of *The Assault on Parenthood*, argues that CAPTA is a distraction. She says the standards for deciding what to do with children who are not being properly cared for by their parents were laid down earlier, with the Family Law Act of 1969. That legislation, Mack writes, "freed family courts from [any] obligation to take into account any presumed rights of parents in decisions regarding child placement."[37] The result was dismal, because it "shifted the burden of proof in child placement decisions from establishing parental 'unfitness' to establishing parental 'fitness,'" Mack declares.[38]

For all the talk of using removal as a threat, or weapon of last resort, there are opposing pressures and incentives faced by child-welfare and -protection workers that become evident when scanning the myriad other reasons children are removed from their parents. It becomes obvious that as complicated and important a problem as obesity may be for American children, it is equally important to recognize that the child-welfare system has too many problems and is already stretched too thin to be able to offer effective relief in this area.

"American parents today take for granted the existence of government agencies that have *carte blanche* to monitor their family lives, censor their child-rearing habits, and even take their children away from them," writes Mack in her exceptional study.[39]

Liberty Justice Center staff attorney Jeffrey Schwab describes what happens as accusations of neglect fall upon specific groups, instead of across all parents.

> Arbitrary application of laws like child neglect by [Department of Child and Family Services] tends to disproportionately affect single-parent families, immigrants and ethnic minorities. The vast majority of women the Family Defense Center assists . . . are single mothers or have a partner who was not indicated, and almost all are ethnic minorities or immigrants.[40]

These observers are obviously critics of child protection. What about those who support the system and the notion that pediatric obesity ought to be tackled by these agencies? Listen to Shauneen Garrahan and Andrew Eichner, who echo Schwab's observation about interventions even as they come to the opposite conclusion: "The history of child abuse laws in the United States indicates a general progression towards greater government involvement in the family sphere when negligent parental actions put the health of a child at risk. The development of child protection laws nationwide indicates a trend towards earlier and more aggressive intervention."[41]

It is within this landscape of "earlier and more aggressive intervention," where government agencies nearly have "*carte blanche* to monitor" family life and where application of the law falls more on some groups than others, that we have to understand the movement to help overweight children. What other sorts of child protection have these state service agencies been engaged in, and have they been successful? Are we looking at adding another burden onto an already well-run honorable sys-

tem or a morass of mission creep and unaccountable bureaucracy that can't handle its current caseload let alone additional
responsibilities?

FAULTS IN THE SYSTEM: 1. DEFINING ABUSE

The challenge for child welfare has always been the same: define the parameters of the mission and then effectively go about
alleviating the problem. But as a look at a century of evidence
suggests, this simple formula has always been at odds with certain other realities. As historian Linda Gordon recounts in her
study of Boston child welfare from 1880 to 1960,

> Family violence is not a fixed social illness which, like
> tuberculosis, can have its causal microorganism identi-
> fied and then killed. Rather, its definitions have changed
> substantially since it first appeared as a social problem.
> Most of the discussion of family violence today assumes
> that what makes it problematic and requires social ac-
> tion is self-evident. Yet what was considered spanking
> a century ago might be considered abusive today, and
> the standards for what constitutes child neglect have
> changed greatly.[42]

Gordon's observation about the malleability of definitions
of abuse and neglect could not be more appropriate for the
present day. Take the case of mother Toya Graham. By most
definitions, she abused her son. Out in the open, she hit and
slapped him, and she did both repeatedly and with as much
force as she could muster. Her son hid from her, cowered, and
tried to turn away. She wouldn't have that, so she yanked on
his clothes and kept hitting him. For this abusive display, Graham was labeled Mother of the Year by more than a few media
onlookers. Why? Because Graham was hitting her son in the

middle of the Baltimore police riots. She identified him from among the throng, though his face was covered, and she walked out into the street to physically assault him and drag him home.

Graham is a hero to many parents because she hit her son "related to the purpose of safeguarding or promoting the welfare of the minor,"[43] which is part of the definition of acceptable physical parental discipline as set by the Massachusetts high court in June 2015, when the judges reversed a decision against a dad who spanked his two-year-old daughter in public. The court affirmed the right of parents to discipline their kids within specific boundaries and asserted that parents have a right to mount an affirmative defense should they get charged with battery—as happened in this case.

While Massachusetts is narrowing the definition of abuse by redefining standards of corporal punishment, child protection typically broadens its scope. Take Vermont, for example, which in 2015 decided to be bold and admit that its idea of child protection was now going to be focused on alleviation of poverty (which is obviously a much bigger challenge), and it wasn't going to side with parents. "The change to state statute puts 'the best interest of the child' ahead of reunification of a child with his or her parents."[44] When Georgia changed its child-welfare system in 2015, the stated goal was building "a better future for this state by developing the best child welfare agency in the world. It is a lofty goal," explained Bobby Cagle, director of Georgia's Division of Family and Children Services. After all, he said, "[o]ne in five Georgians will come into contact with our agency over the next five years."[45] But why are so many Georgians going to be involved in the system at all, and is this a pattern of citizen-government interaction we want to promote?

Gordon describes the evolving understanding of child abuse in political terms, as a matter of shifting power structures. The "definition of what constitutes unacceptable domestic violence, and appropriate responses to it, developed and then varied according to political moods and the force of certain political movements," she argues.[46]

FAULTS IN THE SYSTEM: 2. OVERBURDENED

When I discussed these issues with Professor Yodit Betru, who spends her days training social workers at the University of Pittsburgh, she admitted that attitudes about family and what's in the best interest of the child have always been mutable. "We started off [with the] orphan train movement [which] sent kids out to the country," Betru said. Since such a system became unsustainable and even undesirable, foster care came next. There are inherent risks with this system as well. As Betru explained, the foster-care system is expensive, and studies show significant limitations beyond the cost to government.

In 1995, before a Senate subcommittee about federal child-protection policy, Carol Lamb Hopkins reported that her state of California had a 70 percent foster-care error rate that was burning a hole in the state budget. "The foster care cost to the State of California alone, for the 63,207 children who should not be there is $303,394,500 per year. Projected nationally that is three billion dollars," she testified.

Not much has changed in the intervening decades. "Children in foster care are 75 percent more likely to be maltreated, four times more likely to be sexually abused, and are more likely to receive inadequate health care and develop behavioral and emotional problems," reported Elizabeth Ralston in 2012. She then extrapolated that adding obesity cases to this mix is a bad idea. "Unless remaining in the home places a child in grave danger, it is unlikely that foster care is a better alternative for an obese child."[47]

Betru also describes what sounds like a serious systemic problem with present-day child-protection services, namely, that the system works at cross-purposes. "Concurrent planning," she explains, is when a substantiated abuse or neglect case is opened and the "case [is] assigned two tracks—to adopt the kid out or to preserve the family—at the same time." So each case is assigned two diametrically opposed goals. How is that supposed to work efficiently?

It is also apparent when examining federal mandates about child protection—especially 1997's Adoption and Safe Families Act (ASFA)—that family preservation isn't Washington's priority. Consider two critics of the law, who each from their opposing vantage points agree that "fixing foster care" by terminating biological parents' rights and adopting out more children was the purpose of the legislation. In *Shattered Bonds: The Color of Child Welfare*, Northwestern University law professor Dorothy Roberts argues ASFA establishes "a preference for adoption as the means of reducing the exploding foster care population."[48] Elizabeth Bartholet, professor at Harvard Law School, criticizes ASFA for not having gone far enough toward adoption. She argues in her book *Nobody's Children: Abuse and Neglect, Foster Drift, and the Adoption Alternative* that the law leaves "too much room for those in the child welfare system who are committed to family preservation to resist and evade [the law's] apparent purpose."[49]

The government's current position seems largely based on the notion that any intervention is going to be better than no intervention and that, almost without exception, no resulting harm is worth the risk of inaction. This too often leaves parents as the bad guys.

FAULTS IN THE SYSTEM: 3. KIDS VS PARENTS

Betru says that blaming parents can come easily, depending on the problem. When I spoke to lawyer Jennifer Ani, she explained how often police and child-welfare workers make judg-

ments against parents for *legal* behavior. Ani lives and works in a
part of the country where medical marijuana is legal and prevalent. She has witnessed too many cases, she told me, of children
removed and parents accused of being inadequate guardians
because of the presence of marijuana in their homes. In some
cases, parents have been considered criminals because there was
cannabis in or around the home—irrespective of whether the
adults were growing, distributing, or using, all of which can be
legal activities. Think what you will about the value of pot as
medicine, it is legal in California (and dozens of other states),
and there is no law that says parents are unfit because of it. "We
can't pit kids versus parents as a social policy," Ani argues.

As for obesity, Betru believes it is a mistake not to treat
it as a symptom of a larger problem. Since removing a child
is supposed to be a solution of last resort, Betru explains that
she and her colleagues "try to teach this from an institutional
perspective.... [It's] the stance that we come from as social
workers." She worries, though, about all the people working in
child protection who are not properly trained. "If you are not
taught within that theory, you are not going to have a lot of
empathy for the parents," she said in our interview. Such a lack
of empathy can lead to real trouble when those child-protection
workers have the power to break up families.

Twenty years ago, in 1995, when Hopkins testified before
a Senate subcommittee, she ably identified many of the same
problems.

> Currently there is no uniform screening, training, cer-
> tification, or assessment of protection workers. Work-
> ers are given tremendous responsibility and awesome
> power but, for far too many, no training whatsoever.
> Again, there is a definition problem. Protection work-
> ers may be high school graduates, they may have their

B.A. in physical education, they may never have taken a single course in social work. In too many cases it is only the work they do which defines them as "social workers."

[W]ould we turn over schools to untrained, randomly selected adults, call them "teachers," give them inadequate resources, keep adding students, make it impossible for the parents to complain or hold anyone accountable, and then expect learning to occur without fairly frequent disasters?

In March 2003 the Government Accountability Office basically agreed with Hopkins and Betru when it reported on the need among child-welfare agencies to recruit and retain experienced staff. The importance of social workers being properly trained was a major conclusion of the report. But even the best-trained professionals can fall victim to what Betru warns is a constant concern, when social workers bring their own prejudices and emotional baggage to the problems they are trying to help solve for their clients.

Betru worries that the visibility of obesity causes visceral reactions. And her concerns are echoed by Dr. Melinda Sothern, who for 20 years has worked with obese children. Though the Louisiana-based exercise physiologist and author of *Trim Kids* has seen only about a dozen obese children removed from their homes, Sothern has noticed a marked change in attitude. "I've seen less and less willingness on the professional side to understand how hard it is on the parents' side, especially from younger professionals," she says. And she brings up another concern as well: "[Child protection] laws have changed, so a lot of times [child protection personnel] worry that if they don't report parents, they'll get in trouble."[50]

Better training isn't the solution, according to Diane

Redleaf, who works tirelessly on behalf of parents as executive director of the Family Defense Center in Chicago. From her perspective, the problem is systemic. Though she agrees that training isn't as good as it could be, "we also have policy disagreements with the Department of Children & Family Services as to where the line between reasonable parenting and neglect should be set. We think DCFS intervenes far too readily as a matter of policy." Redleaf also sees that what services are available are often wrong for the given situation. "I think there are ... too many investigators and too few service-providing caseworkers at the child welfare agency. We have a punitive investigatory model. Services to deflect cases out of the system are not available." And as a result, she disagrees that spending more money on investigations or training is a good solution.

There is a further complication: How do we define a family? Mack believes the child-welfare system is poisoned by the attitude that children are to be protected from their parents, as opposed to being helped from within their families. And Gordon, whose research deals with the era of social services delivered before the establishment of the welfare state (as well as after), says that conditions improved with state control, exactly for the reasons Mack describes.

Gordon *favors* the children-first, children-always philosophy. By her lights, dealing with families is political. "The effect of social workers' involvement was sometimes to change existing family power relations, usually in the interest of the weaker family members."[51] Weaker here means children, not parents, and sometimes wives, not husbands, and Gordon advocates for that feminist view while acknowledging how some people see the family differently. "When critics of social control perceive social work simply as unwanted intervention ... it is in large part because they conceive of the family as a homogeneous unit."[52]

This is not an insignificant disagreement. Child-welfare workers have a very different mission if they view families as homogeneous units (irrespective of structure) with rights and responsibilities. If families are viewed through the more segmented prism—divided between the alleged power inequity between members—then child protection naturally becomes kids versus parents. After years of working in child welfare, NYU Law professor Martin Guggenheim came to the conclusion that Gordon has it right. "Child welfare's purpose in the latter part of the twentieth century was dramatically narrowed to protecting children from harm inflicted upon them by their parents,"[53] Guggenheim declares. Note his terminology: Child welfare's *purpose* is protecting kids *from* their parents.

According to Guggenheim, the change from helping families to protecting children's rights began in the 1960s, when "medical professionals focused public attention on evidence that many physical injuries to children were apparently inflicted by parents."[54] From there, Guggenheim explains,

> [t]he burgeoning children's rights movement encouraged policymakers to focus on the separate human rights of children to be raised in safety, even if that meant separating them from their birth families. This fueled, and was fueled by, a nascent societal consensus that children were independent persons with rights of their own, even when enforcement of those rights came at the expense of their parents.[55]

Child-welfare workers aren't the only ones who interpret the law this way. During a 2009 case of removal for pediatric obesity, the court argued that "parents do not have absolute rights to raise their children without state involvement and that parental rights are secondary to the child's best interests."[56]

FAULTS IN THE SYSTEM: 4. NO TRANSPARENCY

A final consideration is the child-welfare system's longstanding problem with accountability and a lack of transparency.

In 1992, after the San Diego Grand Jury spent nine months investigating the child-dependency system, the concluding report was a stinging rebuke: More accountability is essential. As the resulting "Families in Crisis" report states,

> The Jury asked almost every professional who testified what they would do to improve the condition of the Juvenile Dependency System. . . . [T]here was an almost unanimous consensus among attorneys, therapists, physicians, judges, law enforcement, social workers, and clients that there needs to be a more effective accountability link between prescribed standards and practice and between mandated intervention services and appropriations. Therefore, there is a demand for a more effective system of checks and balances.[57]

These days, transparency is an equally thorny problem. Betru's concern is that caseworkers are engaging with individual families whose privacy should not be violated. There is an "overall tension," Betru says, between caseworkers' "micro level work with macro level implications. They can share the process but not the specifics [of any single case]." The tension between the macro implications and the micro-level work with individual families is often, unfortunately, sorted out through litigation, with thousands of parents suing the authorities, claiming their rights as parents have been violated. Betru argues that this is a "necessary form of social movement" because, "as much as we like to think that we are introspective and [analyze whether we are engaged in] best practice," in reality, "people don't like change."

According to the editors of *Welfare of Children: Lessons Learned from Class Action Litigation*, over 40 years of class-action lawsuits have improved and reformed child-welfare practice and policies across the country.[58] "Approximately 70 class action lawsuits are pending or have governed some aspect of child welfare practice in nearly 30 states, and almost 20 states are currently working to implement consent decrees and/or other court orders related to the reform of their child welfare systems."[59] As the editors explain, the need for the lawsuits as an effective lever to force reform is recognized across the spectrum.

> Despite the best efforts of administrators and child welfare workers, the poor outcomes for many children and families involved with these systems and the scores of daily press accounts of children at risk speak powerfully to the limitations, scarce resources and dysfunctions in many of these systems ... [and] many advocates have concluded that the monitoring by federal agencies and state legislative bodies lacks the necessary force to effectuate comprehensive reform.[60]

OBESITY IS THE LATEST EXTREME

State child-welfare agencies haven't been very good about self-examination or reform, however. Instead, four decades of class-action lawsuits against child-welfare systems attest to the reality that far too many families have endured investigations, removals, and trials for alleged wrong-doing that turn out in many cases to have been either mistaken or due to an overbroad

understanding of abuse and neglect. As Hopkins declared in
her 1995 Senate testimony,

> The definition has been expanded to include neglect
> due to poverty, cultural differences in child rearing, law-
> ful corporal punishment, failure to protect, truancy, and
> emotional abuse. . . . [A]s the definition kept expanding,
> the face of "child abuse" was expanded sufficiently to
> become the face of every family, at one time or another.
>
> I could share anecdotal stories about the destruc-
> tion of families, the insensitivity of social workers, the
> collusion of juvenile court judges, which might well
> cause you to decide that the damage done to children
> and families in the name of child protection far out-
> weighs the good.

Miscarriages of justice are the work of many hands, from
overzealous police, child-protection and -welfare workers, mandated reporting requirements (for more, see Chapter 1 and conclusion), along with health and school professionals. Has the
situation changed since 1995, when Hopkins offered her dire
assessment? Ask the parents of two Illinois girls who endured
removal due to just one such error. When their then-13-month-
old daughter stopped putting weight on her left leg, her parents
decided to take her to the emergency room rather than wait to
see their pediatrician the next day. That choice led to a 15-week
nightmare of accusations by the Department of Children and
Family Services that the child had been abused. The family's two
children were removed, and the parents had to fight in court to
get them back, even as the state admitted the original charges
filed against them did not support the conclusion of abuse. The
children were kept away from their parents while DCFS got a
second chance to refile their petition. It was advocacy by the
Family Defense Center that finally reunited the family.

In 2013, FDC executive director Diane Redleaf confirmed in an op-ed for the *Chicago Sun-Times* just how often her organization has dealt with similar situations. "Our cases often involve a parent who turned her head at the same moment a child fell, or a false allegation made by a disgruntled spouse in a bitter divorce proceeding."[61] And Redleaf argued that what she was seeing as a parent advocate, the local DCFS was seeing even more often. "Such situations account for more than two-thirds of the DCFS caseload," she declared.

When I interviewed Redleaf, she offered a general assessment of the current challenge. "Parents have been stigmatized and made powerless in this system," she explained. She argues that organizations like hers exist "to provide legal counsel" and advocate for parents whose "rights are violated and where laws on the books are the problem." But Redleaf also criticized DCSF for picking the wrong battles. She wants "DCFS to renew its efforts to deflect cases based on poverty into support services" so that DCFS can focus on cases of true abuse and neglect. This is important because "children deserve protection from abusive parents and caregivers," and that "starts with having a clear definition of abuse and neglect and an ability to recognize which cases should be investigated and which families should be left alone. Not all Hotline calls are credible, and only a fraction of DCFS calls involve actual or serious threats of harm to a child."[62]

Redleaf is not alone. She has colleagues across the country fighting for parents whose families have been trampled by child protection. When I spoke with Captain Mommy Jennifer Ani, she explained how she'd gotten into the business of parent advocacy after her own daughter was born. Before becoming a mom, she had worked in the mortgage industry, but that all changed when she was in the hospital after giving birth.

"I hit all the red flags," she admits. "Single mom, unemployed," though Ani says the fact that she owned her home worked in her favor. "I agreed to get visited by the [public health] nurse," Ani says. When I asked why she even needed to agree to such scrutiny, she replied as if I was being naïve. If she hadn't agreed to the home visit, she would have been viewed with suspicion and likely marked for a visit from child protection. The home visit went smoothly, and she never heard anything else about it, but the experience, Ani says, "is a big part of the reason I went into this area of the law. I want to provide some support for parents who faced similar circumstances." These days she fights a lot of cases where parents who have a legal right to grow or use cannabis for medicinal purposes are threatened or have lost custody of their kids. "I have two goals: get the kids home, and get them out of the system," Ani declares.

Years of watching how child-welfare workers operate have turned Ani into a critic. She argues that they begin with a bias, but they have to make sure they have "proof" that they were right to remove the child, since they'll have to justify their reasoning to a judge. "Social workers have so much discretion and immunity to remove a child," Ani explained to me in our phone interview. Then, she says, when you get to court, "they have to back up why they took the kid."

Ani sounds exactly like Hopkins, who 20 years earlier testified about the same troubles with the California system. She'd been deputy foreman of the San Diego County grand jury that reviewed the county's juvenile dependency system. She'd also served as a member of the San Diego District Attorney's ad hoc Committee of Child Abuse. As Hopkins explained,

> Most Americans, and even most attorneys, are unaware that accused parents have no right to a trial by jury . . . or that rank hearsay is admissible to withhold children from their families for days, weeks, months, years, for-

ever; that the burden of proof is the same or less than that required to forfeit the family car. I have witnessed egregious perjury, and abuse of power.... Families are thrust into closed courtrooms where all the rules favor the efforts to destroy the family unit. Families are terminated entirely in swift, secret, hardly intelligible proceedings. Confidentiality is used as sword and shield. Families are told that confidentiality is to protect them and their children. More often it is used to protect child protection services from the public scrutiny which would come in these cases.[63]

At the time, the San Diego district attorney was moved to investigate the county's child-welfare system because of an infamous tragedy. In 1989, eight-year-old Alicia Wade was abducted from her home in the middle of the night and violently raped. Worse yet was the state's treatment of her father, who was falsely accused of the crime. *Three years later*, after the case was finally sorted out and the shattered Wades moved away to pick up the pieces, a thorough investigation of the child-welfare system ensued, with Hopkins helping to expose what turned out to be a callous, failed system. The Wade fiasco was exacerbated by its proximity to a series of daycare-worker trials during which children were abused by psychologists and prosecutors who were more focused on convictions than truth.

It would be great to think that this is all ancient history. Instead, it is more accurate to say that while satanic worship among daycare workers has been discredited, there are other hysterias that have taken hold among child-health and -welfare advocates.

As Walter Olson argues, moreover, the pressure to overdo it derives from more sources than child-protection agencies. "Regulators already begin with incentives to do more rather than less—the surest way for them to catch heat is for an injury to occur that they could have prevented. . . . But don't overlook the third parties, such as the organized public health profession. The campaign to require hot dogs to be cut into small pieces before serving to kids isn't coming from a nervous bureaucrat or an obsessed mom, but from the super-respectable (and extremely nannyish) American Academy of Pediatrics," he explained to me.

If only the influence of the AAP were limited to fanaticism over hot dogs and choking hazards (or breastfeeding, as we learned in Chapter 2). In reality, in the two decades following the daycare scandals, another scientifically based hysteria took hold: shaken baby syndrome (SBS).

As Northwestern University law professor Deborah Tuerkheimer explains in her exposé *Flawed Convictions: "Shaken Baby Syndrome" and the Inertia of Injustice*, the AAP's 1993 statement on SBS was based on the "medical presumption of child abuse" that remained in effect for more than two decades and unfortunately took on "remarkable legal significance as proof of guilt."[64] Shaken baby syndrome prosecutions of parents and child-care workers were based on a triad of evidence—bleeding beneath the outermost layer of membranes that surround the brain, bleeding in the retina, and brain swelling—that for two decades basically ensured convictions. And this "proof" of SBS was reinforced by the AAP and pressed on prosecutors across the country to "educate" those who would be bringing justice down on the heads of these "abusers," Tuerkheimer explains.

Finally, and all too slowly, SBS convictions are now being reexamined and in many cases thrown out. As Debbie Cenziper reported in the *Washington Post*, "16 convictions have been overturned since 2001. . . . In Illinois, a federal judge who recently freed a mother of two after nearly a decade in prison called Shaken Baby Syndrome 'more an article of faith than a proposition of science.'"[65]

Tuerkheimer blames the legal system for being unable to change course. "From prosecutorial decisions, to evidentiary rulings, to judicial review—we see a drive to push forward rather than revisit. A diagnosis of SBS sets in motion systemic confirmation, first in the clinical realm, and then the legal. The course of injustice is almost immovable," she writes.[66] Perhaps her efforts—along with the work of journalists like Cenziper and filmmakers like Meryl and Susan Goldsmith, whose documentary *The Syndrome* has been boycotted and protested—will keep moving the needle in favor of provable science. In the meantime, however, as Tuerkheimer complained to CBSNews .com, too many "innocent parents and caregivers remain incarcerated and, perhaps more inexplicably, prosecutions based solely on the 'triad' symptoms continue even to this day." Tuerkheimer is convinced that "the cautionary tale of Shaken Baby Syndrome shows that our system is too inclined to stay the course, and awful injustices can result."[67]

There's another cautionary tale, to borrow Tuerkheimer's phrase, about how the child-welfare system and legal apparatus views parents. It is much easier to accept the "scientific" proof of SBS, given the already well-established precedent that parents are prime suspects in their children's troubles. Perhaps SBS wouldn't have been such a popular diagnosis, and perhaps we could have avoided the rash of convictions, if the table hadn't already been set for viewing parents as perpetrators. How much less often would child-protection workers and legal operatives default to removing kids if they didn't carry into their work an anti-parent bias?

FOR CHILDREN, CURE IS WORSE THAN THE DISEASE

Jerri Gray gave some thought to whether it was useful to take her son Alexander away from her. She understood that he lost weight while in the custody of her sister, but the pain of separation was terrible. "Even though good has come out of this as far as him losing weight, he told me just last week, 'Mommy, I want to be back with you so bad.' They've done damage by pulling us apart," Gray said.[68]

Though too many families have been forced apart by overzealous child-protection workers, there are people involved with trying to help kids deal with weight issues who admit there is a problem with jumping straight to this solution. Melinda Sothern, the author of the book *Trim Kids*, says that getting her patients to shed weight isn't as easy as it may seem. She had to argue with social workers whose first instinct was to remove one boy in her care. "They were saying, 'This mother must be feeding him to death. We need to remove him.' I said, 'Guys, before you do that, we need to look at more options—he's obese, but he's fit, enrolled in sports. He can run. His breathing has improved.'"[69]

Removal from parents is terrible for the child, even one who is very young and even if it is for a limited time. "Children at [three years of] age are very susceptible to high levels of stress, that's a biological fact. . . . [T]he neural networks that are developing most rapidly at that time tend to be most susceptible to the biology of stress," Dr. Robert Anda said. He argues that "removing any child from a parent at that age has to be considered carefully."[70]

Some researchers believe that the timing and quality of a removal can be devastating. "If there were some moments that were traumatizing, it gets imprinted on our psyche," explains Michaela L. Zajicek-Farber, an associate professor in the School of Social Service at Catholic University of America. "When we interpret policy with a black and white response, and we don't consider context of human behavior, people often get hurt," she said.[71]

According to a 2011 Citizens Review Panel report on the

District of Columbia's Child and Family Services Agency, the problem was too many unnecessary removals—three-quarters of the total, in fact. "CFSA's child removal decisions must balance the need to protect children from serious abuse or neglect with the need to protect children from the significant emotional trauma that comes from the government separating them from their families," the report advised.[72] And the manner in which kids were removed was equally problematic. "We've had kids that thought they were kidnapped," said Judith Sandalow, executive director of the Children's Law Center. "If a kid is just learning to talk, for example, they might stop talking for a while," she said.[73]

DESIGNED TO FAIL

Removals are traumatic and even destructive, but such concerns must be balanced against the crisis to be solved—in this case, pediatric obesity. If the state is going to take custody of obese kids, then at least we're sure it's an effective solution, right? Not so fast.

"The impact of . . . removing the child from the home is completely unknown in terms of both efficacy in achieving physical outcomes (e.g. weight loss and health improvement) and the potential for permanent damage to the family unit and the child's emotional well-being,"[74] argued clinical psychologist Martin Binks in 2011. Binks' criticism of removals went further, too. "The assumption that placement in foster care, for a limited time, can have any meaningful long-term impact on the child's weight trajectory is unsubstantiated. . . . However, even if we assume that a foster care placement will be able to effectively provide a healthy and structured food and activity environment (which is doubtful), the impact of this non-professional, limited scope 'intervention' on weight also remains unknown."[75]

University of Pennsylvania bioethicist Art Caplan agrees with Binks. He argues that, even if foster care did work, there is no feasible way the child-welfare system (as flawed as it is) could handle every case of pediatric morbid obesity. Caplan also rejects the notion that risks to kids are imminent.

> The risk of death from obesity is real, but it is way down the road for kids. There is no proven cure for obesity. The ability to treat a child with diet or a lifestyle change who does not want to be "treated" by strangers is a long shot at best. The number of kids involved— an estimated 2 million children with body-mass index above the 99th percentile—would quickly swamp already overwhelmed social service departments. And, no matter what you do with overweight children, sooner or later they are going back home where their often overweight parents will still be.[76]

And if healthy skepticism and reasonable criticism of the removal scheme weren't enough, the doctor who authored the paper that legitimized removals doesn't think it'll work every time. "State intervention is no guarantee of a good outcome, but to do nothing is also not an answer," said Dr. Ludwig, who directs the Optimal Weight for Life program at Children's Hospital of Boston. "It should only be used as a last resort," he cautioned. "It's also no guarantee of success, but when we have a 400-pound child with life threatening complications, there may not be any great choices."[77]

There is a significant gap, however, between Ludwig's assertion of scarcity of good choices and relying on the child-welfare system to provide an effective solution. Moreover, there is sincere disagreement about what causes obesity—given similar circumstances, not all children put on an unhealthy amount of weight. "Defining childhood obesity as abuse would place a tremendous burden on parents—and an unfair one," wrote Phil Yam in *Scientific American*. He was responding to the various articles endorsing removal as a solution. Yam argued instead that low-cost, highly caloric foods heavily marketed to children were a significant piece of the problem. "Even the U.S. government could be blamed," Yam continued, "considering that the Department of Agriculture promotes the consumption of U.S. foods."[78]

Caplan worries that removals put too much blame on parents. Obese children are victims of advertising, marketing, peer pressure, and bullying, which are all things parents can't control, Caplan suggests. "If you're going to change a child's weight, you're going to have to change all of them," Caplan says.[79] Dr. Dana Rofey of the University of Pittsburgh, whose weight-management clinic is regularly called on during custody battles in which one parent blames the other for making a child obese, agrees with Caplan. "It's unfair to blame solely the parents, when there's a myriad of other factors influencing a child's weight," she says. Contributing factors include not just genetic predisposition and socioeconomic status but also environmental factors, like whether children have access to parks and playgrounds. Rofey also sees children of all ages sneaking extra food behind their parents' backs.[80]

The complexity of "solving" pediatric obesity only multiplies when one scans even a small sampling of the research. If you think there is a single ingredient in kids' diets that is making them fat—soda, fast food, high-fructose corn syrup—think again. If you believe the increase in obesity, as measured by BMI, is just a few decades old, you ought to take a look at the work of John Komlos and Marek Brabec, who have found that BMI has been rising for more than a century.[81] Even the übernannies over at the Center for Science in the Public Interest have their insights. Margo Wootan, director of nutrition policy, said a reduction of just 78 calories a day could have a significant impact. "The whole obesity epidemic can be explained by an extra 100 to 150 calories a day," she said.[82] Got that, parents? Cut you kids' calories by a smidge, and you might protect them from an unhealthy weight.

Of course, all of these alternate explanations are just maybes. There is no certainty about what causes or what will cure obesity. What is certain is there are enough pressures and problems with the child-welfare system without using it to try to help obese kids get to a healthier weight. Such attempts to exploit the foster-care and legal system only provide evidence that the nanny state lacks compassion for parents and families, while it knowingly harms innocent children by employing inefficient and ineffective methods.

Conclusion

"What if they come after us?" said Mr. Bucket, speaking for the first time.

"What if they capture us?" said Mrs. Bucket.

"What if they shoot us?" said Grandma Georgina.

"What if my beard were made of green spinach?" cried Mr. Wonka. "Bunkum and tummyrot!" You'll never get anywhere if you go about what-iffing like that. Would Columbus have discovered America if he'd said 'What if I sink on the way over? What if I meet pirates? What if I never come back?' He wouldn't even have started! We want no what-iffers around here, right Charlie? Off we go, then!"

> —CHARLIE AND THE GREAT GLASS ELEVATOR,
> BY ROALD DAHL

THIS EXCHANGE from a 1972 classic reads like it was written as a parody of how modern regulations are written, especially when it comes to children. As we've learned, the worry-warts at the Consumer Product Safety Commission, for example, warn parents every day in anxiety-inducing newsletters about too many toys and children's products that *may* cause harm or that have *potential* risks that *could* result in a kid getting hurt. But the problem isn't the warnings; the problem is that they are inefficient and ineffective, and they end up pressuring private businesses into bankruptcy.

Cities ban running in playgrounds and sledding in public parks because someone *could* get hurt, but what they are really afraid of are lawsuits. Schools step between parents and kids when they examine students at school and report the health data back to parents who never volunteered to have the school collect or disseminate their child's information. All this is done on the basis of *potential* health concerns. And there are police officers who conduct paralysis-inducing thought experiments with parents. As we saw, Lenore Skenazy was asked by an officer about the *possible* risks to her son riding alone on the Long Island Rail Road: "What if two people were trying to abduct him?"

Who, then, are our modern-day Willie Wonkas? They are the Captain Mommies, some whom we've now met, who confront the what-if brigade by shouting, "Leave my family alone!"

In 2005, then–prime minister Tony Blair accurately highlighted how the regulatory state can go too far. "There is usually a seductive logic to any new regulation," he argued when speaking to the Institute for Public Policy Research. He continued,

> There is almost always a case that can be made for each specific instrument. The problem is cumulative. All these good intentions can add up to a large expense, with suffocating effects. Sometimes, we need to pause for a moment and think whether we will not do more damage with a hasty response than was done by the problem itself.[1]

Here in the US, Philip Howard understands well enough how this happens so consistently, especially as regards the protection of children. As Howard argues in his book *The Rule of Nobody*,

> Government regulators feel under pressure for more rules—from politicians to "do something," from the

public to avoid last year's scandal, from special interests to accommodate all kinds of hidden agendas, and from fellow bureaucrats to outdo each other. So regulators try to imagine everything that might happen, write a regulation for just that situation, and then toss it onto the pile. The more, the better. Any activity in society that might affect other people needs a rule. . . . [The problem is that] law that aspires to completeness doesn't leave room for questions of priority and practicality.[2]

The consequence is that what-iffers use regulation to prevent potential hazards, usually irrespective of impact, efficiency, or effectiveness. And this paternalism is so pervasive and well entrenched that by now it is a real question whether it is even possible to reduce its scope, let alone get rid of it entirely. Parents are therefore likely to be punished for asserting their authority, as the government continues to proclaim—both explicitly and implicitly—that it can and should parent in place of mom and dad. As pervasive as the problem we've already described is, the reach of the nanny state is felt elsewhere and with consequences that are just as troubling. We'll look at two examples in particular, namely, sex-offender registries and mandated-reporter rules. When it comes to these other areas of life, parents are less directly able to confront the system, even as the impact on their kids may be significant. It is also useful to look at the experience of overregulation and the most extreme instances of nanny-state intrusiveness from Scotland and the UK to understand how other democracies are dealing with these same issues.

TEENAGERS TRAPPED BY REGISTRIES

Les Anderson and his wife, Amanda, can tell you all about the problems with sex-offender registries. In a July 2015 piece for

the *New York Times,* Julie Bosman wrote about the Andersons'
19-year-old son Zachary, who because of one *consensual* sexual
liaison will be listed on the sex-offender registry in his home
state of Indiana for 25 years. He will be required to be in regular contact with the authorities; he must allow searches of his
home every 90 days; and he must live far from schools, parks,
and other public places. Nor can he go shopping at the mall or
be in a house with youngsters. He can't live at home because his
teenage younger brother lives there.[3] And all this, again, after a
single consensual sexual encounter.

What is obvious to everyone is that Anderson does not
fit the profile of the pedophiles, child molesters, and abusers
that the sex-offender registries were designed to monitor. In
the three decades since the registries became commonplace, the
number of listed offenders has grown to nearly 850,000. And
registrants today "go beyond adults who have sexually assaulted
other adults or minors. Also listed are people found guilty of
lesser offenses that run the gamut from urinating publicly to
swapping lewd texts," explained Bosman.[4] When asked about
the Anderson case, one former Michigan judge was adamant.
"I think it's utterly ridiculous to take teenage sex and make it
a felony. This guy is obviously not a pedophile," said Judge
William Buhl. "The whole registry is a horrible mistake."[5]

Jill Levenson says nationally the registries include 6 percent
of people aged 26 or younger whose crimes mirror Anderson's.
As the professor of social work at Barry University in Miami
wrote at CNN.com,

> For those of us who are parents, most can imagine
> the horror of learning that our child has been sexually
> abused. But I'm sure we can also relate to the fear of
> learning that a young adult has engaged in a moment
> of bad judgment or poor impulse control and is facing

life-altering consequences. Who among us would want the single worst decision we made as a teenager to define us for 25 years or maybe even forever?[6]

The registries were designed to keep track of criminals after their release from jail and to protect the public. It allows one to look at the local registry to determine whether there is a pedophile in your neighborhood. It also means that one can publicly shame those who have been convicted of a specific category of sexual crimes. But, like other examples of legislative solutions for complex problems, the sex-offender registry has ballooned beyond its original intentions and now ensnares those who have engaged in behaviors that, while perhaps morally questionable, are not actually crimes.

"Current sex offender registries grew out of a series of heinous crimes against children," explains the activist organization Reforming Sex Offender Laws, Inc. (RSOL). "Their original intent was to protect minors against strangers who, having committed serious sex offenses previously, were seen at high risk of doing so again."[7] But over the decades, the registries have become more and more divorced from their original intent. "Depending upon the state," says RSOL,

> an individual may be placed on the registry for public urination, streaking, exposing their genitals, or hiring a prostitute. An increasing number are individuals who as children or teenagers themselves had sex with a willing, but younger, partner, or who sent sexually-oriented images of themselves or their partners via their phone or computer.[8]

There is little evidence that the current iterations of sex-offender registries actually accomplish the intended goals, and some evidence seems to suggest the opposite. As the authors

Jeffrey Sandler, Naomi Freeman, and Kelly Socia concluded from their study of the outcomes from New York State's Sex Offender Registration Act,

> Results provide no support for the effectiveness of reg-
> istration and community notification laws in reducing
> sexual offending by: (a) rapists, (b) child molesters, (c)
> sexual recidivists, or (d) first-time sex offenders. Analy-
> ses also showed that over 95 percent of all sexual offense
> arrests were committed by first-time sex offenders,
> casting doubt on the ability of laws that target repeat
> offenders to meaningfully reduce sexual offending.[9]

In other words, registries don't seem to work; there is no evidence that being listed reduced incidences of repeat offenses, nor does it seem to serve any public-safety goals to list first-time youth offenders like Zachary Anderson. And according to a 2013 policy paper by Human Rights Watch called *Raised on the Registry*, no reasoning can justify the kind of damage done. "Youth sex offenders on the registry," the report concludes,

> experience severe psychological harm. They are stig-
> matized, isolated, often depressed. Many consider sui-
> cide, and some succeed. They and their families have
> experienced harassment and physical violence. They
> are sometimes shot at, beaten, even murdered; many
> are repeatedly threatened with violence.... Youth sex
> offenders on the registry are sometimes denied access
> to education because residency restriction laws prevent
> them from being in or near a school. Youth sex offender
> registrants despair of ever finding employment.[10]

As the Human Rights Watch report states, families may also come under negative scrutiny because of a child's inclusion on the sex-offender registry. "Public registries provide no measurable protection for children or the general public, yet endanger the well-being of children and family members of registrants," argue the sex-offender-registry reformers at RSOL.[11]

Levenson agrees that current standards are too expansive and argues that the categories of offenders included on these registries ought to be reconsidered.

> Juveniles should be removed from registries, and young-adult offenders should be reassessed to determine whether deviant sexual disorders motivated their crimes, or simply poor judgment. Risk-assessment tools, which have been well-researched and are designed specifically to classify sex offenders into risk categories, should be used to estimate the likelihood of future offenses. Discretion should be returned to judges (in most cases, if someone is convicted of specific statutes, registration is mandatory, regardless of whether a judge feels it should apply) so that punishments fairly fit the crimes.[12]

EVERYONE IS A MANDATED REPORTER

Problems with sex-offender registries mirror the inefficiencies inherent in mandated-reporter rules, which in recent years have also begun including people who were never before considered potential reporters. Mandated reporters are citizens and professionals the state designates as legally required to report suspicions of abuse. Recent legislation expanding the definition of who must serve as a mandated reporter also highlights the trouble that comes when regulations attempt to solve a problem best dealt with by other means.

Pennsylvania has just been dealing with this issue because of the sensational and devastating Jerry Sandusky child-abuse scandal at Penn State University. Maribeth Roman Schmidt has argued that the Sandusky revelations along with other local abuse cases led to an explosion of new reporting rules, without any corresponding reform of the procedures for what happens after a report is filed. These cases, Schmidt argues, show that "Pennsylvania needs to implement paradigm-shifting changes to ensure that reports are properly investigated. Reports that are ignored do no good."[13]

The problem Schmidt describes is twofold. For years, accusations against Sandusky were filed with the state, but the abuse continued. Now those who work with undergraduates must undergo background checks and fingerprinting before being cleared to perform their jobs at a university, a remedy that is both ineffective and sows distrust. The irony is that after establishing that you are not a potential threat to minors, you are required by the same law to serve as a mandated reporter.

When I interviewed Carnegie Mellon University history professor Caroline Acker about the new rules, she argued that the law is too broadly written and will effectively prevent good, qualified people from teaching at Pennsylvania universities. Such qualified people might include, she noted, "harm-reduction professionals who were once drug users or sex workers and who served prison sentences." Those who "earned graduate degrees in public health [and] are able to combine their first-hand knowledge of marginal populations [with] their education to work creatively in outreach to these populations," Acker explained, are superbly qualified but would be barred from teaching undergraduates according to Act 153.[14]

Dana Mack argues that one significant problem with mandated-reporting rules is the too-broad wording of the legal statutes related to abuse allegations and the adoption of mandated-reporting laws, not only for professionals such as doctors and teachers, but also for laymen. Many of these statutes include threats of prosecution for those who fail to report and, on the flipside, prosecutorial immunity for accusers—even false ones. Often, too, those enlisted to serve as reporters have been conscripted without being offered proper training or even having the option of declining the responsibility.

Diane Redleaf agrees that mandated reporting has gone too far and the laws are too vague, which has led to "a flooding of the system" in Illinois, where she runs the Family Defense Center. "The idea of 'when in doubt, report,'" she explained during our interview,

> and "when in doubt, find abuse or neglect," contributes to this massively overblown system that hurts more children than it helps. Pairing down the duty of mandated reporting to "likely abuse" instead of plausible suspicion and limiting it to doctors and psychologists (and addressing the problem that psychologists may have to report people as soon as they have sought treatment, which . . . deters treatment and doesn't address root causes of child abuse), would be very helpful in turning the system into one that addresses serious abuse better but leaves average, good parents alone.

But will more background checks and reporting rules make everyone safer? The reality is that evildoers will find a way to avoid detection, regardless of these rules. And for all our years with these supposed safety measures, there is little evidence that we are safer as a result. What these rules have accomplished, on the other hand, is to sow the seeds of mistrust throughout the community. "It's almost as if you're presumed guilty until you demonstrate your innocence rather than the other way around," says St. Joseph's University sociology professor Robert Moore.[15]

ACTIONS ACROSS THE POND

Why not turn to the government? This is a serious question, given the extent of child poverty and the number of at-risk kids nationwide. So what if some parents find it intrusive that child-protection services or police criminalize their reasonable behavior? After all, aren't there millions of other children who have been provided needed support? Of course there are. Certainly support services are needed for some citizens. But not for all.

It might be a useful comparison to look at how some other countries implement similar—and even more extreme—policies. Some seem to challenge the very notion of independent rights of parents and families.

For a perfect example of how government can go to extremes, just look at Scotland. In 2004, the government started researching how to improve the delivery of all manner of services—health, education, police, housing, and social work—to vulnerable children and families. Facing an overly complex welfare bureaucracy, they wanted to streamline and integrate all the organizations (both public and nonprofits) that engage with children and, in addition, to become involved earlier instead of waiting for some disastrous event to trigger action. They also bought into the ideology—familiar to Americans—that children need special protection (from their parents and everyone else). The result was the 2014 Children and Young People (Scotland) Act, which includes a much-debated provision that every child in the country will, at birth, be designated an educator or health worker (a "named person"), who is responsible for their well-being until they turn 18.

In 2015, as implementation started, so did all manner of problems. (Shocker!) By now there is an array of groups fighting against the invasion of privacy and government overreach and trying to roll back the legislation, so far unsuccessfully.

Frank Furedi, emeritus professor of sociology at the University of Kent in the England, worries that legislation is not the only trouble with the named-person law. He wonders about the mentality that doesn't see a problem with overriding the rights of parents by requiring that a stranger monitor every child's life. In 2014, Furedi explained his concerns.

> Scotland's minister for Children and Young People, Aileen Campbell, thinks that this erosion of parental authority is OK and offers reassurance with the not very reassuring words that "we recognize that parents also have a role." "Also"? If the experience of the past 15 years is anything to go by, political intervention in child rearing is likely to become more prescriptive and intrusive.[16]

Meanwhile, Furedi has seen the same thing happening in England, though never going so far as the named-person concept. Over the most recent decades, and especially when a new Labor government was elected in 1997, with Tony Blair at its head, there has been a steady growth of regulation and legislative intrusions into the lives of British kids and their parents.

In his 2004 book *The Nanny State*, Robert Huntington noted similar thinking among British politicians. He records how, at a major public-policy conference in 2003, just after the initial establishment of the Minister for Children, its head Margaret Hodge caused a small firestorm when she declared, "If parenting is so important, and has such an important impact on children, we cannot abandon it to the vagaries of the individual."

When the howls of protest subsided and concerned citizens demanded to know if she had made a mistake and would retract her comments, Hodge doubled down. "For me, it's not a question of whether we should intrude in family life, but how and when." Hodge offers the perfect example of nanny-state thinking, and British kids are the losers. "Their childhoods are being robbed by a mean Nanny that refuses to let them go out and play, preventing them from exploring the world and making their own discoveries about it as children are supposed to," Huntington declares.[17]

Mean nanny or nice nanny, the voices against the overbearing, intrusive state have grown louder in the UK. We have already seen Furedi's comments. Simon Hills declared in his 2006 book *Strictly No!* that the British were steadily being overrun,[18] and Josie Appleton's London-based Manifesto Club also advocates against "the hyperregulation of everyday life."[19] And Tim Gill in his 2007 book *No Fear* admitted that

> [c]hildhood is becoming undermined by risk aversion. Activities and experiences that previous generations of children enjoyed without a second thought have been relabeled as troubling or dangerous, while the adults who still permit them are branded as irresponsible.[20]

The Labor government did indeed try to mitigate some of these extremes by reforming aspects of its regulatory policies and procedures. Prime Minister Blair publicly complained about unreasonable fear of risk, using the example of a small town that removed playground equipment without there having been any harm to children. "In August 2006," Gill also notes,

> the Health and Safety Executive launched a campaign with the strapline "Get a Life" that was highly critical of petty health and safety concerns. The campaign declared that sensible risk management was not about creating a totally risk-free society. Rather it was (to quote the HSE website) about "balancing benefits and risks, with a focus on reducing real risks—both those which arise more often and those with serious conse-

quences." The HSE initiative argued convincingly that some so-called "health and safety" stories were myths or distortions, while others were convenient excuses to justify unpopular decisions or cover up management failures.[21]

In the mid-2000s, after a decade of growth, it seems the nanny state was trying to get the balance right between regulation, reasonable standards, and liberty. But even the reforms were based on the foundational assumption that government is responsible for protecting children from harm. And as *The Economist* remarked, the state's record of accomplishment was dismal. "For although taking children from their parents may sometimes be the least bad thing to do," the editors noted,

> the government is, in aggregate, a deadbeat, feckless parent. Children who have been in care are 50 times more likely to go to prison than those who have not, according to calculations by Policy Exchange, a think-tank. They are also 66 times more likely to see their own children taken into care. This is not for lack of money: the average bill for taking a child under the state's wing is £38,000 ($61,400) per year. Better, then, to employ a latter-day Mary Poppins to nanny a family into staying together.[22]

Instead of accepting failure, blowing up the bureaucratic system, and starting over, the Labor government piloted a program that the subsequent Conservative government embraced as a vast improvement. Instead of having a "named person law," as in Scotland, that assumes every child needs an advocate, separate from their family, to protect their rights and well-being, the British government decided to try prioritizing families instead.

The model, which began in Westminster in November 2008, is the Family Recovery Programme, and in 2011 one of the local councilors, Nickie Aiken, described it as a huge success. "The project builds a dedicated team centered around the family," she wrote in *The Guardian*,

> with a single contact acting as the gateway to all public services on offer. Our team typically works intensively with a family for six to 12 months; we phase in support to avoid overloading the family with too much information and change at any one point.... We seek the family's consent to work with them, and in turn these families adhere to strict "contracts with consequences." This provides the stick in addition to the carrot—the families understand that they could face a raft of potential consequences if they do not use the help on offer to make the changes they need.[23]

It is valuable that the program is centered on the family as a whole unit and focused on those on the verge of losing a child to state care or losing their home or liberty. It is also worth appreciating that the effort is designed to simplify the bureaucracy and insists that parents agree to participate and face consequences for failure to adhere to the rules.

Natasha Bishopp, head of the Family Recovery Programme, explained it was a challenge at first to build up trust and acceptance of the new project. "They've usually had many years of public services intervening in their lives against their will," Bishopp stated. "But where we're different is that we focus on what they want to achieve as well as what we need them to do."[24] The very fact that the program is voluntary is a step in the right direction. If parents don't sign the contract, they can't participate. In this way, the government is embracing voluntary rather than mandated transactions and treating parents as adults, rather than as the enemy.

After three years, by various measures, families had improved their lives, and Aiken declared the program a success. "More than 80 percent of children have shown increased school attendance," Aiken explained. Neighbors were happier, domestic-violence complaints were down, and crime rates were substantially lower. The program was even thought to have saved taxpayers millions, mainly due to efficiencies of pooling services.[25]

Two elements that are central to the Family Recovery Programme—a voluntary contract and treating families as a single unit—are largely missing from the American model of social services. It isn't that there are no models for a holistic approach to families among American agencies. Rather, such thinking isn't in the mainstream of theory or practice. Far more common across government agencies is the assumption that children need individual protection as separate entities from their families. It is precisely this concept at the center of so much that is the problem with regulation and nanny-state paternalism.

Experimenting with voluntary contractual agreements between service agencies and families might also go a way toward improving attitudes on both sides: the attitudes of providers toward their clients and of families toward government oversight. And voluntary agreements and contracts have one other value that is missing from Washington-centered, one-size-fits-all problem solving: trust. When people are reduced to lists of rules, protocols, and mandates, without room for personal judgment, discretion, and control, they lose their incentive to perform at the highest level and their sense of personal commitment to the goal.

Of course, the Family Recovery Programme doesn't answer the question of whether it is a good idea for government to be this involved in the everyday lives of families. Certainly, for those who adhere to the quaint idea that being a parent gives you the authority to raise your own children, the level of intervention is disquieting. But for now, in the UK at least, it seems clear that the question of whether government should intervene between parents and children has been settled.

Back here at home, that conversation has yet to really begin, though every Captain Mommy (and Daddy) is hoping it will start soon. It is hard to understand why it hasn't happened yet.

Acknowledgments

Thanks beyond thanks to my husband, Ben Schachter, and my parents, Ruth Wisse and Leonard Wisse, for love, faith, support, and inspiration.

Thanks to Lenore Skenazy for providing source material and encouragement in the earliest stages, and to Adam Bellow for backing the initial concept.

Thank you to Glenn Hartley, Roger Kimball, Katherine Wong, Lauren Miklos, and Sam Schneider for nurturing and publishing the final product.

Thank you Billy Wisse and Maud Kozodoy for careful reading and constructive suggestions. Thanks go to Emily Schultheis for careful editing and Catherine Taylor for proofreading. And to Elizabeth Becker, thank you.

Thank you to all those who agreed to be interviewed: Alina Adams, Yodit Betru, Sara Burrows, Philip K. Howard, Mike Lanza, Nancy Nord, Lori Levar Pierce, Diane Redleaf, Lenore Skenazy, and Walter Olson.

Thank you to all those friends and family who sent along stories, photos, clips, or references that fed my passion for this subject, including Sonia and Theresa Schachter, Jacob Wisse and Rebecca Lieberman, Jordan Fishbach, Joshua Swedarsky, Adam Shear, Debby Gilboa, and Rachel Kranson.

Thank you to Danielle Kranjec, Debby Gilman, Naomi Schaefer Riley, Tevi Troy, and Tamar Jacoby, for friendship, time, interest, and advice.

Notes

INTRODUCTION

1. C.S. Lewis, *God in the Dock: Essays on Theology and Ethics* (Cambridge, UK: Wm. B. Eerdmans Publishing Co., 1972), 292.
2. Mari-Jane Williams, "Harvey Karp Talks about Recent Daycare Swaddling Bans in Three States," *Washington Post*, November 26, 2013, accessed February 24, 2015, http://www.washingtonpost.com/lifestyle/on -parenting/harvey-karp-talks-about-recent-day-care-swaddling-bans-in -three-states/2013/11/26/58c12200-55f2-11e3-8304-caf30787c0a9_story.html.
3. Sara Burrows, "Preschooler's Homemade Lunch Replaced with Cafeteria 'Nuggets,'" *Carolina Journal*, February 14, 2012, accessed April 7, 2015, www.carolinajournal.com/articles/displaystory.html?id=8762.
4. Frank Furedi, "How Much Independence Should Children Have?" *The Independent*, July 21, 2014, accessed March 2, 2016, http://www .independent.co.uk/life-style/health-and-families/features/how-much -independence-should-children-have-9619918.html.
5. Dana Mack, *The Assault on Parenthood: How Our Culture Undermines the Family* (New York: Simon & Schuster, 1997).
6. Barry Schwartz and Kenneth Sharpe, *Practical Wisdom: The Right Way to Do the Right Thing* (New York: Riverhead Books, 2010), 29.
7. Dan Kennedy, "The Wrong Arm of the Law," review of *Three Felonies a Day: How the Feds Target the Innocent*, by Harvey Silverglate, *The Guardian*, November 17, 2009, accessed March 2016, http://www.theguardian .com/commentisfree/cifamerica/2009/nov/17/silverglate-three-felonies -book.
8. Common Good is a nonpartisan reform coalition that offers Americans a new way to look at law and government, http://commongood.org/.
9. Philip K. Howard, *The Rule of Nobody* (New York: W.W. Norton & Co., 2014), 62.
10. Harvey Silverglate, "What You Don't Know *Can* Hurt You," *Reason*, July 2011, accessed March 2, 2016, http://reason.com/archives/2011/06/21 /what-you-dont-know-can-hurt-yo.

11. "New Jersey Court Finds Mother Who Left Child Alone in Car Outside Middlesex Mall Was Abusive," News 12 New Jersey, January 15, 2014, accessed March 2, 2016, http://newjersey.news12.com/news/new -jersey-court-finds-mother-who-left-child-alone-in-car-outside -middlesex-mall-was-abusive-1.6802894.

12. Scott Greenfield, "Car Alone," *Simple Justice* blog, February 3, 2014, accessed March 28, 2016, http://blog.simplejustice.us/2014/02/03/car -alone/.

13. Schwartz and Sharpe, *Practical Wisdom*, 42.

14. John F. Kennedy, "The Soft American," *Sports Illustrated*, Dec. 26, 1960, 15–17.

15. Ibid.

16. Ibid.

17. Tim Gill, *No Fear: Growing Up in a Risk-Averse Society* (London: Calouste Gulbenkian Foundation, 2007), 23.

18. Furedi, "How Much Independence Should Children Have?"

19. Daniel Gilbert, "If Only Gay Sex Caused Global Warming," *Los Angeles Times*, July 2, 2006, accessed March 2, 2016, http://articles.latimes.com /2006/jul/02/opinion/op-gilbert2.

20. David Boaz, "Obesity and 'Public Health?'" CATO Institute *Commentary* blog, published July 20, 2004, accessed March 2, 2016, http://www .cato.org/publications/commentary/obesity-public-health.

21. Ibid.

22. *Jimmy Kimmel Live!*, video, February 27, 2015, accessed March 28, 2015, https://www.youtube.com/watch?v=QgpfNScEd3M.

23. Maimuna S. Majumder et al., "Substandard Vaccination Compliance and the 2015 Measles Outbreak," *JAMA Pediatrics* 169 (2015): 494–95, doi:10.1001/jamapediatrics.2015.0384.

24. Kennedy, "The Soft American," 15–17.

CHAPTER 1: ARRESTING CAPTAIN MOMMY

1. "Is Having Grit the Key to Success?" NPR *TED Radio Hour*, last modified February 27, 2015, http://www.npr.org/2013/11/01/240779578 /is-having-grit-the-key-to-success.

2. Corey Adwar, "Support Grows Online for Mom Who Lost Custody of Daughter after Letting Her Play Alone at a Park," *Business Insider*, July 16, 2014, accessed February 5, 2016, http://www.businessinsider.com /debra-harrell-arrested-for-allegedly-letting-daughter-play-alone-at -park-2014-7.

3. Lizzie Widdicombe, "Mother May I?" *New Yorker*, February 23, 2015, accessed March 2, 2016, http://www.newyorker.com/magazine/2015/02 /23/mother-may.

4. Jake Edmiston, "Florida Mother Arrested for Neglect after Letting Seven-Year-Old Son Walk Alone to Park 800 Metres Away," *National Post*, July 31, 2014, accessed March 2, 2016, http://news.nationalpost.com/2014/07/31/florida-mother-arrested-for-neglect-after-letting-seven-year-old-son-walk-alone-to-park-800-metres-away/.

5. Erica Quiroz, "LaPort Mother Sues City, Neighbor after Child Abandonment Arrest," *Houston Chronicle*, last modified September 23, 2012, accessed April 2015, http://www.chron.com/default/article/LaPorte-mother-sues-city-neighbor-after-child-3887670.php.

6. Cameron Langford, "Child Endangerment, My Eye, Mom Says," Courthouse News Service, September 7, 2012, accessed Feb 11, 2016, http://www.courthousenews.com/2012/09/07/50051.htm.

7. Johnson City Police Department, "Felony Arrest—Child Neglect," news release, June 8, 2012, accessed February 2016, http://jcpd.blogspot.com/2012/06/fw-press-release-april-l-lawson.html.

8. Laura Halm, "Mom Speaks Out about Neglect Charges," WCYB.com, June 8, 2012, accessed March 2, 2016, http://www.wcyb.com/Mom-Speaks-Out-About-Neglect-Charges/15240294.

9. Telephone interview with Lori Levar Pierce, November 2012.

10. Mike Jones, "Police Say Dad Left Kids at Park to Shower," *Chartiers Valley Patch*, April 12, 2012, accessed March 3, 2016, http://patch.com/pennsylvania/chartiersvalley/police-say-dad-left-kids-at-park-while-he-shopped-showered.

11. Charles Eisenstein, "Disorderly Conduct," *Charles Eisenstein* blog, undated, http://charleseisenstein.net/disorderly-conduct/.

12. ABC News, "Silver Spring Parents Charged with 'Child Neglect' for Allowing Kids to Walk Home Alone," WJLA.com, March 8, 2015, accessed March 3, 2016, http://www.wjla.com/articles/2015/03/silver-spring-parents-charged-with-child-neglect-for-allowing-kids-to-walk-home-alone-112094.html.

13. Donna St. George, "'Unsubstantiated' Child Neglect Finding for Free-Range Parents," *Washington Post*, March 2, 2015, accessed March 3, 2016, http://www.washingtonpost.com/local/education/decision-in-free-range-case-does-not-end-debate-about-parenting-and-safety/2015/03/02/5a919454-c04d-11e4-ad5c-3b8ce89f1b89_story.html.

14. Hanna Rosin, "CPS Finds 'Free Range' Parents Responsible for Unsubstantiated Child Neglect. Now What?" *Slate*, March 2, 2015, accessed March 8, 2016, http://www.slate.com/blogs/xx_factor/2015/03/02/meitiv_decision_cps_finds_free_range_parents_responsible_for_unsubstantiated.html.

15. Caitlin Fuller and Diane Redleaf, *When Can Parents Let Children Be Alone? Child Neglect Policy and Recommendations in the Age of Free Range and Helicopter Parenting* (Chicago: Family Defense Center, 2015), 34.

16. Lenore Skenazy, "A Principal Calls CPS after Mom Lets Daughter, 10, Ride City Bus to School," *Free-Range Kids* blog, November 15, 2012, accessed March 30, 2016, http://www.freerangekids.com/a-principal -calls-cps-after-mom-lets-daughter-10-ride-city-bus-to-school/.

17. Lenore Skenazy, "Mom Arrested for Letting Her 13-Y.O. Babysit Siblings," *Free-Range Kids* blog, June 6, 2012, accessed March 30, 2016, http://www.freerangekids.com/mom-arrested-for-letting-her-13-y-o -babysit-siblings/.

18. Conor Friedersdorf, "This Widow's 4 Kids Were Taken after She Left Them Home Alone," *The Atlantic*, July 16, 2014, accessed March 30, 2016, http://www.theatlantic.com/national/archive/2014/07/this-widows-4 -kids-were-taken-because-she-left-them-home-alone/374514/.

19. Radley Balko, "And Now: The Criminalization of Parenthood," *Washington Post*, July 14, 2014, accessed March 30, 2016, http://www.washington post.com/news/the-watch/wp/2014/07/14/and-now-the-criminalization -of-parenthood/.

20. Ibid.

21. Schwartz and Sharpe, *Practical Wisdom*, 110.

22. Ibid.

23. Kari Anne Roy, "It's All Fun and Games Until Your Neighbor Decides that She Is the Boss of Fun and Games," *Haiku of the Day* blog, September 9, 2014, accessed March 30, 2016, http://www.haikuoftheday .com/haiku_of_the_day/2014/09/it-was-a-monday-late-morning-hot ter-than-hot-we-were-not-even-24-hours-home-from-vacation-and -i-was-going-through-the-pil.html.

24. Kari Anne Roy, "How Letting My Kid Play Alone Outside Led to a CPS Investigation," *Dallas Morning News*, September 25, 2014, accessed March 8, 2016, http://www.dallasnews.com/opinion/sunday-commen tary/20140925-the-vilification-of-outdoor-play.ece.

25. Ibid.

26. Tracy Cutchlow, "Would You Call 911 on Another Parent?" *Washington Post*, March 3, 2015, accessed March 8, 2016, https://www.washington post.com/news/parenting/wp/2015/03/03/would-you-call-911-on -another-parent/.

27. Kim Brooks, "The Day I Left My Son in the Car," *Salon*, June 3, 2014, accessed March 8, 2016, http://www.salon.com/2014/06/03/the_day_i _left_my_son_in_the_car/.

28. Petula Dvorak, "'Free-Range' Kids and Our Parenting Police State," *Washington Post*, April 13, 2015, accessed March 8, 2016, https://www .washingtonpost.com/local/free-range-kids-and-our-parenting-police -state/2015/04/13/42c30336-e1df-11e4-905f-cc896d379a32_story.html.

29. Schwartz and Sharpe, *Practical Wisdom*, 110.

30. Ibid.

31. Philippe Petit, "Kid on Wire: Let Children Take Risks and Learn to Trust Their Own Intuition," *Big Think* blog, March 2015, accessed March 30, 2016, http://bigthink.com/videos/philippe-petit-teaching -kids-intuition.

32. Peter Gray, "Meet Danielle Meitiv: Fighting for Her Kids' Rights," *Psychology Today*, April 11, 2015, accessed March 30, 2016, https://www .psychologytoday.com/blog/freedom-learn/201504/meet-danielle-meitiv -fighting-her-kids-rights.

33. Margorie Ingall, "Ethical Parenting Is More Than Possible. It Is Essential, for Parents and Children Alike," *Tablet Magazine*, October 31, 2013, accessed March 8, 2016, http://www.tabletmag.com/jewish-life-and -religion/148942/ethical-parenting.

34. Laura Pappano, " 'Grit' and the New Character Education," *Harvard Education Letter* 29 (2013), accessed March 8, 2016, http://hepg.org/hel -home/issues/29_1/helarticle/grit%E2%80%9D-and-the-new-character -education

35. Roy, "How Letting My Kid Play Alone Outside Led to a CPS Investigation."

36. Michael Brendan Dougherty, "Why It May Be Impossible to Raise 'Free Range Kids,' " *The Week*, March 30, 2015, accessed March 8, 2016, http://theweek.com/articles/546752/why-may-impossible-raise-free -range-kids.

37. Judith Rodin, "Realizing the Resilience Dividend," *Huffington Post*, January 22, 2014, accessed March 8, 2016, http://www.huffing tonpost.com/judith-rodin/realizing-the-resilience_b_4643821 .html.

38. Jane E. Brody, "Parenting Advice from 'America's Worst Mom,' " *New York Times*, January 19, 2015, accessed March 8, 2016, http:// well.blogs.nytimes.com/2015/01/19/advice-from-americas-worst -mom/?_r=0.

39. Lenore Skenazy, "The Free-Range Kids & Parents Bill of Rights," *Free-Range Kids* blog, February 10, 2015, accessed March 8, 2016, http://www.freerangekids.com/the-free-range-kids-parents-bill -of-rights/.

40. Julie Lythcott-Haims, *How to Raise an Adult: Break Free of the Overparenting Trap and Prepare Your Kid for Success* (New York: Henry Holt and Company, 2015), Kindle edition.

41. Greg Lukianoff and Jonathan Haidt, "The Coddling of the American Mind," *The Atlantic*, September 2015, accessed March 8, 2016, http:// www.theatlantic.com/magazine/archive/2015/09/the-coddling-of-the -american-mind/399356/.

42. Ibid.

43. Furedi, "How Much Independence Should Children Have?"

44. Mack, *The Assault on Parenthood*, 242.
45. Ibid., 244.
46. Ibid.

CHAPTER 2: BREAST IS BEST, *OR ELSE*

1. Suzanne Barston, *Bottled Up: How the Way We Feed Babies Has Come to Define Motherhood, and Why It Shouldn't* (Berkeley: University of California Press, 2012).
2. *Fearless Formula Feeder* blog, www.fearlessformulafeeder.com.
3. Naser Kalantari and Arezoo Haghighian Roudsari, "Breastfeeding Promotion in Iran: Opportunities and Challenges," *Journal of Comprehensive Pediatrics* 4 (2013): 165–66.
4. "Latch On NYC: A Hospital-Based Initiative to Support a Mother's Decision to Breastfeed," New York City Department of Health and Mental Hygiene, May 2012, http://www.nyc.gov/html/doh/downloads /pdf/ms/initiative-description.pdf.
5. Peggy O'Mara, "Choice Is a Red Herring," *Peggy O'Mara* blog, April 15, 2013, accessed January 13, 2016, http://www.peggyomara.com/2013/04/15 /choice-is-a-red-herring/.
6. "New York City Health Department Launches 'Latch On NYC' Initiative to Support Breastfeeding Mothers," New York City Department of Health and Mental Hygiene, May 2012, accessed March 8, 2016, http:// www1.nyc.gov/site/doh/about/press/pr2012/pr013-12.page.
7. Ibid.
8. Gayle Tzemach Lemmon, "A Woman's Right to Choose (Not to Breastfeed)," *The Atlantic*, July 31, 2012, accessed March 8, 2016, http://www .theatlantic.com/health/archive/2012/07/a-womans-right-to-choose -not-to-breastfeed/260530/.
9. Nursing Mothers Counsel of Oregon, "Portland, Oregon First City in the Nation to Eliminate Hospital Discharge Bags Containing Infant Formula Sample Packs," press release, August 7, 2007, http://www .breastfeedingor.org/wp-content/uploads/2012/10/press_Portland1.pdf.
10. John George, "Six Philadelphia Maternity Wards Ban Baby Formula Giveaways," *Philadelphia Business Journal*, last modified August 1, 2014, http://www.bizjournals.com/philadelphia/blog/health-care/2014/08 /philadelphia-hospital-maternity-wards-ban-industry.html.
11. Ban the Bags, accessed January 13, 2016, http://banthebags.org/.
12. Don Sapatkin, "Phila. Hospitals to Stop Giving Free Formula to New Mothers," *Philadelphia Inquirer*, August 2, 2012, accessed March 8, 2016, http://articles.philly.com/2014-08-02/news/52332150_1_breast-feeding -rate-new-mothers-marsha-walker.
13. Ibid.

14. "Ten Steps to Successful Breastfeeding," Baby-Friendly USA, http://
www.babyfriendlyusa.org/about-us/baby-friendly-hospital-initiative
/the-ten-steps.

15. Jim Langabeer et al., "An Economic Cost Analysis of Becoming a Baby
Friendly Hospital," August 28, 2009, http://www.breastfeedingor.org
/wp-content/uploads/2012/10/baby_friendly_cost_analysis.pdf.

16. "Breastfeeding State Laws," National Conference of State Legislatures,
last modified December 22, 2015, http://www.ncsl.org/research/health
/breastfeeding-state-laws.aspx.

17. Bonnie Rochman, "What Mitt Romney Has to Do with Breast-Feeding
and Infant Formula," *Time*, July 17, 2012, accessed March 30, 2016, http://
healthland.time.com/2012/07/17/what-mitt-romney-has-to-do-with
-breast-feeding-and-infant-formula/.

18. Andrew Kitchenman, "More NJ Hospitals Encourage Breastfeeding
through 'Baby Friendly' Initiative," *NJ Spotlight*, June 10, 2014, accessed
March 31, 2016, http://www.njspotlight.com/stories/14/06/09/more-nj
-hospitals-encourage-breastfeeding-through-baby-friendly-initiative/.

19. Joan B. Wolf, *Is Breast Best? Taking On the Breastfeeding Experts and the
New High Stakes of Motherhood* (New York: New York University Press,
2011), 11.

20. Arthur I. Eidelman and Richard J. Schanler, "Breastfeeding and the Use
of Human Milk," *Pediatrics* 129 (2012): e827.

21. "Breastfeeding: Maternal and Infant Aspects," ACOG Committee
Opinion, February 2007, accessed January 15, 2016, http://www.acog.org
/Resources-And-Publications/Committee-Opinions/Committee-on
-Health-Care-for-Underserved-Women/Breastfeeding-Maternal-and
-Infant-Aspects.

22. "Nutrition Program Facts," USDA Food and Nutrition Service, last
modified April 2014, http://www.fns.usda.gov/sites/default/files/WIC
-Fact-Sheet.pdf.

23. Nicholas Kirstof, "Malachi's World," *New York Times*, June 18, 2015,
accessed July 2015, A31, http://www.nytimes.com/2015/06/18/opinion
/nicholas-kristof-malachis-world.html.

24. "Breastfeeding Benefits," Healthcare.gov, https://www.healthcare.gov
/coverage/breast-feeding-benefits/.

25. Sarah Kliff, "The Breast Pump Industry is Booming, Thanks to Obama-
Care," *Washington Post*, January 4, 2013, accessed January 15, 2015, http://
www.washingtonpost.com/blogs/wonkblog/wp/2013/01/04/the-breast
-pump-industry-is-booming-thanks-to-obamacare/.

26. Barston, *Bottled Up*, 99.

27. "Maternal, Infant, and Child Health," HealthyPeople.gov, accessed
March 9, 2016, https://www.healthypeople.gov/2020/topics-objectives
/topic/maternal-infant-and-child-health.

28. "HHS FY2015 Budget in Brief," U.S. Department of Health and Human Services, accessed March 9, 2016, http://www.hhs.gov/about /budget/fy2015/budget-in-brief/ios/index.html.

29. "Breastfeeding," WomensHealth.gov, accessed March 9, 2016, http:// www.womenshealth.gov/breastfeeding/.

30. "It's Only Natural: Mother's Love, Mother's Milk," WomensHealth.gov, accessed March 9, 2016, http://womenshealth.gov/itsonlynatural/.

31. Toby Harnden and Liza Meckler, "Michelle Obama Urges Women to Breastfeed," *The Telegraph*, February 15, 2011, accessed March 9, 2016, http://www.telegraph.co.uk/news/worldnews/michelle-obama/8326566 /Michelle-Obama-urges-women-to-breastfeed.html.

32. "The Surgeon General's Call to Action to Support Breastfeeding 2011," U.S. Department of Health and Human Services, accessed January 2015, http://www.surgeongeneral.gov/library/calls/breastfeeding/calltoaction tosupportbreastfeeding.pdf.

33. Katherine R. Shealy et al., *The CDC Guide to Breastfeeding Interventions* (Atlanta: U.S. Department of Health and Human Services, Centers for Disease Control and Prevention, 2005).

34. Harriet Hall, "Breastfeeding Is Good but Maybe Not THAT Good," *Science-Based Medicine*, April 13, 2010, accessed March 31, 2016, http:// www.sciencebasedmedicine.org/breastfeeding-is-good-but-maybe-not -that-good/.

35. Wolf, *Is Breast Best?*, xii.

36. Ibid., 21.

37. Ibid., 24.

38. Cynthia G. Colen and David M. Ramey, "Is Breast Truly Best? Estimating the Effect of Breastfeeding on Long-Term Child Wellbeing in the United States Using Sibling Comparisons," *Social Science & Medicine* 109 (2014): 55–65.

39. Anne L. Wright and Richard L. Schanler, "The Resurgence of Breastfeeding at the End of the Second Millenium," *The Journal of Nutrition* 131 (February 2001): 421S, http://jn.nutrition.org/content/131 /2/421S.full.

40. Wolf, *Is Breast Best?*, 38.

41. M. S. Kramer et al., "Effects of Prolonged and Exclusive Breastfeeding on Child Height, Weight, Adiposity, and Blood Pressure at Age 6.5 Y: Evidence from a Large Randomized Trial," *American Journal of Clinical Nutrition* 86 (December 2007): 1717–21, http://www.ncbi.nlm.nih.gov /pubmed/18065591.

42. Wolf, *Is Breast Best?*, preface.

43. Ibid., 37.

44. Ibid., 94.

45. Ansa Varughese, "Babies at Risk of Obesity Due to Parents Overfeed-

ing," *Medical Daily*, May 22, 2013, accessed March 9, 2016, http://www.medicaldaily.com/babies-risk-obesity-due-parents-overfeeding-246144.

46. Emily Oster, "Everybody Calm Down about Breastfeeding," FiveThirtyEight.com, May 20, 2015, accessed March 9, 2016, http://fivethirtyeight.com/features/everybody-calm-down-about-breastfeeding/.

47. Ibid.

48. Ibid.

49. Suzanne Barston, "Q&A with Joan Wolf, Author of 'Is Breast Best?'" *Fearless Formula Feeder* blog, February 7, 2011, accessed December 2014, http://www.fearlessformulafeeder.com/2011/02/qa-with-joan-wolf-author-of-is-breast-best/.

50. Wolf, *Is Breast Best?*, 86–87.

51. Adam Smith, *An Inquiry into the Nature and Causes of the Wealth of Nations*, Edwin Cannan, ed. (London: Methuen & Co., 1904), http://www.econlib.org/library/Smith/smWN.html.

52. Hanna Rosin, "The Case against Breast-Feeding," *The Atlantic*, April 2009, accessed January 20, 2016, http://www.theatlantic.com/magazine/archive/2009/04/the-case-against-breast-feeding/307311/?single_page=true.

53. Barston, *Bottled Up*, 102.

54. Ibid.

55. Interview with Suzanne Barston, December 2014.

56. Amy Tuteur, "Viewpoint: The Breast-Feeding Police Are Wrong about Formula," *Time*, May 13, 2013, accessed January 20, 2016, http://ideas.time.com/2013/05/13/viewpoint-the-breastfeeding-police-are-wrong-about-formula/.

57. Barston, *Bottled Up*, 11.

58. Suzanne Barston, "FFF Friday: 'She Assured Me that All I Had to Do Was Try Hard Enough,'" *Fearless Formula Feeder* blog, January 10, 2015, accessed January 20, 2016, http://www.fearlessformulafeeder.com/2015/01/fff-friday-she-assured-me-that-all-i-had-to-do-was-try-hard-enough/.

59. Suzanne Barston, "FFF Friday: 'It Feels Like This Is Something for Which I Must Beg Forgiveness,'" *Fearless Formula Feeder* blog, December 19, 2014, accessed January 20, 2016, http://www.fearlessformulafeeder.com/2014/12/fff-friday-it-feels-like-this-is-something-for-which-i-must-beg-forgiveness/.

60. Sally Fallon, *Nourishing Traditions: The Cookbook that Challenges Politically Correct Nutrition and Diet Dictocrats* (Washington, DC: NewTrends Publishing, Inc., 2007), 599.

61. Sarah, "Homemade Baby Formula (Recipe and Video How-To)," *Healthy Home Economist* blog, accessed March 9, 2016, http://www

.thehealthyhomeeconomist.com/video-homemade-milk-based-baby
-formula/.

62. Stacie Billis, "Move Over Lactation Consultants, We Need Formula
Consultants," *Huffington Post*, October 9, 2012, accessed March 9, 2016,
http://www.huffingtonpost.com/stacie-billis/baby-formula_b_1761575
.html.

CHAPTER 3: DAYCARE NANNIES

1. White House, Office of the Press Secretary, "Remarks by the President
in State of the Union Address," January 20, 2015, http://www.white
house.gov/the-press-office/2015/01/20/remarks-president-state-union
-address-january-20-2015.

2. Child Care Aware of America, *Parents and the High Cost of Child Care*
(Arlington, VA: Child Care Aware of America, 2014), 8, http://www
.arizonachildcare.org/pdf/2014-child-care-cost-report.pdf.

3. "It's Your Children's Bureau," Social Security Administration, accessed
March 2016, https://www.ssa.gov/history/childb2.html.

4. Child Care Aware of America, *Parents and the High Cost of Child
Care*, 9.

5. Ibid.

6. Ibid.

7. Alissa Quart, "Crushed by the Cost of Child Care," *New York Times*,
August 17, 2013, accessed March 9, 2016, http://opinionator.blogs
.nytimes.com/2013/08/17/crushed-by-the-cost-of-child-care/?_r=2.

8. Ibid.

9. Jeffrey A. Tucker, "Why Is Daycare Scarce and Unaffordable?" Foundation for Economic Education, January 28, 2015, accessed January 20, 2016,
http://fee.org/blog/detail/why-is-day-care-scarce-and-unaffordable.

10. Howard, *The Rule of Nobody*, 55.

11. Ibid.

12. Kristy Kennedy, "Unwrapping the Controversy over Swaddling," American Academy of Pediatrics *Gateway* blog, May 27, 2013, accessed March
2016, http://www.aappublications.org/content/34/6/34.

13. Susan T. Mahan and James R. Kasser, "Does Swaddling Influence
Developmental Displasia of the Hip?" *Pediatrics* 121 (January 2008),
doi:10.1542/peds.2007-1618.

14. Melinda Wenner Moyer, "No, Swaddling Will Not Kill Your Baby,"
Slate, last modified March 13, 2013, accessed March 9, 2016, http://www
.slate.com/articles/double_x/the_kids/2013/03/swaddling_debate_is
_swaddling_safe_or_does_it_increase_sids_risk.html.

15. Gary A. Emmett, "Can We Settle the Swaddling Controversy?" *Phila-*

delphia Inquirer, June 27, 2013, accessed March 9, 2016, http://www.philly
.com/philly/blogs/healthy_kids/Can-we-settle-the-swaddling-contro
versy.html.

16. Telephone interview with employee at the National Resource Center for
Health and Safety in Child Care and Early Education, October 2013.

17. Harvey Karp, "Ban on Swaddling: A Bad Idea, Coming to Your Town,"
BabyCenter blog, March 20, 2013, accessed March 9, 2016, http://blogs
.babycenter.com/mom_stories/ban-on-swaddling-a-bad-idea-coming
-to-your-town/.

18. Wolf, *Is Breast Best?,* 89.

19. Task Force on Sudden Infant Death Syndrome, "The Changing Concept of Sudden Infant Death Syndrome," *Pediatrics* 116 (2005): 1251,
doi:10.1542/peds.2005-1499.

20. Catherine Pearson, "Swaddling Ban: Why Are Day Cares Banning
Baby Burritos?" *Huffington Post,* April 4, 2013, accessed March 9, 2016,
http://www.huffingtonpost.com/2013/04/03/swaddling-ban_n_2885662
.html.

21. Ibid.

22. Associated Press, "Probation for Sisters Who 'Abused' Daycare Infants
by Swaddling," *Huffington Post,* January 7, 2015, accessed March 9, 2016,
http://www.huffingtonpost.com/2015/01/07/sisters-swaddling-abuse_n
_6430416.html.

23. Pearson, "Swaddling Ban."

24. Ibid.

25. Tennille Tracy, "Proposal Aims for Healthy Food at Day Care," *Wall
Street Journal,* January 15, 2015, accessed March 4, 2015, http://www
.wsj.com/articles/proposal-aims-for-healthier-food-at-day-care-centers
-1421342014.

26. "Child Care Facilities Licensing," Arizona Department of Health
Services, accessed March 9, 2016, http://azdhs.gov/licensing/childcare
-facilities/index.php.

27. Ibid.

28. "Licensing Rules for Child Care Centers and Homes," Michigan
Department of Licensing and Regulatory Affairs, accessed March 9,
2016, http://www.michigan.gov/lara/0,4601,7-154-63294_5529_49572
_50051---,00.html.

29. "New York Day Care Licensing Requirements," Daycare.com, accessed
March 2016, http://www.daycare.com/newyork/new-york-daycare
-center-licensing-requirements.html.

30. Katharine Mieszkowski and Jennifer LaFleur, "California Day Care
Centers Stay Open Despite Long Lists of Violations," *Reveal* blog, January 24, 2015, accessed March 9, 2016, http://www.revealnews.org/article
/california-day-care-centers-stay-open-despite-long-lists-of-violations/.

31. Drew DeSilver, "Rising Cost of Child Care May Help Explain Increase in Stay-at-Home Moms," Pew Research Center *Fact Tank* blog, April 8, 2014, accessed March 9,2016, http://www.pewresearch.org/fact-tank /2014/04/08/rising-cost-of-child-care-may-help-explain-increase-in -stay-at-home-moms/.

32. D'Vera Cohn, Gretchen Livingston, and Wendy Wang, "After Decades of Decline, a Rise in Stay-at-Home Mothers," Pew Research Center, April 8, 2014, accessed March 31, 2016, http://www.pewsocialtrends .org/2014/04/08/after-decades-of-decline-a-rise-in-stay-at-home -mothers/.

33. Allison Linn, "Opt Out or Left Out? The Economics of Stay-at-Home Moms," *CNBC Personal Finance* blog, May 12, 2013, accessed March 31, 2016, http://www.cnbc.com/id/100727292.

34. Tim Hoover, "Early State Proposal Would Ramp Up Rules for Child Care Centers to Earn License," *Denver Post*, July 12, 2011, accessed March 31, 2016, http://www.denverpost.com/ci_18459206.

35. "Rule Manual Volume 7 Child Care Facility Licensing," Colorado Department of Human Services, accessed March 30, 2016, http://www.sos .state.co.us/CCR/GenerateRulePdf.do?ruleVersionId=4073.

36. Madeline Novey, "County Grapples with High Cost of Child Care," *Coloradoan*, August 9, 2014, accessed March 30, 2016, http://www .coloradoan.com/story/news/local/2014/08/09/county-grapples-high -cost-child-care/13835305/.

37. Child Care Aware of America, *Parents and the High Cost of Child Care*.

38. Ibid., 6.

39. Ibid., 20.

40. "The Average Cost for Child Care by State," *Boston Globe*, July 2, 2014, accessed March 2, 2016, https://www.bostonglobe.com/2014/07/02/map -the-average-cost-for-child-care-state/LN65rSHXKNjr4eypyxToWM /story.html.

41. Christopher Ingraham, "Start Saving Now: Day Care Costs More than College in 31 States," *Washington Post*, April 9, 2014, accessed March 9, 2016, http://www.washingtonpost.com/blogs/wonkblog/ wp/2014/04/09/start-saving-now-day-care-costs-more-than-college -in-31-states/.

42. Jonathan Cohn, "The Hell of American Day Care," *The New Republic*, April 15, 2013, accessed March 30, 2016, https://newrepublic.com/article /112892/hell-american-day-care.

43. Randal Heeb and M. Rebecca Kilburn, *The Effects of State Regulations on Childcare Prices and Choices* (Rand Corporation, 2004), 1, https:// www.rand.org/content/dam/rand/pubs/working_papers/2004/RAND _WR137.pdf.

44. V. Joseph Hotz and M. Rebecca Kilburn, *Regulating Child Care:*

The Effects of State Regulations on Child Care Demand and Cost (RAND Corporation, 1995), 1, http://www.rand.org/pubs/drafts /DRU956.html.

45. Jordan Weissman, "Why Is Childcare Getting So Expensive?" *The Atlantic*, November 12, 2013, accessed March 30, 2016, http://www .theatlantic.com/business/archive/2013/11/why-is-childcare-getting -so-expensive/281394/.

46. Katharine B. Stevens, "Here Come the Child-Care Cops," *Wall Street Journal*, December 21, 2014, accessed March 30, 2016, http://www.wsj .com/articles/katharine-stevens-here-come-the-child-care-cops -1419205984.

47. Tucker, "Why Is Day Care Scarce and Unaffordable?"

48. Stevens, "Here Come the Child-Care Cops."

49. Bridget K. Hamre and Robert C. Pianta, "Student-Teacher Relation-ships," in *Children's Needs III: Development, Prevention, and Intervention*, ed. George G. Bear and Kathleen M. Minke (Washington: National Association of School Psychologists, 2006), 59–71.

50. Hotz and Kilburn, *Regulating Child Care*, 1.

51. Cohn, "The Hell of American Day Care."

52. Ibid.

53. Hotz and Kilburn, *Regulating Child Care*, 3.

54. Ibid., abstract.

55. David M. Blau, "Unintended Consequences of Child Care Regulations," *Labour Economics*, 14 (2007): 513–38, http://www.unc.edu/depts/econ /profs/blau/Unintended%20consequences%20of%20child%20care%20 regulations2.pdf.

56. David S. Fallis and Amy Brittain, "In Virginia, Thousands of Day-Care Providers Receive No Oversight," *Washington Post*, August 30, 2014, ac-cessed March 30, 2016, http://www.washingtonpost.com/sf/investiga tive/2014/08/30/in-virginia-thousands-of-day-care-providers-receive -no-oversight/.

57. Hotz and Kilburn, *Regulating Child Care*, abstract.

58. Howard, *The Rule of Nobody*, 14.

59. Ibid., 4.

60. Heeb and Kilburn, *The Effects of State Regulations on Childcare Prices and Choices*, 1.

61. Howard, *The Rule of Nobody*, 59.

62. Ibid., 71.

63. Ibid., 145.

64. Ibid., 47.

65. John Braithwaite and Valerie Braithwaite, "The Politics of Legalism: Rules versus Standards in Nursing Home Regulation," *Social & Legal*

Studies 4 (1995): 311, https://www.anu.edu.au/fellows/jbraithwaite
/_documents/Articles/politicsoflegalism_95.pdf.

66. Anthony L. Fisher, "Elder Care Doesn't Have to Resemble Prison,"
Reason, February 6, 2015, accessed March 9, 2016, http://reason.com
/archives/2015/02/06/elderly-care-in-the-age-of-choice.

67. Ibid.

68. Ibid.

69. Betsy Z. Russell, "Lawmakers Ease Day Care Rules," *The Spokesman
Review*, May 15, 2011, accessed March 9, 2016, http://www.spokesman
.com/stories/2011/may/15/lawmakers-ease-day-care-rules/.

CHAPTER 4: SCHOOL STATISTS

1. "Healthy Schools," LetsMove.gov, accessed May 2015, http://www.lets
move.gov/healthy-schools.

2. "The ED*Facts* Initiative," U.S. Department of Education, accessed May
2015, http://www2.ed.gov/about/inits/ed/edfacts/index.html.

3. "New Meal Pattern Requirements and Nutrition Standards," USDA
Food and Nutrition Service, accessed March 9, 2016, http://www.fns
.usda.gov/sites/default/files/LAC_03-06-12_0.pdf.

4. "The School Day Just Got Healthier," USDA Food and Nutrition Service, accessed March 9, 2016, http://www.fns.usda.gov/sites/default/files
/School_Meals_Summary.pdf.

5. Ibid.

6. "Dietary Guidelines for Americans," U.S. Department of Agriculture
and U.S. Department of Health and Human Services, accessed March
2015, http://www.health.gov/dietaryguidelines/dga2010/dietaryguide
lines2010.pdf.

7. Ibid.

8. Ibid.

9. "Dietary Guidelines for Americans 2010," U.S. Department of Agriculture and U.S. Department of Health and Human Services, accessed
March 30, 2016, http://www.health.gov/dietaryguidelines/dga2010
/dietaryguidelines2010.pdf.

10. Kyle Olson, "Students Slam Michelle O Lunch Rules: 'The Trash Cans
Are More Full than My Stomach,'" EAGnews.org, January 5, 2015, accessed March 9, 2016, http://eagnews.org/students-slam-michelle-o
-lunch-rules-the-trash-cans-are-more-full-than-my-stomach/.

11. School Nutrition Association, "SNA Survey Reveals Serious Challenges
with School Meal Standards," press release, December 4, 2014, https://
schoolnutrition.org/PressReleases/SNASurveyRevealsSeriousChal
lengeswithSchoolMealStandards/.

12. Helena Bottemiller Evich, "Behind the School Lunch Fight," *Politico*, June 4, 2014, accessed March 30 2016, http://www.politico.com/story /2014/06/michelle-obama-public-school-lunch-school-nutrition -association-lets-move-107390.

13. Jacob Tierney, "Lunch Programs Eat Away at Western Pennsylvania School Districts' Funds," *Pittsburgh Tribune-Review*, April 19, 2015, ac- cessed March 9, 2016, https://www.pressrush.com/author/8652211/jacob -tierney.

14. Tennille Tracy, "School Cafeterias Try Haute Cuisine," *Wall Street Jour- nal*, December 14, 2014, accessed March 9, 2016, http://www.wsj.com /articles/school-cafeterias-try-haute-cuisine-1418588555.

15. Greg Reinbold, "Southwest Greensburg Chef Moves from Restaurant into W.Pa. Schools," *Pittsburgh Tribune-Review*, February 23, 2015, ac- cessed March 9, 2016, http://triblive.com/news/westmoreland/7765774-74 /hudak-chef-greensburg#axzz3a1nmP6bt.

16. Ibid.

17. Arthur Delaney, "Food Stamp Recipients More Likely to Be Obese, Study Finds," *Huffington Post*, May 5, 2015, accessed May 22, 2015, http:// www.huffingtonpost.com/2015/05/05/food-stamps-obesity_n_7204824 .html.

18. Ibid.

19. "Diet Quality of Americans by SNAP Participation Status: Data from the National Health and Nutrition Examination Survey, 2007–2010— Summary," USDA Food and Nutrition Service, May 2015, accessed March 30, 2016, http://www.fns.usda.gov/sites/default/files/ops /NHANES-SNAP07-10-Summary.pdf.

20. Ibid.

21. "History of Firsts," *The Children's Aid Society*, accessed March 9, 2016, http://www.childrensaidsociety.org/about/history/history-firsts.

22. Ellen S. Woodward, "Hot Lunches for a Million School Children" (speech, National Archives, Works Progress Administration Papers), accessed March 9, 2016, http://newdeal.feri.org/works/wpa02.htm.

23. Gordon W. Gunderson, "National School Lunch Act," USDA Food and Nutrition Service, last modified August 26, 2015, accessed March 9, 2016, http://www.fns.usda.gov/nslp/history_5#APPROVED.

24. Ricardo Lopez, "USDA to Buy Meat from Drought-Stricken Livestock Farmers," *Los Angeles Times*, August 13, 2012, accessed March 9, 2016, http://articles.latimes.com/2012/aug/13/business/la-fi-mo-usda-to-buy -meat-from-farmers-drought-20120813.

25. Neal Barnard, "The Dairy Product Industry Needs to Stop Milking School Lunches," Physicians Committee for Responsible Medicine, *Dr. Barnard's Blog*, July 24, 2012, accessed March 29, 2016, http://www

.pcrm.org/nbBlog/index.php/the-dairy-product-industry-needs-to
-stop-milking-school-lunches.

26. Ibid.

27. Nia-Malika Henderson, "How Michelle Obama Lost in the Budget
Bill," *Washington Post*, December 10, 2014, accessed March 9, 2016,
http://www.washingtonpost.com/blogs/the-fix/wp/2014/12/10/how
-michelle-obama-lost-in-the-budget-bill/.

28. James Nye, "Teacher Sends Father a Stern Note Scolding Him for
His Daughter's 'Unhealthy' Pack Lunch of 'Chocolate, Marshmallows,
a Cracker and a Pickle'—Unfortunately for the School, Dad's a Doctor," *Daily Mail*, last modified January 25, 2015, accessed March 9, 2016,
http://www.dailymail.co.uk/news/article-2923657/School-apologizes
-teacher-sends-doctor-curt-letter-pack-daughter-proper-lunch
-tomorrow.html.

29. Tribune Media Wire, "Mom Says School Wouldn't Let Daughter Finish
Lunch Because It Was Not 'Nutritious,'" WNEP News, April 28, 2015,
accessed March 9, 2016, http://wnep.com/2015/04/28/mom-says-school
-wouldnt-let-daughter-finish-lunch-because-it-was-not-nutritious/.

30. Daisy Luther, "Feds to Parents: No Lunches from Home without Doctor's Note, School Lunch Only," REALfarmacy.com, November 15, 2013,
accessed May 2015, http://www.realfarmacy.com/no-lunches-from
-home-without-doctors-note-school-lunch-only/.

31. Monica Eng and Joel Hood, "Chicago School Bans Some Lunches
Brought from Home," *Chicago Tribune*, April 11, 2011, accessed March
9, 2016, http://articles.chicagotribune.com/2011-04-11/news/ct-met-
school-lunch-restrictions-04112011 0410_1_lunch-food-provider-public
-school.

32. Sara Burrows, "Preschooler's Homemade Lunch Replaced with Cafeteria 'Nuggets,'" *Carolina Journal*, February 14, 2012, accessed November 17,
2014, https://www.carolinajournal.com/news-article/preschoolers-home
made-lunch-replaced-with-cafeteria-nuggets/.

33. Ibid.

34. Carolina Journal Staff, "Chicken Nugget Furor Prompts Bipartisan
Congressional Letter to Federal Cabinet Leader," *Carolina Journal*,
February 16, 2012, accessed November 17, 2014, https://www.carolina
journal.com/news-article/chicken-nugget-furor-prompts-bipartisan
-congressional-letter-to-federal-cabinet-leader/.

35. Nutrition Nannies Facebook page, https://www.facebook.com/Nutri
tionNannies/info?tab=page_info.

36. Ruben Navarrette, "'Fat Letters' from Schools to Parents Are Wrong,"
CNN.com, last modified September 24, 2013, accessed March 9, 2016,
http://www.cnn.com/2013/09/24/opinion/navarrette-fat-letters/.

37. Rachel Bertsche, "Mom Claims School Fat-Shamed 6-Year-Old,"
    Yahoo Parenting, February 9, 2015, accessed March 9, 2016, https://www
    .yahoo.com/parenting/mom-claims-school-fat-shamed-6-year-old-the
    -mother-110557012432.html.

38. Michelle Castillo, " 'Fat Letters' Outrage Some California Parents,"
    CBSNews.com, October 24, 2013, accessed March 9, 2016, http://www
    .cbsnews.com/news/fat-letters-outrage-some-california-parents/.

39. Edmund DeMarche, "New York Mom Fuming after Daughter Gets
    School Letter Calling Her Overweight," FoxNews.com, May 23, 2014,
    accessed March 9, 2016, http://www.foxnews.com/us/2014/05/23/new
    -york-mom-fuming-after-daughter-gets-school-letter-calling-her
    -overweight/.

40. Joe Tacopino et al., "This Kid Is Fat (According to the City of New
    York)," *New York Post*, May 22, 2014, accessed March 9, 2016, http://
    nypost.com/2014/05/22/nyc-says-this-girl-is-fat/.

41. Julie Deardorff, "BMI Measuring in Schools Proves Weighty Issue,"
    Chicago Tribune, May 17, 2013, accessed March 9, 2016, http://articles
    .chicagotribune.com/2013-05-17/health/ct-met-bmi-backlash-20130517
    _1_bmi-childhood-obesity-rates-muscular-people#sthash.P9YoIM3c
    .dpuf.

42. Tacopino et al., "This Kid Is Fat."

43. "Facts and Concerns about School-Based BMI Screening, Surveillance
    and Reporting," Eating Disorders Coalition, accessed March 2016,
    http://eatingdisorderscoalition.org.s208556.gridserver.com/couch
    /uploads/file/School%20Based%20BMI.pdf.

44. Ibid.

45. Allie Bidwell, "Massachusetts Schools to Stop Sending 'Fat Letters,' "
    US News & World Report, October 17, 2013, accessed March 9, 2016,
    http://www.usnews.com/news/articles/2013/10/17/massachusetts-schools
    -to-stop-sending-fat-letters.

46. Michael Friedman, "The Psychological Consequences of 'Fat Letters,' "
    Psychology Today, January 7, 2014, accessed March 9, 2016, https://www
    .psychologytoday.com/blog/brick-brick/201401/the-psychological-con
    sequences-fat-letters.

47. Navarrette, " 'Fat Letters' from Schools to Parents Are Wrong."

48. A. J. Nihiser et al., "Body Mass Index Measurement in Schools," *Journal
    of School Health* 77 (2007): 651–71, http://www.cdc.gov/HealthyYouth
    /obesity/BMI/pdf/BMI_execsumm.pdf.

49. Deardorff, "BMI Measuring in Schools Proves Weighty Issue."

50. Ibid.

51. Joanne P. Ikeda et al., "BMI Screening in Schools: Helpful or Harmful,"
    Health and Education Research 21 (2006): 764, http://her.oxfordjournals
    .org/content/21/6/761.full.

52. Deardorff, "BMI Measuring in Schools Proves Weighty Issue."

53. "Study of Nutrition and Wellness Quality in Child Care Settings," Abt website, accessed March 30, 2016, http://abtassociates.com/Projects/2015 /Study-of-Nutrition-and-Wellness-Quality-in-Child-C.aspx.

54. "Agency Information Collection Activities: Proposed Collection; Comment Request-Study on Nutrition and Wellness Quality in Childcare Settings (SNAQCS)," USDA Food and Nutrition Service, March 23, 2015, accessed January 25, 2016, https://www.federalregister.gov/articles /2015/03/23/2015-06592/agency-information-collection-activities-pro posed-collection-comment-request-study-on-nutrition-and.

55. Emma Brown, "D.C. Parents Push for More Recess," *Washington Post*, August 31, 2013, accessed March 9, 2016, http://www.washingtonpost .com/local/education/dc-parents-push-for-more-recess/2013/08/30 /467e52a0-10c6-11e3-bdf6-e4fc677d94a1_story.html.

56. "Education and Health in Schools: A Survey of Parents," NPR, Robert Wood Johnson Foundation, Harvard School of Public Health, September 2013, accessed March 30, 2016, http://media.npr.org/documents/2013 /dec/rwjf_npr_harvard_edpoll.pdf.

57. Kathy Speregen, "Physical Education in America's Public Schools: Physical Education and School Performance," University of Michigan, April 19, 2013, http://sitemaker.umich.edu/356.speregen/physical _education_and_school_performance (site discontinued).

58. Ibid.

59. Maanvi Singh, "To Get Kids Exercising, Schools Are Becoming Creative," NPR, last modified December 13, 2013, accessed March 8, 2016, http://www.npr.org/blogs/health/2013/12/06/249247319/to-get-kids -exercising-schools-are-becoming-creative?live=1.

60. Ibid.

61. Gary Horvath, "Moon Teen Helping Others Jump to Better Health at Swickley Valley YMCA," *Pittsburgh Tribune-Review*, April 29, 2015, accessed March 8, 2016, http://triblive.com/news/8123439-74/jeremy -rope-ymca.

62. Nanci Hellmich, "Report: More PE, Activity Programs Needed in Schools," *USA Today*, May 23, 2013, accessed March 8, 2016, http://www.usatoday.com/story/news/2013/05/23/physical-education -schools/2351763/.

63. Erica Lue, "Cutting Physical Education and Recess: Troubling Trends and How You Can Help," National PTA, Learning First Alliance, September 3, 2013, accessed March 8, 2016, http://www.learningfirst.org /cutting-physical-education-and-recess-troubling-trends-and-how-you -can-help.

64. Hellmich, "Report: More PE, Activity Programs Needed in Schools."

65. Ibid.

CHAPTER 5: THE WAR ON FUN

1. Furedi, "How Much Independence Should Children Have?"
2. Gill, *No Fear*, 10.
3. Ibid., 19.
4. Abby W. Schacher, "Meet the Consumer Product Alarmist Commission," *Pittsburgh Tribune-Review*, March 22, 2014, accessed March 30, 2016, http://triblive.com/opinion/featuredcommentary/5794673-74/cpsc-government-toy#axzz3dEedpU5Z.
5. Cass Sunstein, *Risk and Reason: Safety, Law, and the Environment* (Cambridge UK: Cambridge University Press, 2002), 289.
6. "Who We Are—What We Do for You," U.S. Consumer Product Safety Commission, accessed January 25, 2016, http://www.cpsc.gov/en/Safety-Education/Safety-Guides/General-Information/Who-We-Are---What-We-Do-for-You/.
7. "About CPSC," U.S. Consumer Product Safety Commission, accessed January 25, 2016, http://www.cpsc.gov/en/About-CPSC/.
8. "Feds Seize 'Potentially Dangerous' Playground Toys at Port of Savannah," *Savannah Morning News*, July 27, 2015, accessed March 3, 2016, http://savannahnow.com/crime/2015-01-27/feds-seize-potentially-dangerous-playground-toys-port-savannah.
9. "Marin Mountain Bikes Recalls Children's Bicycles Due to Fall Hazard; Handlebars Can Loosen," U.S. Consumer Product Safety Commission, February 10, 2015, accessed March 3, 2016, http://www.cpsc.gov/en/Recalls/2015/Marin-Mountain-Bikes-Recalls-Childrens-Bicycles/.
10. Ryan Jaslow, "Bumbo Baby Seats Recalled Again Over Risk of Falling, Skull Fractures," CBSNews.com, August 15, 2012, accessed March 3, 2016, http://www.cbsnews.com/news/bumbo-baby-seats-recalled-again-over-risk-of-falling-skull-fractures/.
11. David Harsanyi, *Nanny State: How Food Fascists, Teetotaling Do-Gooders, Priggish Moralists, and Other Boneheaded Bureaucrats Are Turning America into a Nation of Children* (New York: Broadway Books, 2007).
12. Ibid., 145.
13. Ibid., 144.
14. U.S. Consumer Product Safety Commission, "Baby Girl Dies in Bath Ring; CPSC Chairman Warns of Drowning Hazard," press release, December 6, 1994, http://www.cpsc.gov/en/Newsroom/News-Releases/1995/Baby-Girl-Dies-In-Bath-Ring-CPSC-Chairman-Warns-Of-Drowning-Hazard/.
15. Philip K. Howard, *Life without Lawyers: Restoring Responsibility in America* (New York: W. W. Norton and Company, 2009), 36.
16. Nancy Nord, "The Irrational Federal War on Buckyballs," *Wall Street*

Journal, November 12, 2013, accessed March 8, 2016, http://www.wsj
.com/articles/SB10001424052702303914304579191764269660456.

17. Jim Epstein, "The Feds vs. Craig Zucker," *Reason*, March 2014, accessed
March 8, 2016, http://reason.com/archives/2014/02/20/the-feds-vs-craig
-zucker.

18. *CBS This Morning*, video, August 20, 2012, https://www.youtube.com
/watch?v=WpoB-xuUtZo.

19. Gibson Dunn, "The CPSC's Latest Attempts to Expand Its Enforcement Authority," Gibson Dunn client alert, last modified July 31, 2013,
accessed March 3, 2016, http://www.gibsondunn.com/publications
/pages/CPSC-Latest-Attempts-to-Expand-Enforcement-Authority
.aspx.

20. Email interview with Nancy Nord, August 1, 2015.

21. Harsanyi, *Nanny State*, 147.

22. Office of the Governor, "Gov. Blagojevich Signs Legislation Making
Illinois First in the Nation to Ban Dangerous Child Toy; Provides New
Resource to Parents to Keep Kids Safe," press release, June 8, 2005,
accessed March 8, 2016, http://www3.illinois.gov/PressReleases
/ShowPressRelease.cfm?SubjectID=1&RecNum=4021.

23. Glenn Blain, "Classic Kids Games Like Kickball Deemed Unsafe by
State in Effort to Increase Summer Camp Regulation," *New York Daily
News*, April 19, 2011, accessed March 3, 2016, http://www.nydailynews
.com/new-york/classic-kids-games-kickball-deemed-unsafe-state-effort
-increase-summer-camp-regulation-article-1.110822.

24. Ibid.

25. Howard, *Life without Lawyers*, 41.

26. Hanna Rosin, "The Overprotected Kid," *The Atlantic*, April 2014,
accessed March 8, 2016, http://www.theatlantic.com/features/archive
/2014/03/hey-parents-leave-those-kids-alone/358631/.

27. Ibid.

28. "Playground Safety," U.S. Consumer Product Safety Commission,
accessed March 3, 2016, http://www.cpsc.gov/en/Safety-Education
/Safety-Guides/Sports-Fitness-and-Recreation/Playground-Safety/.

29. Rosin, "The Overprotected Kid."

30. Ibid.

31. Kay Randall, "Child's Play," University of Texas at Austin, January
2007, accessed March 8, 2016, http://www.utexas.edu/features/2007
/playgrounds/.

32. Kate Briquelet, "City Shells Out $20M over Kids' Playground Injuries,"
New York Post, March 1, 2015, accessed March 8, 2016, http://nypost
.com/2015/03/01/city-shells-out-20m-over-kids-playground-injuries/.

33. Kirstin Cole, "Exposing the Hidden Dangers of NYC Playgrounds,"

PIX11, last modified May 7, 2015, accessed March 8, 2016, http://pix11
.com/2015/05/07/some-nyc-playgrounds-have-unsafe-design-poor
-maintenance-report/.

34. Ibid.
35. Harsanyi, *Nanny State*, 139.
36. Ibid., 140.
37. Howard, *Life without Lawyers*, 45.
38. Ibid., 46.
39. Ibid.
40. David Mitchell and Julie Hayden, "7-Year-Old Playing an Imaginary
    Game at School Gets Suspended for Real," Fox31 Denver, last modified
    February 4, 2013, accessed March 8, 2016, http://kdvr.com/2013/02/04
    /7-year-old-playing-an-imaginary-game-at-school-gets-suspended-for
    -real/.
41. Nicole Hensley, "Texas Boy Suspended for Saying He Could Make
    Classmate 'Disappear' with 'Lord of the Rings' Sorcery," *New York Daily
    News*, January 31, 2015, accessed March 8, 2016, http://www.nydailynews
    .com/news/national/texas-boy-suspended-bringing-ring-power-school
    -article-1.2099103.
42. Jacqueline Burt Cote, "27 Normal Things Every '80s Kid Did in School
    That Would Never Fly Today," *The Stir* blog, May 18, 2015, accessed
    March 8, 2016, http://thestir.cafemom.com/being_a_mom/185828/11
    _normal_things_every_80s.
43. Sandy Louey, "Recess Gets Regulated: Worried about Safety, Schools
    Restrict Traditional Games," *Sacramento Bee*, August 22, 2004, accessed
    March 3, 2016, http://www.bridges4kids.org/articles/2004/8-04/SacBee
    8-22-04.html.
44. Harsanyi, *Nanny State*, 151.
45. Louey, "Recess Gets Regulated."
46. "New Hampshire School Bans Students from Playing 'Tag,'"
    FoxNews.com, October 11, 2013, accessed March 8, 2016, http://www
    .foxnews.com/us/2013/10/11/new-hampshire-school-tells-parents-that
    -rules-ban-tag/.
47. Associated Press, "Mass. Grade School Bans Tag, Other Chase Games,"
    NBCNews.com, October 19, 2006, accessed March 8, 2016, http://www
    .nbcnews.com/id/15316912/ns/us_news-education/t/mass-grade-school
    -bans-tag-other-chase-games/#.VYLPa_lVikp.
48. Ibid.
49. Emily Bazar, "'Not It!' More Schools Ban Games at Recess," *USA Today*,
    last modified July 27, 2006, accessed March 8, 2016, http://usatoday30
    .usatoday.com/news/health/2006-06-26-recess-bans_x.htm.
50. Monica Scott, "Zeeland Teachers Set 'No Tag, No Chasing' Policy

for Kindergarteners," MLive.com, last modified October 4, 2013, accessed March 8, 2016, http://www.mlive.com/news/grand-rapids /index.ssf/2013/10/zeeland_teachers_no_tag_no_cha.html.

51. Ryan Jaslow, "N.Y. School Bans Balls at Recess, Cracks Down on Tag Games over Safety Fears," CBSNews.com, October 8, 2013, accessed March 8, 2016, http://www.cbsnews.com/news/ny-school-bans-balls -at-recess-cracks-down-on-tag-games-over-safety-fears/.

52. Louey, "Recess Gets Regulated."

53. Harsanyi, *Nanny State*, 139.

54. "About Playworks," Playworks, accessed March 8, 2016, http://www .playworks.org/about#sthash.SblRd7WE.dpuf.

55. Tim Cushing, "Schools Ban Tag, Cartwheels and 'Unstructured Play': The Inevitable Outcome of Unrealistic Promises and Expectations," *Techdirt* blog, October 10, 2013, accessed March 8, 2016, https://www .techdirt.com/articles/20131007/16154124788/schools-ban-tag-cartwheels -unstructured-play-inevitable-outcome-unrealistic-promises-expecta tions.shtml.

56. Ibid.

57. Ibid.

58. Graeme Paton, "Schools Banning Conkers and Leapfrog over Safety Fears," *Telegraph*, April 19, 2011, accessed March 8, 2016, http://www .telegraph.co.uk/education/educationnews/8458526/Schools-banning -conkers-and-leapfrog-over-safety-fears.html.

59. Furedi, "How Much Independence Should Children Have?"

60. Cushing, "Schools Ban Tag, Cartwheels and 'Unstructured Play.'"

61. Dani Isdale, "The School with No Rules," SBS Dateline, October 20, 2014, accessed March 3, 2016, http://www.sbs.com.au/news/article /2014/10/20/school-no-rules.

62. Marika Hill, "School Ditches Rules and Loses Bullies," Stuff.co.nz, January 26, 2014, accessed March 3, 2016, http://www.stuff.co.nz /national/education/9650581/School-ditches-rules-and-loses-bullies.

63. Ibid.

64. Grant Schofield, "Playing without Rules, but with Consequences," *The Science of Human Potential* blog, February 3, 2014, accessed March 8, 2016, http://profgrant.com/2014/02/03/playing-without-rules-but-with -consequences/.

65. Judith Kieff, "The Silencing of Recess Bells," *Childhood Education* 77 (2001): 319–20.

66. Peter Grey, "Spread the Word; Feb. 4 Is Global School Play Day," *Psychology Today*, January 20, 2015, accessed March 8, 2016, https://www .psychologytoday.com/blog/freedom-learn/201501/spread-the-word-feb -4-is-global-school-play-day.

67. Peter Grey, "The Play Deficit," *Aeon*, September 18, 2013, accessed March 8, 2016, http://aeon.co/magazine/culture/children-today-are-suffering-a-severe-deficit-of-play/.

68. "NR Interview: What about Our Boys?" *National Review Online*, September 16, 2013, accessed March 8, 2016, http://www.nationalreview.com/article/358589/what-about-our-boys-interview.

69. Howard, *Life without Lawyers*, 43–44.

70. Richard Louv, *Last Child in the Woods: Saving Our Children from Nature-Deficit Disorder* (Chapel Hill, NC: Algonquin Books, 2005), 9.

71. Petit, "Kid on Wire."

72. Cushing, "Schools Ban Tag, Cartwheels and 'Unstructured Play.'"

73. KaBOOM! is a national nonprofit organization dedicated to bringing balanced and active play into the daily lives of all kids, particularly those growing up in poverty in America, http://kaboom.org.

CHAPTER 6: OBESITY POLICE

1. Telephone interview with Yodit Betru, June 2015.

2. Lindsey Tanner, "Should Parents Lose Custody of Super Obese Kids?" Associated Press, January 20, 2012, accessed March 8, 2016, http://news.yahoo.com/parents-lose-custody-super-obese-kids-200342454.html.

3. Telephone interview with Yodit Betru, June 2015.

4. Linda Gordon, *Heroes of Their Own Lives: The Politics and History of Family Violence, Boston 1880–1960* (Urbana and Chicago: University of Illinois Press, 1988), 6.

5. Ron Barnett, "S.C. Case Looks on Child Obesity as Child Abuse. But Is It?" *USA Today*, July 23, 2009, accessed March 3, 2016, http://usatoday30.usatoday.com/news/health/weightloss/2009-07-20-obesityboy_N.htm.

6. Keither Ecker, "Mother Loses Custody of Obese Son," Lawyers.com, December 27, 2011, accessed March 3, 2016, http://blogs.lawyers.com/2011/12/mother-loses-custody-of-obese-son/.

7. Rachel Dissell, "County Places Obese Cleveland Heights Child in Foster Care," *The Plain Dealer*, last modified November 28, 2011, accessed March 8, 2016, http://blog.cleveland.com/metro/2011/11/obese_cleveland_heights_child.html.

8. Alyssa Newcomb, "Obese Third Grader Taken from Mom, Placed in Foster Care," ABCNews.com, November 27, 2011, accessed March 8, 2016, http://abcnews.go.com/blogs/health/2011/11/27/obese-third-grader-taken-from-family-placed-in-foster-care/.

9. Ibid.

10. Dan Harris and Mikaela Conley, "Childhood Obesity: A Call for Par-

ents to Lose Custody," ABCNews.com, July 14, 2011, accessed March 8, 2016, http://abcnews.go.com/Health/childhood-obesity-call-parents-lose-custody/story?id=14068280.

11. Lindsey Murtagh and David S. Ludwig, "State Intervention in Life-Threatening Childhood Obesity," *Journal of American Medical Association* 306 (2011): 206, doi:10.1001/jama.2011.903.

12. Ibid.

13. Ibid.

14. Martin Binks, "The Debate Surrounding Removal of Severely Obese Children from the Home: An Editorial Commentary," The Obesity Society, accessed August 2011, http://www.obesity.org/home.

15. Murtagh and Ludwig, "State Intervention in Life-Threatening Childhood Obesity."

16. Ibid.

17. Todd Varness et al., "Childhood Obesity and Medical Neglect," *Pediatrics* 123 (2009), accessed March 8, 2016, doi:10.1542/peds.2008-0712.

18. Ibid.

19. Shauneen M. Garrahan and Andrew W. Eichner, "Tipping the Scale: A Place for Childhood Obesity in the Evolving Legal Framework of Child Abuse and Neglect," *Yale Journal of Health Policy, Law, and Ethics* 12 (2012): 340, accessed March 8, 2016, http://digitalcommons.law.yale.edu/yjhple/vol12/iss2/3.

20. Melissa Mitgang, "Childhood Obesity and State Intervention: An Examination of the Health Risks of Pediatric Obesity and When They Justify State Involvement," *Columbia Journal of Law and Social Problems* 44 (June 2011): 587, accessed March 8, 2016, http://connection.ebscohost.com/c/articles/66729732/childhood-obesity-state-intervention-examination-health-risks-pediatric-obesity-when-they-justify-state-involvement.

21. Tanner, "Should Parents Lose Custody of Super Obese Kids?"

22. Kristen E. Brierley, "Family Law—Childhood Morbid Obesity: How Excess Pounds Can Tip the Scales of Justice in Favor of Removing a Child from the Home and/or Termination of Parental Rights," *Western New England Law Review* 35 (2013): 12, accessed March 8, 2016, http://www1.wne.edu/assets/170/Brierley_FINAL_51313_Croppedocr.pdf.

23. Shawna Boothe and Caroline Ackerman, "Courts Struggle with the Growing Problem of Child Obesity: Is It Neglect Justifying Removal from the Home?" IICLE—New Perspectives Flashpoints, Schiff Hardin LLP (January 2014), 3, http://www.schiffhardin.com/Templates/media/files/publications/PDF/Boothe--Shawna---Courts-Struggle-with-Growing-Problem-of-Child-Obesity---IICLE---Jan-2014.pdf.

24. Maria L. LaGanga, "For Obese Girl, Battle of Blame Comes Too Late," *Los Angeles Times*, December 26, 1997, accessed March 3, 2016, http://articles.latimes.com/1997/dec/26/news/mn-2357.

25. Mike Ellis, "Parents Being Prosecuted for Young Son's Obesity," *Indianapolis Star*, November 29, 2000, accessed March 3, 2016, https://groups.google.com/forum/#!topic/misc.consumers/BVawV1QTgzw.

26. Abigail Darwin, "Childhood Obesity: Is It Abuse?" *Children's Voice* 17 (2008): 26, accessed March 8, 2016, http://www.ellennotbohm.com/JulyAug08_Voice_ChildhoodObesity.pdf.

27. Ibid.

28. Darwin, "Childhood Obesity: Is It Abuse?"

29. Elizabeth Ralston, "KinderLARDen Cop: Why States Must Stop Policing Parents of Obese Children," *Seton Hall Law Review* 42 (2012): 1783–1820, http://scholarship.shu.edu/cgi/viewcontent.cgi?article=1454&context=shlr.

30. Boothe and Ackerman, "Courts Struggle with the Growing Problem of Child Obesity," 4.

31. Ralston, "KinderLARDen Cop," 1795.

32. Ibid.

33. Boothe and Ackerman, "Courts Struggle with the Growing Problem of Child Obesity," 4.

34. Ralston, "KinderLARDen Cop," 1798.

35. KJ Antonia, "Should the State Remove Fat Kids from Their Homes?" *Slate*, July 13, 2011, accessed March 8, 2016, http://www.slate.com/blogs/xx_factor/2011/07/13/two_harvard_researchers_advocate_putting_extremely_obese_kids_in.html?wpisrc=twitter_socialflow.

36. Stephanie Sciarani, "Morbid Childhood Obesity: The Pressing Need to Expand Statutory Definitions of Child Neglect," *Thomas Jefferson Law Review* 32 (2010): 318, http://www.tjeffersonlrev.org/print/32/2/morbid-childhood-obesity-pressing-need-expand-statutory-definitions-child-neglect.

37. Dana Mack, *The Assault on Parenthood: How Our Culture Undermines the Family* (New York: Encounter Books, 1997), 86.

38. Ibid.

39. Ibid., 62.

40. Jeffrey Schwab, "Leaving Children Alone Can Come with Lifelong Consequences for Illinois Families," *Illinois Policy*, July 2, 2015, accessed March 29, 2016, https://www.illinoispolicy.org/leaving-children-alone-can-come-with-lifelong-consequences-for-illinois-families/.

41. Garrahan and Eichner, "Tipping the Scale."

42. Gordon, *Heroes of Their Own Lives,* 2.

43. Eugene Volokh, "Parents Have a Right to Reasonably Spank Their Children, Says Massachusetts High Court," *Washington Post*, June 26,

2015, accessed March 29, 2016, https://www.washingtonpost.com/news /volokh-conspiracy/wp/2015/06/26/parents-have-a-right-to-reasonably -spank-their-children-says-massachusetts-high-court/.

44. Elizabeth Hewitt, "Shumlin Signs Child Protection Reform Bill into Law," VTDigger.org, June 15, 2015, accessed March 29, 2016, http:// vtdigger.org/2015/06/15/shumlin-signs-child-protection-reform-bill -into-law/.

45. Bobby Cagle, "Cagle: Building a Better Child Welfare System in Georgia," *Athens Banner-Herald*, June 19, 2015, accessed March 29, 2016, http://onlineathens.com/opinion/2015-06-19/cagle-building-better-child -welfare-system-georgia.

46. Gordon, *Heroes of Their Own Lives*, 3.

47. Ralston, "KinderLARDen Cop," 1814.

48. Dorothy Roberts, *Shattered Bonds: The Color of Child Welfare* (New York: Basic Civitas Books, 2001), 109.

49. Elizabeth Bartholet, *Nobody's Children: Abuse and Neglect, Foster Drift, and the Adoption Alternative* (Boston: Beacon Press, 1999), 193.

50. Gaelle Faure, "Should Parents of Obese Kids Lose Custody?" *Time*, October 16, 2009, accessed March 31, 2016, http://content.time.com /time/health/article/0,8599,1930772,00.html.

51. Gordon, *Heroes of Their Own Lives*, 296.

52. Ibid.

53. Martin Guggenheim. *What's Wrong with Children's Rights* (Cambridge: Harvard University Press, 2005), Kindle edition.

54. Ibid.

55. Ibid.

56. Brierley, "Family Law—Childhood Morbid Obesity," 129.

57. Grand Jury, County of San Diego, to Honorable John Burton, Assemblyman, April 20, 1992, http://www.liftingtheveil.org/burton.htm.

58. Judith Meltzer, Rachel Molly Joseph, and Andy Shookhoff, eds., *For the Welfare of Children: Lessons Learned from Class Action Litigation* (Washington, DC: Center for the Study of Social Policy, 2012).

59. Ibid., preface.

60. Ibid., vi.

61. Diane L. Redleaf, "DCFS's Real Crime? Breaking Up Families," *Chicago Sun-Times*, Nov. 24, 2013, accessed March 31, 2016, http://www.family defensecenter.net/wp-content/uploads/2015/02/DCFSs_real_crime __Breaking_up_families_-_Chicago_Sun-Times.pdf.

62. Ibid.

63. "Testimony of Carol Lamb Hopkins before the Senate Committee on Labor and Human Resources Subcommittee on Children and Families," 104th Congress (May 25, 1995), http://liftingtheveil.org /hopkins.htm.

64. Deborah Tuerkheimer, *Flawed Convictions: Shaken Baby Syndrome and the Inertia of Injustice* (Oxford: Oxford University Press, 2014), Kindle edition.

65. Debbie Cenziper, "Prosecutors Build Murder Cases Based on Disputed Shaken Baby Syndrome Diagnosis," *Washington Post*, March 20, 2015, accessed March 31, 2016, http://www.washingtonpost.com/graphics /investigations/shaken-baby-syndrome/.

66. Tuerkheimer, *Flawed Convictions*.

67. Deborah Tuerkheimer. "Questionable Convictions in 'Shaken Baby' Cases?" CBSNews.com, February 26, 2015, accessed March 31, 2016, http://www.cbsnews.com/news/questionable-convictions-in-shaken -baby-cases/.

68. Tanner, "Should Parents Lose Custody of Super Obese Kids?"

69. Faure, "Should Parents of Obese Kids Lose Custody?"

70. Janice D'Arcy, "Safeway Shoplifting Arrest and Unforeseen Conse- quences," *Washington Post*, November 2, 2011, accessed March 8, 2016, http://www.washingtonpost.com/blogs/on-parenting/post/safeway -shoplifting-arrest-and-unforeseen-consequences/2011/11/02/gIQA Ie6XgM_blog.html.

71. Ibid.

72. Teresa Tomassoni, "D.C. Child Welfare Agency Often Acts Too Quickly to Remove Children, Study Says," *Washington Post*, October 5, 2011, accessed March 8, 2016, http://www.washingtonpost.com/local/dc -child-welfare-agency-often-acts-too-quickly-to-remove-children-study -says/2011/09/29/gIQAIGweOL_story.html.

73. Ibid.

74. Binks, "The Debate Surrounding Removal of Severely Obese Children from the Home."

75. Ibid.

76. Arthur Caplan, "Obesity Alone Is No Reason to Remove Kids from Their Homes," NBCNews.com, July 14, 2011, accessed March 29, 2016, http://www.nbcnews.com/id/43727876/ns/health-health_care/t/obesity -alone-no-reason-remove-kids-their-homes/#.VZLZkPlViko.

77. Dan Harris and Mikaela Conley, "Childhood Obesity: A Call for Par- ents to Lose Custody," ABCNews.com, July 14, 2011, accessed March 30, 2016, http://abcnews.go.com/Health/childhood-obesity-call-parents -lose-custody/story?id=14068280.

78. Veronique Greenwood, "Debate: Should the State Take Severly Obese Children from Their Families?" *Discover*, July 14, 2011, accessed March 30, 2016, http://blogs.discovermagazine.com/80beats/2011/07/14/debate -should-the-state-take-severely-obese-children-from-their-families/# .VZREAflVikp.

79. Tanner, "Should Parents Lose Custody of Super Obese Kids?"

80. Faure, "Should Parents of Obese Kids Lose Custody?"

81. John Komlos and Marek Brabec, "The Trend of BMI Values among US Adults," CESifo Working Paper Series No. 2987, March 24, 2010, accessed March 29, 2016, http://papers.ssrn.com/sol3/papers.cfm ?abstract_id=1573500.

82. Stephanie Strom, "Food Companies Have Cut Back on Calories, Study Says," *New York Times*, January 9, 2014, accessed March 29, 2016, http:// www.nytimes.com/2014/01/09/health/food-companies-have-cut-back -on-calories-study-says.html?_r=0.

CONCLUSION

1. Tony Blair, "Full Text: Tony Blair's Speech on Compensation Culture," *The Guardian*, May 26, 2005, accessed March 30, 2016, http://www.the guardian.com/politics/2005/may/26/speeches.media.

2. Howard, *Rule of Nobody*, 33.

3. Julie Bosman, "Teenager's Jailing Brings a Call to Fix Sex Offender Registries," *New York Times*, July 4, 2015, accessed March 8, 2016, http:// www.nytimes.com/2015/07/05/us/teenagers-jailing-brings-a-call-to-fix -sex-offender-registries.html?_r=0.

4. Ibid.

5. Ibid.

6. Jill Levenson, "Does Youthful Mistake Merit Sex-Offender Status?" CNN.com, August 6, 2015, accessed March 30, 2016, http://www.cnn .com/2015/08/06/opinions/levenson-sex-offender-registry-reform/.

7. "Registries' Reach Has Expanded Exponentially (RSOL's First Asser- tion)," Reform Sex Offender Laws, accessed March 30, 2016, http:// nationalrsol.org/wp-content/uploads/2015/07/RSOL-First-Assertion .pdf.

8. Ibid.

9. Jeffrey C. Sandler, Naomi J. Freeman, and Kelly M. Socia, "Does a Watched Pot Boil? A Time-Series Analysis of New York State's Sex Of- fender Registration and Notification Law," *Psychology, Public Policy, and Law* 14 (2008): 284–302, http://dx.doi.org/10.1037/a0013881.

10. Human Rights Watch, "Raised on the Registry: The Irreparable Harm of Placing Children on Sex Offender Registries in the US," Human Rights Watch, May 2013, accessed April 1, 2016, http://www.hrw.org /sites/default/files/reports/us0513_ForUpload_1.pdf.

11. "Assertions," Reform Sex Offender Laws, accessed April 1, 2016, http://nationalrsol.org/about-us/assertions/.

12. Levenson, "Does Youthful Mistake Merit Sex-Offender Status?"

13. Maribeth Roman Schmidt, "Tutko Grand Jury Report Underlines the

Need for Reform at Child Welfare Agencies," PennLive.com, June 11, 2015, accessed April 1, 2016, http://www.pennlive.com/opinion/2015/06 /tutko_grand_jury_report_underl.html.

14. Abby W. Schachter, "This Perverse Law Won't Flag Child Abusers," *Pittsburgh Tribune*, April 25, 2016, accessed April 1, 2016, http://triblive .com/opinion/featuredcommentary/8207030-74/child-law-pennsylvania #axzz3k1dJhe7c.

15. Ibid.

16. Furedi, "How Much Independence Should Children Have?"

17. Robert Huntington, *The Nanny State* (Hereford, UK: Artnik, 2004), 184.

18. Simon Hills, *Strictly No! How We're Being Overrun by the Nanny State* (Edinburgh: Mainstream Publishing, 2006).

19. "About Us," Manifesto Club, accessed March 2016, http://www.mani festoclub.com/about.

20. Gill, *No Fear*, 10.

21. Ibid., 21.

22. "The Nanny State: What an Experiment in State-Sponsored Parenting Says about British Politics," *The Economist*, October 20, 2012, accessed March 2016, http://www.economist.com/news/britain/21564842-what -experiment-state-sponsored-parenting-says-about-british-politics.

23. Nickie Aiken, "Family Intervention: Tough Love for Better Social Outcomes and Savings," *The Guardian*, September 27, 2011, accessed April 1, 2016, http://www.theguardian.com/local-government-network /2011/sep/27/family-intervention-tough-love.

24. Julie Griffiths, "Pooled Family Intervention Projects Prove Their Worth," *Community Care*, February 4, 2011, accessed April 1, 2016, http://www .communitycare.co.uk/2011/02/04/pooled-family-intervention-projects -prove-their-worth/.

25. Aiken, "Family Intervention."

Selected Bibliography

Barston, Suzanne. *Bottled Up: How the Way We Feed Babies Has Come to Define Motherhood, and Why It Shouldn't.* Berkeley: University of California Press, 2012.

Blau, David M., *Unintended Consequences of Child Care Regulations.* Chapel Hill: University of North Carolina, 2006.

Braithwaite, John, and Valerie Braithwaite. "The Politics of Legalism: Rules versus Standards in Nursing Home Regulation." *Social & Legal Studies* 4 (1995): 307–41.

Child Care Aware of America. *Parents and the High Cost of Child Care.* Arlington, VA: Child Care Aware of America, 2014.

Colen, Cynthia G., and David M. Ramey. "Is Breast Truly Best? Estimating the Effects of Breastfeeding on Long-Term Child Health and Well-being in the United States Using Sibling Comparisons." *Social Science & Medicine* 109 (2014): 55–65.

Connelly, Rachel, and Jean Kimmel. *The Time Use of Mothers in the United States at the Beginning of the 21st Century.* Kalamazoo, MI: W.E. Upjohn Institute for Employment Research, 2010.

Darwin, Abigail. "Childhood Obesity: Is It Abuse?" *Children's Voice* 17 (2008): 24–27.

Fuller, Caitlin, and Diane L. Redleaf. *When Can Parents Let Children Be Alone? Child Neglect Policy and Recommendations in the Age of Free Range and Helicopter Parenting.* Chicago: Family Defense Center, 2015.

Garrahan, Shauneen M., and Andrew W. Eichner. "Tipping the Scale: A Place for Childhood Obesity in the Evolving Legal Framework of Child Abuse and Neglect." *Yale Journal of Health Policy, Law, and Ethics* 12 (2012): 336–70.

Gill, Tim. *No Fear: Growing Up in a Risk-Averse Society.* London: Calouste Gulbenkian Foundation, 2007.

Guggenheim, Martin. *What's Wrong with Children's Rights.* Cambridge, MA: Harvard University Press, 2005.

Harsanyi, David. *Nanny State: How Food Fascists, Teetotaling Do-Gooders, Priggish Moralists, and Other Boneheaded Bureaucrats Are Turning America into a Nation of Children.* New York: Broadway Books, 2007.

Heeb, Randal, and M. Rebecca Kilburn. *The Effects of State Regulation on Childcare Prices and Choices.* Rand Corporation, 2004.

Hills, Simon. *Strictly No! How We're Being Overrun by the Nanny State.* Edinburgh: Mainstream Publishing, 2006.

Howard, Philip K. *Life without Lawyers: Restoring Responsibility in America.* New York: W. W. Norton & Company, 2012.

———. *Rule of Nobody: Saving America from Dead Laws and Broken Government.* New York: W. W. Norton & Company, 2015.

Huntington, Robert. *The Nanny State.* Hereford, UK: Artnik, 2004.

Kearney, Melissa S., and Lesley J. Turner. *Giving Secondary Earners a Tax Break: A Proposal to Help Low- and Middle-Income Families.* Washington, DC: The Hamilton Project, Brookings Institution, 2013.

Kent, George. "WIC's Promotion of Infant Formula in the United States." *International Breastfeeding Journal* 1 (2006).

Lanza, Mike. *Playborhood: Turn Your Neighborhood into a Place for Play.* Menlo Park, CA: Free Play Press, 2012.

Louv, Richard. *Last Child in the Woods: Saving Our Children from Nature-Deficit Disorder.* Chapel Hill, NC: Algonquin Books, 2005.

Lythcott-Haims, Julie. *How to Raise an Adult: Break Free of the Overparenting Trap and Prepare Your Kid for Success.* New York: Henry Holt and Company, 2015.

Mack, Dana. *The Assault on Parenthood: How Our Culture Undermines the Family.* New York: Encounter Books, 1997.

Meltzer, Judith, Rachel Molly Joseph, and Andy Shookhoff, eds. *For the Welfare of Children: Lessons Learned from Class Action Litigation.* Washington, DC: Center for the Study of Social Policy, 2012.

Meyers, John E. B. "A Short History of Child Protection in America." *Family Law Quarterly* 42 (2008): 449–63.

Mitgang, Melissa. "Childhood Obesity and State Intervention: An Examination of the Health Risks of Pediatric Obesity and When They Justify State Involvement." *Columbia Journal of Law and Social Problems* 44 (2011): 553–87.

Murray, Charles. *In Pursuit of Happiness and Good Government.* Indianapolis, IN: Liberty Fund Inc., 2013.

National Institute of Child Health and Human Development. *The NICHD Study of Early Child Care and Youth Development.* U.S. Department of Health and Human Services, National Institutes of Health, 2006.

Phillips, Deborah, and Edward Zigler. "The Checkered History of Federal Child Care Regulation." *Review of Research in Education* 14 (1987): 3–41.

Pimentel, David. "Criminal Child Neglect and the 'Free Range Kid': Is

Overprotective Parenting the New Standard of Care?" *Utah Law Review* 947 (2012): 1–59.

Putnam, Robert D. *Bowling Alone: The Collapse and Revival of American Community*. New York: Simon & Schuster, 2000.

Rodin, Judith. *The Resilience Dividend: Being Strong in a World Where Things Go Wrong*. New York: Public Affairs, 2014.

Schene, Patricia A. "Past, Present, and Future Roles of Child Protective Services." *The Future of Children* 8 (1998): 23–38.

Schwartz, Barry, and Kenneth Sharpe. *Practical Wisdom: The Right Way to Do the Right Thing*. New York: Riverhead Books, 2010.

Silverglate, Harvey. *Three Felonies a Day: How the Feds Target the Innocent*. New York: Encounter Books, 2009.

Skenazy, Lenore. *Free-Range Kids: How to Raise Safe, Self-Reliant Children (Without Going Nuts with Worry)*. San Francisco: Jossey-Bass, 2009.

Tuerkheimer, Deborah. *Flawed Convictions: "Shaken Baby Syndrome" and the Inertia of Injustice*. New York: Oxford University Press, 2014. Kindle edition.

Wolf, Joan B. *Is Breast Best? Taking On the Breastfeeding Experts and the New High Stakes of Motherhood*. New York: New York University Press, 2011.

Index

AAP. *See* American Academy of Pediatrics
abandonment charges, 33–34
Abdallah, Faten, 13
abduction cases, 37, 209
Abt Associates, 142
abuse. *See* child abuse
ACA. *See* Affordable Care Act
Acker, Caroline, 224
Act 153 (background checks, Pennsylvania), 224
Adams, Alina, 48
Adoption and Safe Families Act (ASFA), 199
adventure playgrounds, 160–61, 172
advocacy groups: and breastfeeding, 88; Empower Kids Maryland, 39–40; Family Defense Center (Illinois), 39–40, 206; Human Rights Watch, 222; Reforming Sex Offender Laws, Inc. (RSOL), 221
Affordable Care Act (ACA; Patient Protection and Affordable Care Act), 72, 73–74
African Americans: breastfeeding rates among, 75; obesity among, 76
Agriculture, U.S. Department of. *See* U.S. Department of Agriculture
Aiken, Nickie, 230
allegations/accusations, false, 46, 206, 207, 209, 224, 225
Allen, David B., 187

All Joy and No Fun (Senior), 12
American Academy of Pediatrics (AAP), 187, 210; and blankets in cribs, 102; BMI testing and, 138; breastfeeding recommendations of, 68–69; swaddling recommendations of, 2–3
AmeriCorps, 169
Anderson, Les and Amanda, 219–20, 222
Anderson, Zachary, 219–20, 222
Andis, Cory, 189–90
Ani, Jennifer, 199–200, 207–8
Antonia, KJ, 193
anxiety, sources of parental, 12
Appleton, Josie, 228
arbitrary laws/guidelines, 48
Arizona, daycare rules in, 104
Arons, Stephen, 58
arrests: for abandonment, 33–34; case examples, 33–42; and costs of fighting charges, 34; for endangerment (*see* endangerment charges); and inability to fight charges, 40; and judicial findings, 38–39; and legislation, proposed revisions to, 55–56; for neglect (*see* neglect); and unsupervised children (*see* unsupervised children); wrongful, 33–34
ASFA (Adoption and Safe Families Act), 199
Assault on Parenthood, The (Mack), 8, 58, 194

Association for the Study of Play, 166
Association of Teachers and Lecturers (UK), 170
Australia, regulations for nursing homes in, 117–18
authority, parental. *See* parental discretion/authority

Baby-Friendly Hospital Initiative (BFHI), 66–68, 81
baby seat recall, 152–54
babysitting laws, 40, 42, 94
background checks: for childcare workers, 114; and Pennsylvania Act 153, 224; usefulness of, 225
balanced diet, 15–16
Balko, Radley, 43–44
bans: of Buckyballs, 155–56; children's views of, 149; of flame-resistant clothing, 154; of formula (*see* formula, infant); of games, 166–67; of games in United Kingdom, 170–71; of homemade lunches, 132; of large sodas, 62; parents' demand for, 158; of playground rules in New Zealand, 171–72; of swaddling, 2–3, 97–102; of tobogganing, 158–65; of yo-yo water balls, 156–57, 170
Barber, Diane, 109
Barston, Suzanne, 61, 73–74, 87, 89
Bartholet, Elizabeth, 199
Bartlett, Cheryl, 71
battery charges, 166
behavior: of college students, 56–57; criminalization of, 43–44; criminalizing parents for legal, 199–200; and normality, 37; toward obese children, 192
Betru, Yodit, 181, 182–83, 198
BFHI (Baby-Friendly Hospital Initiative), 66–68
Billis, Stacie, 90
bill of rights for kids and parents, 54–55
Binge Eating Disorder Association, 138

Binks, Martin, 186, 213
Bishopp, Natasha, 230–31
Blagojevich, Rod, 156–57
Blair, Tony, 218, 227, 228
blankets in cribs, 101–2
Blau, David, 114
blogs: *CafeMom*, 166; *Cyclelicious*, 35; *Fearless Formula Feeder*, 61, 89; *Free-Range Kids*, 31; *Simple Justice*, 11
Bloomberg, Michael, 62
BMI. *See* body mass index
Boaz, David, 22
body image, 138–39
body mass index (BMI), 136, 138, 139, 140–41, 215
body shaming, 136–37
Bosman, Julie, 219–20
Bottled Up (Barston), 61
bottle feeding, formula as controlled substance, 62
Brabec, Marek, 215
Bradley, Stormy, 181–82
Braithwaite, John and Valerie, 118
breastfeeding: advocacy organizations, 64–65; barriers to, 88; Bloomberg's mandate on, 62; Breastfeeding Promotion Act, 73–74; breast-or-else dogma, 68, 76–77, 89–90; breast pumping, 72–73, 86–90; Call to Action to Support Breastfeeding, 76; choosing not to breastfeed, 77–79; and decision-making, 64, 79, 80, 82–83, 85, 90; employer mandates about, 12; federal laws and programs, 70–77; generational attitudes toward, 84–85; global initiatives and programs, 66–68; inability to breastfeed, 77–79; *It's Only Natural*, 75; marketing influence on, 65; mastectomy patients and, 76–77; medical associations on, 69–70; myths about, 75; as normal and correct, 66, 69; Michelle Obama on, 75–76; parental discretion for,

77–78; promotion of, 61; pushing on mothers, effects of, 87–88; science of, 79–86; state laws and programs, 68–70; working mothers and, 78–79. *See also* formula, infant

Breastfeeding Promotion Act, 73–74

Brierley, Kristen E., 188–89

Bright, Sandy, 105

Brittain, Amy, 114

Brooks, Alia, 72

Brown, Ann, 153, 154, 155

Buckyballs, 155–56

Buhl, William, 220

Bumbo "Baby Sitter" seat recall, 152–54

Burrows, Sara, 104–5

buses, children riding alone on, 4, 41–42

Cacdac, Laura, 136–37

CafeMom (blog), 166

California: foster-care error rates in, 198; juvenile dependency system in, 208–9; Natomas Elementary School (Sacramento), 168

Call to Action to Support Breastfeeding, 76

Campbell, Aileen, 227

cancer, breastfeeding and, 78–79

Caplan, Art, 214

CAPTA (Child Abuse Prevention and Treatment Act), 194

Captain Mommies and Daddies, 3, 8, 10, 15, 218, 232; of 1970s and '80s, 58; Jennifer Ani, 207–8; Suzanne Barston, 61, 62, 73–74, 87, 89; Stacie Billis, 90; Tammy Cooper, 33–34; on government intervention, 85; Mike Lanza, 19, 168–69, 177–78; Heather Parker, 4, 133–34; Lori Levar Pierce, 35–36; rejection of government parenting standards by, 25; Kari Anne Roy, 45–47, 52–53, 54; Lenore Skenazy, 10, 28–33, 41–42, 54–55; Irene

Trello family, 144–45; Emily Wax-Thibodeaux, 77–78; Laura and Gwendolyn Williams, 137; Craig Zucker, 155–56

Caring for Our Children (HHS), 97, 98–99

Carmona, Elso, 132

Carrel, Aaron L., 187

cars: infant seats in, 152–53; unattended children in, 4, 11, 40, 47–50, 55

"Case Against Breast-Feeding, The" (Rosin), 86

CBS News, 167–68

CDC. *See* Centers for Disease Control

Centers for Disease Control (CDC), 143

Cenziper, Debbie, 210

CFSA (Child and Family Services Agency), 212–13

character traits, for success, 51–52

charges. *See* abandonment charges; arrests; endangerment charges; neglect

Chehab, Lynn Gettleman, 140

child abuse: Child Abuse Prevention and Treatment Act (CAPTA), 194; convictions for, overturned, 210; defining, 193, 196–98; false allegations for, 206; Graham case, 196–97; medical presumptions of, 210; parent-inflicted injuries, 203; Sandusky case, 223–24; swaddling as, 102. *See also* mandated reporters; neglect

child-abuse laws, 195

Child Abuse Prevention and Treatment Act (CAPTA), 194

Child and Family Services Agency (CFSA), 212–13

child care: affordable, 107–8; Conference on the Care of Dependent Children, 91–92; cost of, 92–93, 109–15; cost of, compared to college tuition, 93, 94, 106–7, 108–9;

as national crisis, 93; reasonable
options for, 115–16; siblings as
babysitters, 40, 42, 94; supply and
demand for, 93–94, 111–12. *See also*
daycare centers
Child Care Aware of America, 91, 92;
*Parents and the High Cost of Child
Care*, 107–8
child-dependency system, 204
child development, 175–77
child protective services (CPS):
Child and Family Services
Agency (Washington, DC),
212–13; consequences of reporters calling, 46–47; Department
of Children & Family Services
(Chicago), 202; fundamental
dilemma of child welfare, 182–83;
grounds for investigation by, 55;
"hard lemonade" case (Michigan), 44–45, 49–50; investigations by, 34; parents as mandated
reporters for, 5; Roy case, 46–47;
taking custody of children for
obesity by (*see* obesity, in children); unsubstantiated neglect
and, 38; validity of reports to, 207;
wasting resources of, 45; Wayne
County Child Protective Services, 3; workers for, 194, 199–200,
201, 202–3, 209, 211–12. *See also*
child-welfare systems
childrearing standards. *See* government intervention; standards
Children and Young People (Scotland) Act, 226
Child Welfare League of America,
190
child-welfare systems, 194–95,
200–201; curing obesity by using,
216; failures of, 209; Georgia,
197; interventions by, 202; lack
of transparency of, 204–5; Massachusetts, 197; international (*see*
international welfare systems);
predatory nature of, 22; Scottish,

226–27. *See also* child protective
services
child-welfare workers, 194, 199–200,
201, 202–3, 209, 211–12
Chobani, 131
Citizens Review Panel report,
212–13
Cohn, Jonathan, 109, 113
Colen, Cynthia G., 80
college students, 56–57
college tuition, compared to child-
care costs, 93, 94, 106–7, 108
Colorado: Aurora school lunch, 132;
rules for licensed daycare facilities in, 106–7
Common Good, 9
common sense, 45, 49, 50, 51, 55, 112,
139, 158
communal authority, 8
community, sense of, 54
Conference on the Care of Dependent Children (1909), 91–92
Constitution, U.S.: Fourteenth
Amendment, 7
Consumer Product Safety Commission (CPSC): "Handbook
for Public Playground Safety,"
161–62; home playground equipment safety standards of, 162;
and New Jersey playgrounds,
164; overprotection by, 156–57;
past leaders of, 155; and publicly
funded playgrounds, 161; purpose
of, 20, 150; and recalls, 5, 6, 147,
149, 151–57; warning labels of,
165; warnings of potential risks
by, 217
Cooper, Tammy, 33–34
Corrigan, Christina Ann, 189
court cases. *See* laws/legislation;
litigation
CPS. *See* child protective services
CPSC. *See* Consumer Product Safety
Commission
creativity, 50–51, 175–76
Creativity (Petit), 50

criminalizing parents, 3–4, 6, 10, 12;
    for legal behavior, 200; society's
    role in, 30; for teaching responsi-
    bility, 42–45; for using discretion,
    41–42
criminalizing play, 165–72
crisis response: by neighbors, 54;
    USDA food purchases as, 130
cronyism, political, 131
culture change, affecting law, 54–59
Cumberland County, Tennessee, 4
Cushing, Tim, 169, 170, 178
custody cases, 4; arrest of parents in,
    32–33; effects on children, 212,
    213; effects on families, 208–9;
    for leaving children alone, 4; and
    obesity (*see* obesity, in children);
    outdated laws and, 37; siblings as
    babysitters and, 43
Cutchlow, Tracy, 47
Cyclelicious (blog), 35

daddies. *See* Captain Mommies and
    Daddies
dairy industry, 130–31
danger: actual versus possible, 31;
    assessing for, 148; improper use
    of products and, 152; meaningful,
    153; potential, 95, 101, 155–56
Darwin, Abigail, 190
data collection: flawed, 140–41; and
    health screenings in schools, 136,
    139
Davies, Anthony, 108
daycare centers: costs of complying
    with regulations for, 110–11; costs
    of quality, 92–93, 94, 105; federally
    run, 103–4; and food rules, 95–96;
    fraud protection for consumers
    of, 110; funding for, 111; judgment,
    use of, by, 116; optimal age for
    babies to join, 98–99; overregula-
    tion of, 94–109; *Parents and the
    High Cost of Child Care*, 107–8;
    quality of care in, 14; quality
    standards of, 110; rule writers for,
    14; sleeping positions for infants

in, 97; and staffing issues, 112–13;
    swaddling rules in, 2–3, 97–102.
    See also child care
daycare workers: certification of,
    13; frustrations of, 107; required
    training for, 111; on rules and
    regulations, 104–5; standards set
    by, 13
death: due to failure to act, 194;
    imminent, 188; likelihood of, 154;
    obesity-related, 214; prevent-
    able, 62; product-related, 150–51,
    153–54; SIDS-related, 2, 98–102;
    weight-loss-related, 138
decisions: about breastfeeding, 79, 80;
    government control of, 96; about
    paying for child care, 109–10;
    about staying home with kids,
    105; about swaddling, 101
Department of Child Services. *See*
    child protective services
Department of Health (Massachu-
    setts), 138–39
Department of Health and Human
    Services. *See* U.S. Department of
    Health and Human Services
Department of Health and Safety,
    rules for daycare centers of, 103
Department of Human Services
    (Colorado), 106
DGA (Dietary Guidelines for
    Americans), 124–25
Dierdorff, Julie, 137, 141
Dietary Guidelines for Americans
    (DGA), 124–25
diet/nutrition: dairy products, 130–31;
    and daycare centers, 95–96,
    103–4, 105; Dietary Guidelines
    for Americans, 124–25; free-
    food programs, 129–31; Greek-
    style yogurt, 131; home-packed
    lunches, 4, 131–34; improving, 146;
    malnutrition prevention, 70; in
    nanny-state, 122; National School
    Lunch Program, 16; nut allergies,
    170; Michelle Obama on, 75–76;
    parents versus school lunch,

131–35; restricted-calorie menus, 126; restricted diets, 122; school lunches, one-type-fits-all, 123–28; school lunches, palatability of, 127–28; school lunch menus, 15–16, 122; school mandates, 121; School Nutrition Association, 127; Supplemental Nutrition Assistance Program, 128; USDA study of school meals, 142. *See also* breastfeeding; obesity, in children

Dimyan-Ehrenfeld, Jane, 93
discipline standards, 197
discretion, parental. *See* parental discretion/authority
disease transmission, vaccination compliance and, 23–24
dodgeball, 166–67
domestic violence, 197–98
Dougherty, Michael Brendan, 53
drownings, 154
Duckworth, Angela, 29–30
Dvorak, Petula, 48–49
Dweck, Carol, 30

Early Childhood Environment Rating Scale (ECERS), 107
eating disorders, 138
Eating Disorders Coalition, 138
ECERS (Early Childhood Environment Rating Scale), 107
Economist, The, 229
education: physical, 143–44; sex education in public schools, 140; standards for child-care providers, 112; and USDA nutrition program, 128
Education, U.S. Department of, 143
Eichner, Andrew W., 187, 195
Eisenstein, Charles, 36–37
elder care, 117, 118–19
elementary schools: recess policies in, 166–69; and suspensions for imaginative play, 165–66
Ellmers, Renee, 134
emotional well-being, 56–57, 213

employers: and employee absenteeism, 74; and lactating employees, requirements for, 73; tax incentives for, 73
Empower Kids Maryland, 39–40
endangerment charges: case examples, 34; Connecticut case, 42; Cooper case, 33–34; normal application of, 37; Pierce case, 35–36; playground case (Pittsburgh), 36; Williamson case (Ohio), 43
England. *See* United Kingdom
England, Paula, 105
Evans, Alex, 165

failure, teaching children about, 30
Fallis, David, 114
Fallon, Sally, 89–90
false allegations, 46, 206, 207, 209, 224, 225
families: attitudes toward, 198; damage to, 206–7, 211–12; defining, 202; intrusion into, 227–28; preservation of, 182–83; prioritization of, 229–30; violence in, 182–83
"Families in Crisis" (San Diego, California), 204
Family Defense Center (Illinois), 39–40, 41, 206
Family Law Act, 194
family leave policies, 89
Family Recovery Programme (UK), 230–32
Farley, Thomas, 62
Fearless Formula Feeder (blog), 61, 89
federal programs, breastfeeding, 70–77
first grade, standards of readiness for, 49
Fisher, Anthony L., 118–19
Fitnessgrams, 137–38
flame-resistant clothing, 154
Flawed Convictions (Tuerkheimer), 210
flexible models, nursing homes and daycare, 119
folkways, 84

folk wisdom, 47
food. *See* diet/nutrition
formula, infant: bans on free samples
    of, 64–65, 68–70; as controlled
    substance, 62; demonization of,
    66; government programs for
    providing, 71; industry distribu-
    tion of, 62–63; Latch On NYC
    initiative, 62, 63–64; medical
    associations on, 69–70; and Na-
    tional Alliance for Breastfeeding
    Advocacy, 64–65; recipes for, 90;
    supplemental, 65, 67; WIC pro-
    gram and, 70–71. *See also* breast-
    feeding
Fost, Norman, 187
foster-care system: assumptions
    about placements, 213; effects on
    children of, 198, 213; error rates,
    198; exploitation of, 216; "fixing,"
    199; for obese children, 184, 189,
    191, 214; risks and problems of,
    58, 198
Fourteenth Amendment, U.S. Con-
    stitution, 7
freedom: of choice, 13; lack of, 50–54
freedom for children, developmental
    effects of, 30
Freeman, Naomi, 222
free play, 19, 121, 142, 147, 162, 168–69
Free-Range Kids (blog), 31
Friedersdorf, Colin, 37
Friedman, Michael, 139
Frost, Joe, 162–63
fun. *See* games; physical activity; play;
    playgrounds/parks; toys
funding, for child-care providers, 111
Furedi, Frank, 19, 57–58, 148, 227

Gainey, Nicole, 3–4, 10, 33
Gall, Mary Sheila, 155
games: banning or outlawing, 6, 20,
    147, 149, 158, 170; chase-type, 167;
    criminalizing, 165–72; dodgeball,
    166; government oversight of, 18;
    imaginative, 165; school suspen-
    sions for playing, 175. *See also* play

Garrahan, Shauneen M., 187, 195
Germany, requirements for school
    principals in, 117
Gilbert, Daniel, 20–21
Gill, Tim, 18–19, 148–49, 228–29
global initiatives, breastfeeding,
    66–68
Goldsmith, Meryl, 211
Goldsmith, Susan, 211
Gordon, Linda, 183, 196, 202
Government Accountability Office,
    127
government intervention: and breast-
    feeding (*see* breastfeeding); and
    child abuse, 195–96; and child-
    rearing standards, 7–8, 12–13;
    consequences to adults of, 28–29;
    and custody loss (*see* obesity, in
    children); emotional effects of,
    29; federal lunch programs as, 16;
    federal rules for daycare centers
    as, 103–4; health screenings in
    schools as, 135–42; and home-
    packed lunches, 133; and infant
    formula (*see* formula, infant); and
    obesity (*see* obesity, in children);
    overzealous, 134–35; and preferen-
    tial treatment, 71; problems aris-
    ing from, 8–9; rules-based, 117; in
    Scotland, 227; state control over,
    7; support for, 140; and teaching
    self-reliance and -control, 51–52;
    in United Kingdom, 226–32;
    unrealistic mandates and, 84;
    unsympathetic, 191; and vaccina-
    tions, 24
government mandates: complexity
    of, 9; and immunization, 23–25;
    obstructive, 15; overreactions and,
    11–13, 29, 158, 178; for summer
    camps, 159; and swaddling, 1–2.
    See also regulation; rules
Graham, Toya, 196–97
Gray, Jerri, 183, 211–12
Great Britain. *See* United Kingdom
Greek-style yogurt, 131
Greenfield, Scott, 11

Grey, Peter, 50–51, 173
grit (perseverance), 51–52
growth mindset, 29–30
Guggenheim, Martin, 203

Haidt, Jonathan, 56–57
Hall, Harriet, 78
Hamre, Bridget K., 112
"Handbook for Public Playground Safety," 161–62
"hard lemonade" case (Michigan), 44–45, 49–50
Harmon, Melinda, 14
Harrell, Debra, 3–4, 32, 52
Harsanyi, David, 153, 164
Harvard Educations Letter, 51–52
Harvard University School of Public Health, 143
Head Start, 92; performance standards of, 111–12
Health and Human Services, U.S. Department of (HHS), 74–75, 97, 98–99, 107–8
Health and Safety Executive (UK), 228–29
health and wellness: body mass index, 141; breastfeeding and, 76, 80; government-defined, 122–23; improving, 146; Kennedy fitness programs for, 16–18; potential concerns about, 218; school lunch standards and, 124; screening for obesity, 200–201; standards of, 13. *See also* diet/nutrition; physical activity; weight assessment
health insurance, Patient Protection and Affordable Care Act, 72, 73
health screening, in schools, 135–42
healthy communities, nanny state versus, 45
Healthy Home Economist, The (website), 90
Healthy Hunger-Free Kids Act, 122, 141
Healthy People 2020 Objectives for Maternal, Infant, and Child Health, 74

Heeb, Randal, 116
helicopter (overprotective) parents, 1, 28, 31, 37–38, 56, 154
herd immunity, 23–25
HHS. *See* U.S. Department of Health and Human Services
Hills, Simon, 228
Hodge, Margaret, 227
home-alone children, 48
homeschooling, 58–59
Hopkins, Carol Lamb, 198, 200–201, 208–9
hospitals: Baby-Friendly certification for, 66, 67; distribution of infant formula by, 62–63
Hotz, V. Joseph, 110, 113–14, 115
Howard, Philip K., 9, 13, 96, 115–17, 154, 159, 164, 175, 218–19
How Children Succeed (Tough), 29, 51
Howe, Jim, 4
HSE (Health and Safety Executive; UK), 228–29
Hudak, Scott, 127
Hudson, Janice, 168
Huffington Post, 54, 90, 101, 102
Human Rights Watch, 222
Huntington, Robert, 227
hygiene: daycare rules for, 102–3; definitions of, 12

Illinois: Chicago school lunch, 132; Evanston Township High School, 140; Family Defense Center, 39–40, 41; Hawthorne Elementary School (Elmhurst), 137
imaginative play, 165–72
imminent harm, 181, 185, 187, 188, 192, 194, 214
immunization, 23–25
inadequate supervision. *See* unsupervised children
independent children, 42; inability to raise, 53; as new battleground, 59; opposition to creating, 53; play used to develop, 175–78; and stan-

dards of independence, 48–49;
   trying to raise, 30, 38
infants: sleeping positions for, 97;
   swaddling of, 2–3, 97–102
Infant/Toddlers Environment
   Rating Scale (ITERS), 107
Ingraham, Christopher, 108–9
injuries: charges of battery for, 166;
   inflicted by parents, 203; near,
   170; out-of-proportion risk of,
   151; playground, 163–64; preventable, 210; product-related, 150–51,
   156, 158; recalls without, 5; risk of,
   34, 37, 42; severity of, 157; threat of
   immediate, 52; unreasonable risk
   of, 150, 154
Institute of Medicine, 145
intellectual engagement, 57
international welfare systems: in
   Australia, 117–18; in Germany,
   117; in New Zealand, 98, 171–72;
   in Scotland, 219, 226–27, 229; in
   United Kingdom (see United
   Kingdom)
ITERS (Infant/Toddlers Environment Rating Scale), 107
It's Only Natural, 75

justice system: overreaction by
   authorities in, 11; problems of, 211
juvenile dependency system (California), 204, 208–9
juvenile sex offenders, 219–23

Kaboom!, 179
Karp, Harvey, 2, 98
Kennedy, John F.: fitness focus of,
   16–18; on freedom and public
   good, 24–25
Kieff, Judith, 173
Kilburn, M. Rebecca, 110, 113–14,
   115–16
Kimmel, Jimmy, 23–25
"KinderLARDen Cop" (Ralston),
   191
King, Steve, 134

Kissell, Larry, 134
Kohl, Harold, III, 145–46
Komlos, John, 215
Kristof, Nicholas, 72

lactation consultants, 72, 73
Lamback, Lesa, 32
Lanza, Mike, 19, 168–169, 177–78
Last, Jonathan, 108
Last Child in the Woods (Louv),
   175–76
Latch On NYC, 62, 63
laws/legislation: Adoption and
   Safe Families Act (ASFA), 199;
   Affordable Care Act, 72, 73–74;
   arbitrary application of, 195; badly
   written, 41; bill of rights for kids
   and parents, Skenazy's, 54–55;
   Breastfeeding Promotion Act,
   73–74; Call to Action to Sup-
   port Breastfeeding, 76; chang-
   ing culture by changing, 54–59;
   child-abuse, 195; Child Abuse
   Prevention and Treatment Act
   (CAPTA), 194; child-protection,
   201; Children and Young People
   (Scotland) Act, 226; Family Law
   Act, 194; Healthy Hunger-Free
   Kids Act, 122, 141; and mandated reporter definitions, 223;
   National School Lunch Program,
   122; No Child Left Behind Act,
   145; No Hungry Kids Act, 134;
   Reforming Sex Offender Laws,
   Inc. (RSOL), 221, 223; reforms
   in, 56–58; role of modern, 9; sex-
   offender, 224–25; Sex Offender
   Registration Act (New York),
   222; and student weight and
   height data, collecting, 15; and
   vaccinations (California), 24.
   See also litigation
Lawson, April L., 34–35
Leave It to Beaver (television), 48
legal issues. See laws/legislation;
   litigation

Lemmon, Gayle Tzemach, 64
Let's Move campaign, 122
Levenson, Jill, 220–21
Levin, Susan, 130–31
life skills, 56, 57
Lipin, Lisa, 158
litigation: American culture of,
    18–19; and child custody (*see*
    custody cases); class-action, 205;
    fear of, 19, 147, 166, 178; *Meyer*
    v. Nebraska, 7; by parents, 204;
    and parents of obese children,
    193; and playground injuries,
    162–63; risk of, 164. *See also*
    laws/legislation
Little Village Academy (Chicago),
    132
Long Island Rail Road (LIRR) inci-
    dent, 30–31
Louv, Richard, 175–76, 178–79
Ludwig, David, 185–87, 214
Lukianoff, Greg, 56–57
lunch menus. *See* diet/nutrition
Lythcott-Haims, Julie, 56, 57

MacDonald, Kathleen, 138
Mack, Dana, 8, 58, 194, 202, 224–25
Madigan, Mary Louise, 184
Madsen, Kristine, 141
Majumder, Maimuna, 23–24
Maloney, Carolyn, 73
mandated reporters: after back-
    ground checks, 224; definitions
    of, 223; everyone as, 223–25; par-
    ents as, 5; rules for, 225. *See also*
    child-welfare workers
mandates. *See* government mandates
Manger, Itsik, 26–27
Manning, April, 103–4
Marks, Laura, 142
Maryland: criminalizing parents in,
    41–42; Empower Kids Maryland,
    39–40; interpretation of child-
    related laws of, 40
Masoner, Richard, 35
Massachusetts: acceptable parental

discipline standards in, 197; BMI
    testing in, 138–39; Boston child-
    welfare study, 196; daycare rules
    for hygiene in, 102–3; and tooth-
    brushing requirement in daycare,
    108; and WIC program, 71
Maternity Care Coalition, 65
McLachlan, Bruce, 172
media attention: kidnap/murder
    cases and, 37; problems of, 41
Meitiv, Danielle and Alexander, 3,
    37–40, 50–51
Meyer v. Nebraska, 7
Michigan: daycare centers, rules for,
    104; Zeeland Elementary School
    (Grand Rapids), 167
mission, shared, 53
Missouri, Kirksville Primary School
    lunch, 132
Mitgang, Melissa, 188
mommies. *See* Captain Mommies
    and Daddies
MomsRising, 93
Moore, Robert, 225
morbid obesity. *See* obesity,
    in children
Moyer, Melinda Wenner, 98
murder cases, sensationalized, 37
Murtagh, Lindsey, 185–87

named-person concept, 226, 227, 229
nanny state: and care, standards of,
    148; challenging, 39; control issues
    of, 115–20; criticism of interven-
    tions by, 43–44; effects of threats
    from, 12; elements of, 6; healthy
    communities versus, 45–47; inva-
    sion of, 10; leaving children in
    cars and, 47–50; menu flexibility
    in, 16; one-size-fits-all solutions
    by, 48; overreactions of, 29; pater-
    nalism of, 85–86; reach of, 219;
    risk mitigation by, 13; in schools,
    121; in United Kingdom, 227–28
Nanny State (Harsanyi), 153, 164
Nanny State, The (Huntington), 227

National Alliance for Breastfeeding
  Advocacy, 64–65
National Longitudinal Survey of
  Youth (NLSY), 80
National PTA, 145
National Resource Council (NRC),
  and swaddling rules, 98–100,
  101–2
National School Lunch Program,
  16, 122
Navarette, Reuben, Jr., 135, 139
neglect: accusations of, on particular
  groups, 195; charges of, normal
  application of, 37; charges of,
  unsubstantiated, 38–39; and commonsense laws, 55; definitions of,
  206; Gainey's charges of, 3–4, 10,
  33; Lawson case, 34–35; obesity as,
  22, 189–90. *See also* child abuse;
  mandated reporters
neighbors, as strangers and reporters,
  53–54
New York: and coat hooks in daycare
  centers, 104; formula feeding in,
  62; Greek-style yogurt lobby,
  131; police incident in, 5; Sex
  Offender Registration Act, 222
New York Daily News, 158–59
New Zealand: playground rules, ban
  on, in university study, 171–72;
  SIDS study, 98
Nielsen, Debera, 104
NLSY (National Longitudinal
  Survey of Youth), 80
Nobody's Children (Bartholet), 199
No Child Left Behind Act, 145
No Fear (Gill), 18–19, 148–49, 228
No Hungry Kids Act, 134
Nord, Nancy, 154, 155–56
North Carolina, West Hoke school
  lunch case, 133
no-touch policies, 168
Nourishing Traditions (Fallon), 89–90
Novey, Madeline, 106
NPR (National Public Radio), 49–50,
  143, 144

NRC. *See* National Resource Council
nursing homes, 117–19
nut allergies, 170
nutrition. *See* diet/nutrition
Nutrition Group, 127–28

Obama, Barack, 24, 91, 94, 115
Obama, Michelle, 75–76, 103, 122, 123,
  131, 141
Obamacare. *See* Affordable Care Act
obesity, in children, 15–16, 184; alternative treatments for, 185–86;
  Andis case, 189–90; body mass
  index (BMI) and, 136; breastfeeding as prevention, 71, 76, 83;
  changes in attitudes about, 201;
  Cleveland case, 183–84; Corrigan
  case, 189; criminalization of, 181;
  custody loss and, 183, 189–94;
  definition of, 214–15; D.K. case,
  190–91; foster-care system and,
  184, 189, 191, 214; and fundamental
  dilemma of child welfare, 182–83;
  G.C. case, 190; government logic
  and, 124–25; Jerri Gray case, 183;
  imminent health-risk definition
  of, 185, 192; and judicial reforms,
  205–11; legal literature on removal
  of children, 182; loss of custody
  due to, 21–22; Adela Martinez
  case, 184; milk and, 130–31; overregulation of remedies for, 121;
  parents' behavior toward obese
  children, 192; parents' health
  and, 188–89; as public-health
  issue, 22–23; removing children
  from home and, 181–82, 185–87,
  188, 193, 213–16; screening for,
  200–201; SNAP and, 128; "State
  Intervention in Life-Threatening
  Childhood Obesity," 185; Stop
  Childhood Obesity campaign,
  181–82; as symptom, 200; as systemic problem, 202; unreturned
  children, 191–92. *See also* diet/
  nutrition

obstructive authority, 15
O'Dowd, Mary E., 68
offense taken/given, 164
Ohio, Harrell case, 43
Olson, Walter, 181, 209–10
O'Mara, Peggy, 62–63
Oregon, ban of formula samples, 64
Oster, Emily, 83
outdoor supervision, 148
overprotective (helicopter) parents, 1,
 27, 28, 31, 37–38, 56, 154
overreaction: by authorities in justice
 system, 11; effects of, 44; government mandates as, 12–13; to
 innocent situations, 31; of nanny
 state, 29
overweight kids. *See* diet/nutri-
 tion; obesity, in children; weight
 assessment
Oyfn Veg Shteyt a Boym (There Is a
 Tree That Stands; Manger), 26

pacifiers, WHO on use of, 67
Paranoid Parenting (Furedi), 148
parental discretion/authority: and
 breastfeeding (*see* breastfeeding);
 bureaucracy and, 49; daycare
 rules and, 14; erosion of, 135, 227;
 police citations and, 4; and school
 lunches, 4, 131–35; state intervention and, 6; and swaddling, 2–3,
 14, 97–102
parental-rights vigilantes, 32
parents: attacks on, 10; blaming, 199–
 200, 215; and childrearing standards, 9; criminalization of (*see*
 criminalizing parents); helicopter,
 1, 28, 31, 37–38, 154; as mandated
 reporters, 5; morbidly obese, 188–
 89; and police citations, 5; and
 politicization of parenting, 19;
 punishing, 27–28, 181; reconciling
 values and government by, 25; and
 standards for normal parenting,
 193; state rights to punish, 27–28;
 stressors and anxiety sources for,

12. *See also* Captain Mommies
 and Daddies
Parker, Heather, 4, 133–34
parks. *See* playgrounds/parks
paternalism, effect of, 86
Patient Protection and Affordable
 Care Act. *See* Affordable Care
 Act
PCRM (Physicians Committee for
 Responsible Medicine), 130–31
pedophiles, 220–21
Pennsylvania: Act 153 (background
 checks), 224; cost of child care in,
 108, 109; Department of Public
 Welfare regulation no. 3270.161,
 95–97; mandated reporter rules
 in, 5, 223; regulations on swaddling, 2
Perna, Christopher, 119
perseverance (grit), 51–52
Petit, Philippe, 50, 176
physical activity, 121, 125–26, 139,
 141–44, 167, 213
physical education, 143–44
Physicians Committee for Responsible Medicine (PCRM), 130–31
Pianta, Robert C., 112
Pierce, Lori Levar, 35–36
Pigur, Katja, 65
Plain Dealer, 184
play: benefits of, 52; criminalizing,
 168–69, 170; deficit of, 173–74;
 encouraging, 179; free, 19, 121, 142,
 147, 162, 168–69; government-
 supported programs for, 169;
 imaginative, 165–72; importance
 of, 175–76; improvement of, 177–
 78; for play's sake, 172–79. *See also*
 games; playgrounds/parks; toys
Playborhood (Lanza), 19, 168
playgrounds/parks: eliminating rules
 in, 171–72; equipment recalls and,
 5, 149, 152–57; fun versus safe,
 160–61; "Handbook for Public
 Playground Safety," 161; home
 playground equipment, 162; inno-

vative, 159–60; New Jersey playgrounds, 164; public recreational venues, 158–65; rules in, 218; safety of public equipment, 147–48; supervised children at, 169; unsupervised children at, 32–33, 36; warning signs at, 164

PlayWorks, 169, 170

policies: and contact sports during recess, 167–68; federal child-protection, 198; interpreting, 212; one-size-fits-all, 7–8; parental demands and, 169–70; public, accepting government, 135; and recess, 168; in Scotland, 219, 226–27, 229; and separating children from birth families, 203; zero-tolerance, 4, 165

policy makers. *See* rule writers/policy makers

political cultures, 59, 202

political lines, crossing, 39–40

practical wisdom, 49–50

Practical Wisdom (Schwartz and Sharpe), 8–9, 44–45

Pridgen, G.L., 133

private schools, 5

protection, of children: best practice, 57–58; critics of system of, 195; and guaranteeing safety, 171; need for, 32; overzealous, 148, 156–57; as purpose of child-welfare system, 203; and separation from families, 213

protective services. *See* child protective services

PTA, 145

public good, 12

public health: bureaucracy and, 88–89; obesity as issue of, 22–23; regulatory crusades in, 22; and vaccinations, 23–25

public policy. *See* policies

Puckett, Justin, 132

Quart, Alissa, 93

Raised on the Registry (Human Rights Watch), 222

Ralston, Elizabeth, 191

Ramey, David M., 80

Rand Corporation, 109–15

ratings, daycare center, 107

recalls: Bumbo "Baby Sitter" seat, 152–54; teething toy, 5–6; toys/games/playground equipment, 147, 149, 151–53, 156; without harm done, 152. *See also* Consumer Product Safety Commission

recess: accidents during, 167–68; banning of, 147; government-supported programs for, 169; lack of exercise during, 144; pairing instruction with, 173; regulation of, 121, 143. *See also* play; playgrounds/parks

recreational activities, rules against public, 158–65

Redleaf, Diane, 201–2, 207, 225

Reed, Tom, 166

Reforming Sex Offender Laws, Inc. (RSOL), 221

reforms: difficulty effecting, 27–28; government intervention in daycare, 116; lack of support for, 178–79; legal, 9, 55–58; obese children laws and, 205–11; regulatory, 119–20; and school lunch programs, 127; societal, 20–21

Regino, Anamarie, 184–85

regulation: and cost of child care, 109–15; and daycare centers, 94–109; government (*see* government mandates); and hazard prevention, 219; hyperregulation, 228; increased, effects of, 116; overregulation, 153; of playgrounds and equipment, 161–63; of public recreation, 158–65; speculative risk and, 154; and state child care, 114

relationships, teacher-child, 112

research: Baby-Friendly Hospital

Initiative (BFHI), 67, 81; on bedding-related factors and SIDS, 98; on Boston child welfare, 196; on breastfeeding and obesity, 83; on breastfeeding versus formula feeding, 79–80, 81–82; on child-care costs, 92–93, 109–10; on daycare regulations and quality, 116; flawed data collection and, 140–41; National Longitudinal Survey of Youth (NLSY), 80; on obese children, 215–16; on physical activity and grades, 143; on play for play's sake, 172–79; and playground rules in New Zealand, 171–72; on policing parents of obese children, 191; on pumped breast milk, 88; on relationship between kids and teachers, 112; on school meal nutrition, 142; and school meal programs, 127; on women leaving workforce, 105

Resilience Dividend, The (Rodin), 53–54

responsibility: adult sense of, 53; children's wish for, 50–51; teaching, 42–45

rights: bill of rights for kids and parents, 54–55; of children, 203; of parents, 7, 14, 39–40, 194, 203; protecting, 183; *Raised on the Registry* (Human Rights Watch), 222; state, over women's bodies, 64

risk: acceptable, 154; aversion to, 148–49, 150, 154, 178; of being overweight, 125–26; culture of, 83–85; imminent, 214; importance to kids of, 175; of infant formula, 62–64; of injury to children (*see* endangerment charges); mitigation of, by nanny state, 13; overstating, 156; safety trade-offs with, 159, 168; of SIDS in daycare centers, 98–102; unreasonable, 154; warning labels and, 165

Roberts, Dorothy, 199
Robert Wood Johnson Foundation, 143
Rodin, Judith, 53–54
Rofey, Dana, 215
Roosevelt, Theodore, 91–92
Rosin, Hanna, 18, 38–39, 86, 160–61
Ross, Lainie, 188
Rowe-Finkbeiner, Kristin, 93
Roy, Kari Anne, 45–47, 52–53, 54
RSOL (Reforming Sex Offender Laws, Inc.), 221
Rule of Nobody, The (Howard), 96, 117–18
rules: authority figures following, 45; babysitting, 42; in daycare facilities, 104, 106–7; daycare workers on, 104–5; and food, 95–96; government (*see* government mandates); and mandated reporting, 224–25; and public recreational activities, 158–65; and recess, 168; and school lunches, 103–4; and swaddling, 2–3, 97–102; systems of, 96. *See also* government mandates; policies; regulation; state laws and programs
rule writers/policy makers, 14, 96, 97, 153, 169–70
Russell, Lindsey, 126

safety: and certification, 13; changing notions of, 10–11; children's feelings of, 52; definitions of, 12; extreme measures for, 102–3; guaranteeing, 13, 171; lack of, 31; perfect, 150; and playground equipment, 147–48; and risk trade-offs, 159, 168
Sandalow, Judith, 213
Sandler, Jeffrey, 222
Sandusky, Jerry, 5, 223–24
SBS (shaken baby syndrome), 210–11
Schanler, Richard J., 81
Schmidt, Maribeth Roman, 223–24

Schneiders, Brittney, 166
Schofield, Grant, 172
School Nutrition Association
    (SNA), 127
school rules and regulations: chil-
    dren's health as focus of, 121;
    confidentiality issues and, 138–39;
    Cumberland County, Tennessee,
    4; discretion limitations of, 5; in
    free-food programs, 129–31; and
    health data, 218; in health screen-
    ing, 135–42; and home-packed
    versus school lunch, 131–35; Lake
    County, Florida, 121; need for
    change in, 126–27; and nutrition
    guidelines (see diet/nutrition);
    pick-up policies, 4; and recess,
    121, 143; School Nutrition Asso-
    ciation (SNA), 127; solutions to
    issues of, 142–46; and suspensions
    for imaginative play, 165; weapons
    policies, 170; zero-tolerance poli-
    cies, 4, 165
Schumer, Chuck, 131
Schwab, Jeffrey, 195
Schwartz, Barry, 8–9, 44–45, 49
Science-Based Medicine (website), 78
science of breastfeeding, 79–86
Scotland, 219, 226–27, 229
Seider, Scott, 52
self-reliance, 29, 49, 177–78
self-sufficiency, teaching children, 18
Senior, Jennifer, 12, 84
sex education, 140
sex-offender laws, 224–25
Sex Offender Registration Act (New
    York), 222
sex-offender registry, 219–23
shaken baby syndrome (SBS), 210–11
Sharpe, Kenneth, 8–9, 44–45, 49
Shattered Bonds (Roberts), 199
siblings, as babysitters, 40, 42, 94
sidewalks, 35–36
SIDS (sudden infant death syn-
    drome), 2, 98–101
Silverglate, Harvey, 9
Simon, Russell Max, 39–40

Simon, Scott, 49–50
Simple Justice (blog), 11
Skenazy, Lenore, 10, 28, 30–33, 41–42,
    54–55, 218
Smith, Adam, 85
SNA (School Nutrition Associa-
    tion), 127
SNAP (Supplemental Nutrition
    Assistance Program), 128
Socia, Kelly, 222
social workers. See child-welfare
    workers
societal change, 20–21
socioeconomic status: breast pump-
    ing at work and, 87; and child-
    care costs and, 93, 114–15; infant
    feeding practices and, 80; and
    obesity, 215; and SIDS, 100
Sommers, Christina Hoff, 174–75
Sothern, Melinda, 201, 212
South Carolina, Harrell case, 43
Special Supplemental Nutrition
    Program for Infants and Women,
    70–73
Spencer, Rebecca, 144
Speregen, Kathy, 143–44
standards: acceptable parental disci-
    pline, 197; of care, 148; categories
    of sex offenders, 223; and child-
    abuse definitions, changes to,
    196; for child-care providers,
    112; of childrearing, 7–8, 9, 12–13;
    in daycare, 14, 110; for daycare
    workers, 13; effects of, 119–20;
    and government parenting, 25;
    Head Start Performance Stan-
    dards, 111–12; health, 13; home
    playground equipment safety, 162;
    and imminent harm, 181, 185, 187,
    188, 192, 194, 214; for independent
    children, 48–49; principles- and
    values-based, 117; and school
    lunch, 124; of self-reliance, 49
state laws and programs: adoption
    through federally funded groups,
    13; Arizona, 104; and breastfeed-
    ing, 68–70; California, 168, 198,

208–9; certification for daycare workers, 13; and child care, 114; Colorado, 106–7, 132; Connecticut, 42; Florida, 121; Illinois, 39–40, 41, 132, 137, 140; Maryland, 39–40, 41–42; Massachusetts, 71, 102–3, 108, 138–39, 196, 197; Michigan, 104, 167; New York, 5, 62, 104, 131, 222; North Carolina, 133; Oregon, 64; Pennsylvania, 2, 5, 95–97, 108, 109, 223, 224; South Carolina, 43; Tennessee, 4; Virginia, 114, 132

stay-at-home mothers, 105–6

Stevens, Katharine, 111

Stop Childhood Obesity campaign, 181–82

stress, sources of parental, 12

Strictly No! (Hills), 228

success: character traits for, 51–52; engendering children's, 51

summer camp, 158–59

Sunstein, Cass, 150

supervision, of children: legal age for supervising, 40; Long Island Rail Road (LIRR) incident, 30–31; overzealous, 148; playground incident and, 32–33; unsupervised children, 6, 31, 34–35, 39, 46–47, 56, 173, 179. *See also* unsupervised children

Supplemental Nutrition Assistance Program (SNAP), 128

swaddling, 2–3, 97–102

Swanson School (Auckland, New Zealand), 171–72

Syndrome, The (film), 211

teachers: overzealous, 132; schools as, 51–52

teething toy recall, 5–6

Telegraph (UK), 170

Tenenbaum, Inez, 155

Terry, Mark, 145

Texas, 101

"There Is a Tree That Stands" (Manger), 26–27

Three Felonies a Day (Silverglate), 9

tooth-brushing, 14, 102, 108

Tough, Paul, 29, 51

toys, 5, 20, 62. *See also* bans; play; recalls

Tracy, Tennile, 103–4

transparency, of child-welfare system, 204–5

Trello, Irene, 144–45

trial-and-error learning, 50

Trim Kids (Sothern), 201, 212

trust: in community, 54; parents', in kids, 50

Tryon, Teresa, 35

Tucker, Jeffrey, 93, 111–12

Tuerkheimer, Deborah, 210–11

Turner, Chevese, 138

Turow, Rachel, 102

Tuteur, Amy, 88

unattended children. *See* unsupervised children

UNICEF, 66, 81

United Kingdom (UK), 18–19; Family Recovery Programme, 230–32; games banned in, 170; Health and Safety Executive, 228–29; named-person concept, 227–32; nanny state in, 227–28; Scotland, 219, 226–27, 229

University of California at Berkeley, 140–41

University of Michigan, physical education study, 143–44

University of Texas, study on BFHI cost, 67–68

unsupervised children: in cars, 47–50; case examples, 6, 31, 34–35, 39, 46–47, 56, 173, 179; at home, 48. *See also* supervision, of children

U.S. Census Bureau, 142

U.S. Constitution, Fourteenth Amendment, 7

U.S. Department of Agriculture (USDA): blaming obese children on, 215; calorie-rationing rules, 134; cooking rules for daycare centers, 104; dietary guidelines of, 16; free-food programs of, 129–31; and home-packed lunches, 4, 132–35; School Lunch Program guidelines, 123–24; and school lunch rules, 103–4; school meal quality, 142; Supplemental Nutrition Assistance Program (SNAP), 128; Women, Infants, and Children (WIC) program, 70–73

U.S. Department of Education, 143

U.S. Department of Health and Human Services (HHS), 74–75, 97, 98–99, 107–8

U.S. Department of Health and Safety, rules for daycare centers, 103

vaccinations, 23–25

values, parenting, 25

Varness, Todd, 187

vigilantes, 32

Vilsack, Tom, 129–31, 133–34

vindictive protectiveness, 57

violence. *See* child abuse; domestic violence

Virginia: Richmond school lunch issue, 132; unregulated daycare in, 114

Wade, Alicia, 209

Walk, The (film), 175–76

Walker, Marsha, 64–65

War against Boys, The (Sommers), 174–75

war on fun, 18, 147, 158, 166. *See also* playgrounds/parks

Washington Post, 2, 38, 43–44, 47, 48–49, 73, 77, 108, 114, 210

Watson, Tracy, 137

Wax-Thibodeaux, Emily, 77–78

Wayne County Child Protective Services, 3

Wealth of Nations, The (Smith), 85

Week, The (Dougherty), 53

weight assessment: and being overweight, 125–26; body mass index (BMI), 136, 138, 139, 140–41; laws on, 15. *See also* diet/nutrition; obesity, in children

Weissmann, Jordan, 110–11

Weisz, William, 162

welfare authorities. *See* child protective services

Welfare of Children (Meltzer et al.), 205

What to Expect When No One's Expecting (Last), 108

WIC (Women, Infants, and Children) program, 70–73, 89

Widdicombe, Lizzie, 32

Wiley, Shawna C., 77

Williams, Gwendolyn, 137

Williams, Laura Bruiji, 137

Williamson, Jeffrey, 43

wisdom, practical, 49–50

Wolf, Joan, 69, 79–80, 82

Women, Infants, and Children (WIC) program, 70–73, 89

Won't Back Down (movie), 14–15

Wootan, Margo, 215–16

working mothers/parents: breastfeeding and, 78–79; breast pumping at work, 73–74, 86–90; child care and, 91, 115; leaving workforce, 105

World Health Organization (WHO), 66–68, 67, 69, 81

worst-first thinking, 10

Wrage, Stacie, 103–4

Wright, Anne L., 81

Yam, Phil, 215

Young, Brittany, 127

youth sex offenders, 219–23

Zajicek-Farber, Michaela L., 212

zero-tolerance policies, 4, 165

Zucker, Craig, 155–56